Basic & Respectful E-mailing

Using Outlook Express

Send safe *respectful* e-mail

Receive e-mail safely

Forward safe *respectful* e-mail

Insert and/or attach pictures

Utilize the Address Book more fully

Create and use stationery and signatures

And lots more…

Screen shot(s) reprinted by permission of Microsoft Corporation.

ISBN 0-7414-2120-8

Published by:

INFINITY
PUBLISHING.COM
1094 New Dehaven Street
Suite 100
West Conshohocken, PA 19428-2713
Info@buybooksontheweb.com
www.buybooksontheweb.com
Toll-free (877) BUY BOOK
Local Phone (610) 941-9999
Fax (610) 941-9959

Printed in the United States of America

Printed on Recycled Paper

Published February 2005

Acknowledgements

I am thankful for the opportunity to help all who are new to computers, and/or new to Outlook Express. I believe this book will also serve the more experienced computer user who enjoys a few reminders with fine tuning of their already existing e-mail skills. Personal computers (PCs) allow entry into a wonderful expanding realm where e-mail has become a necessity for many.

I am grateful for electronic mail, affectionately called e-mail that has brought such joy to many while propelling our world to a happier place. Correspondence with friends, relatives, and business associates can be just a mouse click away. I look forward to the day when we can travel as quickly as our e-mail is sent.

I appreciate the many and varied features of Outlook Express — some beyond the scope of this book; yet if studied allow an even greater learning of computers.

I value clients, students, and readers who use Outlook Express as their "e-mail management program" to send and receive their e-mails. This book provides answers not found elsewhere to a multitude of questions asked by many as they embrace this new journey.

I am thankful to and remain in awe of Microsoft Corporation and how they continue to make our computer experiences better every day. Many thanks also to them for permission to reprint screen shots.

Thank you Infinity Publishing for your innovative method of printing and distributing books. You are a dream come true.

Dedication

I dedicate this book specifically to individuals born prior to 1950. I am honored to be of help as you go kicking and screaming into the still vastly unknown world of computers.

Please remember this *can* be fun.

Table of Contents

Introduction

Microsoft's Outlook Express is one terrific way to correspond with anyone in this world right from the desktop of your computer. The only requirement for anyone to receive your e-mail message is that they have access to a computer that can connect to the Internet. It is amazing how the times of letter writing have changed. Thanks to e-mail management programs like Outlook Express, we can send and receive e-mail 24 hours a day, 7 days a week if we so desire.

While instant messaging and newsgroups are hot topics for some and can be dealt with through Outlook Express, this book intentionally does not address either of them in any way. This book is about the e-mail basics; *respectfully* sending and safely receiving, with a few other associated "nice to know" computer topics.

This book is written at the PC beginner level so those knowing very little about computers or e-mail can greatly benefit in a short amount of time. It may offer assistance to Macintosh users, but please understand this book is designed from a Windows computer user perspective.

This material supplements the already existing "HELP" menu included within the Outlook Express program. The intention of this book is extensive clarification.

Chapter 1 teaches you how to be sure you have the latest version of Outlook Express installed on your computer.

Chapter 2 discusses opening Outlook Express. It explains in how to customize the main screen "view."

In order to send and receive e-mail, you must have an account of some sort with an Internet Service Provider (ISP) who, at a minimum provides you a connection to the Internet. This is addressed in Chapter 3, E-mail Accounts — specifically Mail.

In many homes and businesses, more than one individual use the same computer. Outlook Express can keep track of "who-is-who" with regard to e-mail sent and received as well as keeping track of specific e-mail addresses for each user, also known as an identity. This is covered in Chapter 4, Computer User Identities.

Chapter 5 covers the Address Book — backing it up, organizing, printing, and the electronic business card feature.

                                                    Use any and all information at your own risk.

Chapter 6 covers "sending" e-mail that *you* create from scratch. Differences between plain, rich, and HTML text are explained. Using the BCC (blind carbon copy) field is a very nice feature for respectful e-mailing. You learn how to create and add signatures to your messages as well as how to have your own personal stationery with various colors, styles, patterns and backgrounds. You can also add a "digital" business card to outgoing messages. Sending attachments and insertions (pictures, sounds, files, and Web site links) are explained.

Chapter 7 deals with "receiving," "replying to," and "forwarding" e-mail. *Previewing* an e-mail message technically is different from actually *opening* the e-mail. You can create folders to organize messages that you want to keep. You can block messages from *unique* e-mail addresses. Outlook Express can be setup to save names and e-mail addresses of anyone to whom you reply and automatically enter them into the Address Book.

The Appendixes are a bonus section of stand alone information separate from Outlook Express, yet when understood help you interact better with Outlook Express and therefore improve your computer experience in general. They are: Windows Taskbar; Desktop Shortcuts & Icons; Minimize, Maximize, & Close; Block Text, Cut, Copy, & Paste; and Suggested PC Maintenance. A sample of the End The Clutter ETC™ Preferred Subscriber Weekly E-mail Program is included as well.

It is strongly recommended that you have the latest updated version of a reputable Virus Protection software program installed on your system prior to playing with e-mail. It is also important to check for updates for this software daily *before* receiving or sending e-mail. New viruses appear all the time and keeping your software up to date provides you with the latest protection available. You can receive a computer virus in many ways — "previewing" an e-mail, opening an e-mail, opening an attachment, and instant messages to name a few.

This book is written with the "left click" as the primary mouse click.

This book is specifically uses larger print for easier reading. There is ample space for your notes and questions. When a question comes up write it down in this book. If you use a special setting write that in as well. Most of all have fun.

Take a deep breath, relax, and let's get started.

Chapter 1 — Free Updates for Outlook Express

Outlook Express generally comes pre-installed on computers using a Windows Operating System. It is prudent to have the latest version of this program as well as any *updates* as they become available. Updates that are downloaded from the Microsoft Web site manually by the user or automatically by the computer are then immediately installed on your computer. Downloading and installing are two distinct computer processes.

> To "download" in the general sense means to obtain a computer file(s) of some type from a Web site to your computer. To "install" what was downloaded, often can mean that the file(s) must be opened by double left clicking (or one *right* click on the file icon followed by one *left* click on OPEN). After installation, you may be asked to RESTART your computer for the installation to take effect. The term *restart* means shutting the computer down and starting it up again in one step.

To check the availability of free updates for your computer from Microsoft, you must first be connected to the Internet. Latest versions and updates to Outlook Express are just one small part of the many free updates available from Microsoft.

Once you are connected to the Internet, left click once on START; left click once on PROGRAMS (or ALL PROGRAMS), and left click once on WINDOWS UPDATE. This action should take you to the Microsoft site containing the Windows Updates. Please wait; depending on the speed of your connection this can take many minutes.

If for some reason, the above action does not work, open Internet Explorer (the blue "e" icon hopefully located on your desktop or in the "quick launch" area on the taskbar) and type in the following *link* otherwise known as a Web address:

http://v4.windowsupdate.microsoft.com/en/default.asp

Please wait.

When the Microsoft Web site loads it will have a place for you to left click once that says: SCAN FOR UPDATES. Please refer to the figure on the next page.

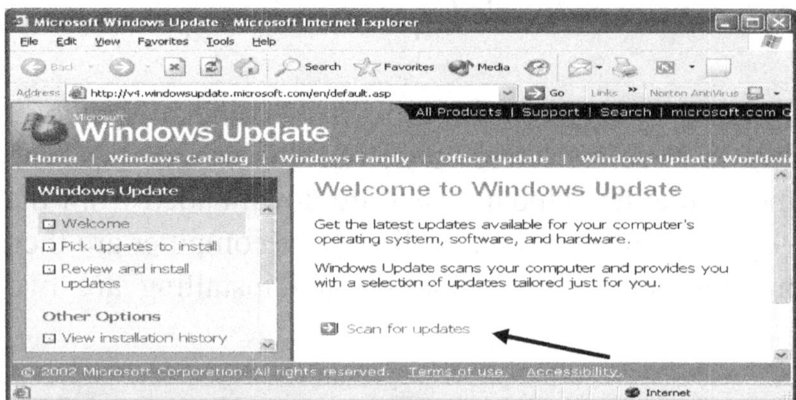

Figure 1 — Windows Update Web site.

After you left click once on SCAN FOR UPDATES, please wait. The next Web page that loads will tell you the updates that are available for *your* computer that you can download and install. Please refer to the figure below.

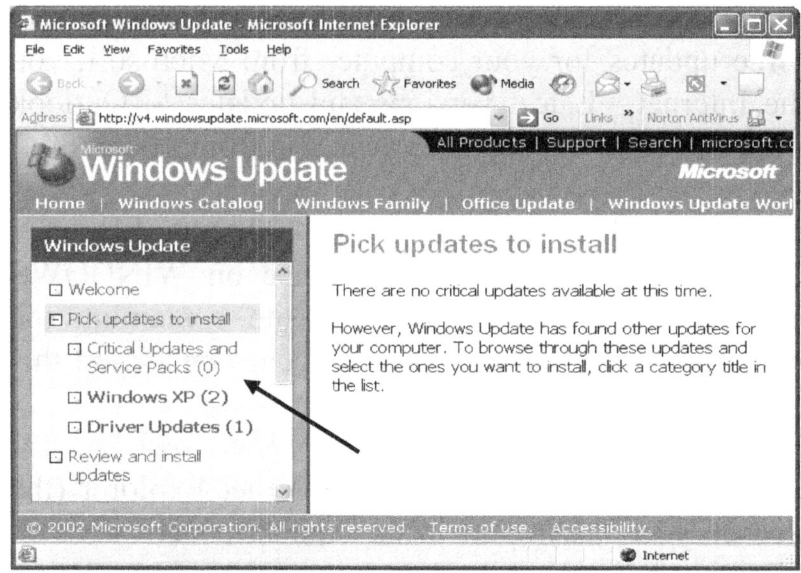

Figure 2 — Critical Updates available for your computer.

This window will be slightly different on every computer based on the operating system you are using and the updates that are available for *your* computer. Updates are often classified as critical and recommended, Windows XP and Driver Updates like in the above example. You want to download any *critical* updates and any updates related to Outlook Express and Internet Explorer. Recommended and other updates are optional.

Some updates must be downloaded and installed one at a time; so you may have to repeat this process several times to get all the updates you need. Follow the computer's lead; it will tell you what has to happen next. Sometimes the files containing the needed updates are very large and the downloading process can take hours if you are using a telephone dial-up method.

To begin the process of downloading, focus on the left side of the Web page window. Left click once where it says "Critical Updates" or where it says "Review and install updates." Please wait.

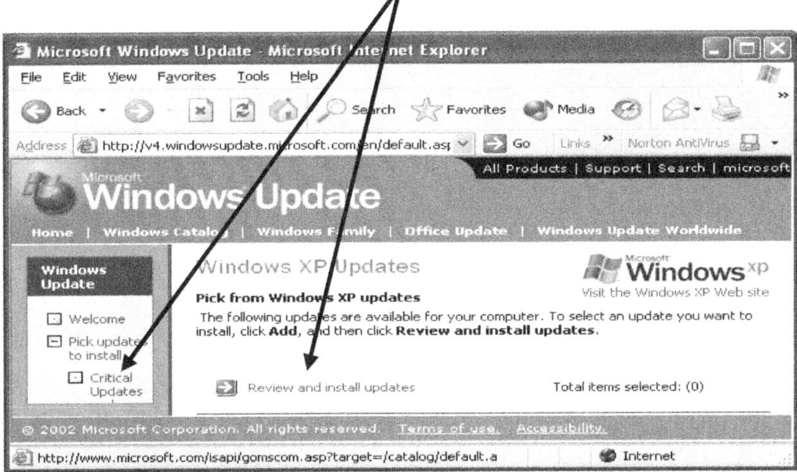

Figure 3 — Critical Updates & Review and install updates.

Follow *all* instructions carefully. If at *any* time you are not comfortable performing this task, please stop and ask for assistance.

After the updates are downloaded and installed, the computer will generally ask you to RESTART. Please agree and left click once on OK or RESTART. If you are not asked to RESTART, it's a good idea to RESTART manually after any update installation. To restart your computer manually, left click once on the START button. Depending upon which Operating System you are using (Windows 95, Windows 98, Windows Me, Windows XP, etc.) you need to find where there is a choice to "SHUT DOWN" or to "TURN OFF COMPUTER." Left click once and this will bring up another window with additional choices for you. In this case you want to choose "RESTART" and then left click once on OK. The computer will shut itself down and then restart. Please wait.

You may have to go through this process a number of times to make sure you have all the available Critical, Outlook Express, and Internet Explorer updates.

Chapter 2 — Opening Outlook Express

There are several ways to open Outlook Express:

1. Use the "Quick Launch" located in your task bar. If you are unfamiliar with the taskbar and its properties please refer to Appendix A.
2. Left click once on the START button, left click once again on PROGRAMS (or on ALL PROGRAMS), and then left click once on OUTLOOK EXPRESS.
3. Double left click on a shortcut icon for Outlook Express that happens to be on your desktop. To learn how to make a shortcut icon for your desktop, please see Appendix B.
4. Right click once on a desktop shortcut icon, and then left click once on OPEN.

A double left click is the same as one right click followed by a left click on OPEN.

When you open Outlook Express, you may or may not see the following window:

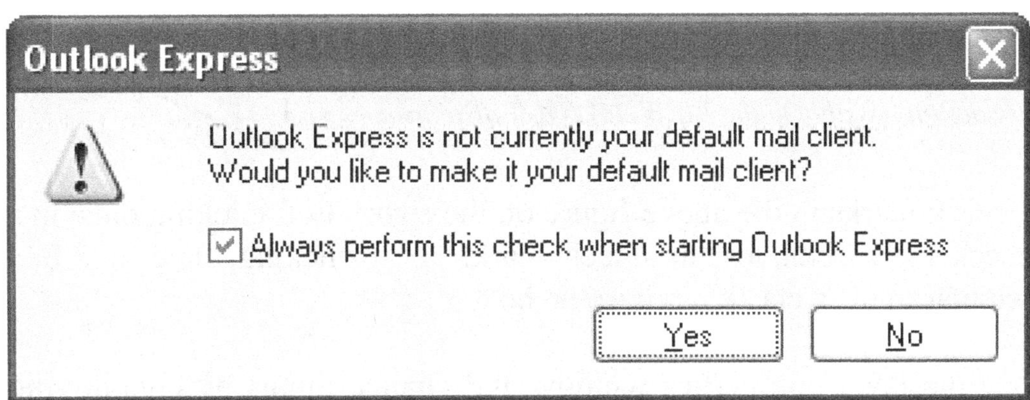

Figure 4 — Default mail program.

The word "default" means a pre-defined setting of some sort. If Outlook Express is the program you want to use for your e-mail, let it be the default program and left click once on YES. If you do not want Outlook Express to be your "default" e-mail program or you are not sure, left click once on NO.

Keep the check mark in the box "Always perform this check when starting Outlook Express" as a precautionary measure.

Main Screen View & Layout

When you open Outlook Express for the first time, the window view that you see might look something like the left figure below. For those who have been in and out of the Outlook Express program many times the *view* may be completely different. You want to make sure the "view" *you* see every time is the "view" that best serves you. In order to do this you need to know your options.

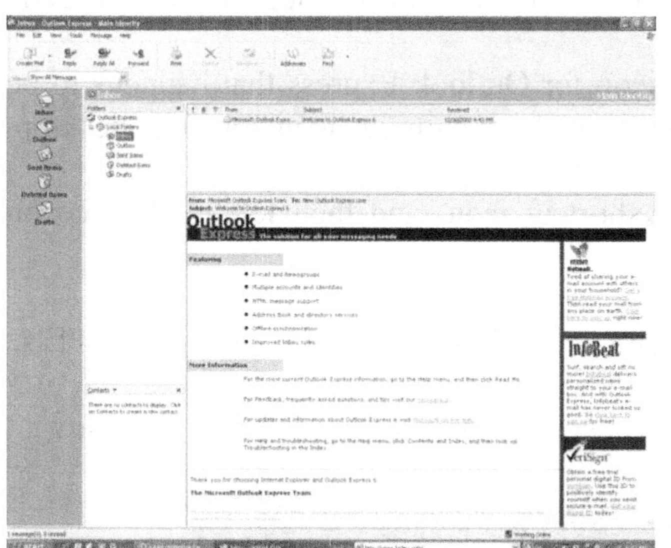
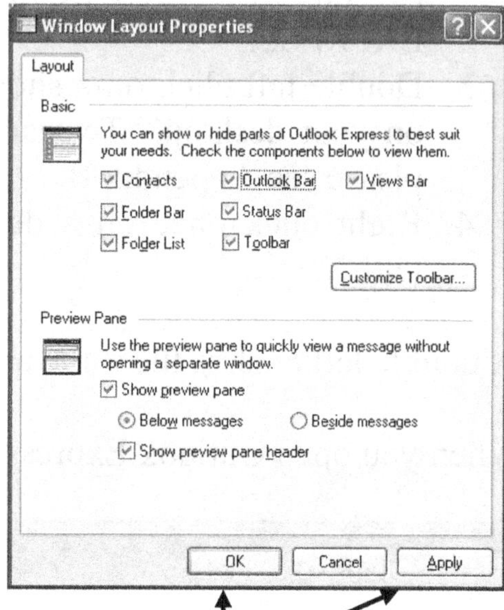

Figure 5 — Every option possible in the VIEW, LAYOUT displayed.

Notice all the check marks in the above figure on the right. Left clicking once in a box with a check mark removes the check mark. Left clicking once in a box without a check mark puts a check mark in the box.

When you open the layout properties window and change things by clicking, no changes take effect until you press the APPLY or OK buttons. Recommend when you are learning that you go into VIEW, LAYOUT and place check marks as they are in the top right figure. Then one by one remove a check mark and immediately left click on APPLY so you can see exactly what that box check mark represented. Don't click on OK until you have the "view" that *you* want. You can change the view whenever you like.

We will go through the choices one by one. Please follow along on your computer if you like. Open Outlook Express and then left click once on VIEW, LAYOUT.

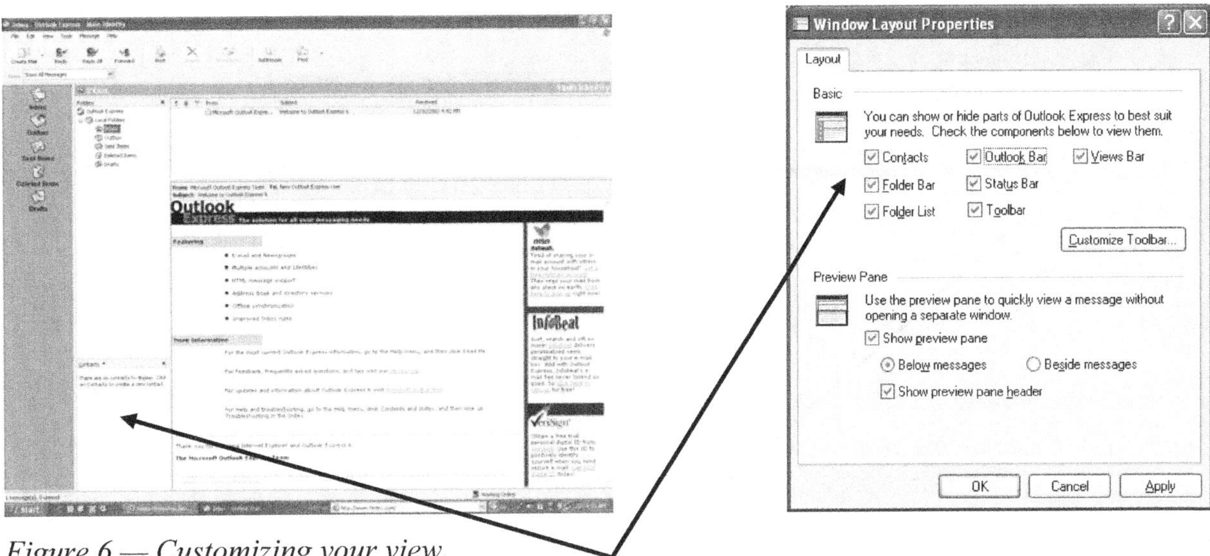

Figure 6 — Customizing your view.

Contacts

You can choose to have your contacts showing or not. Some people want them showing and others do not. Contacts are the people you have entered into the Address Book which is covered in Chapter 5.

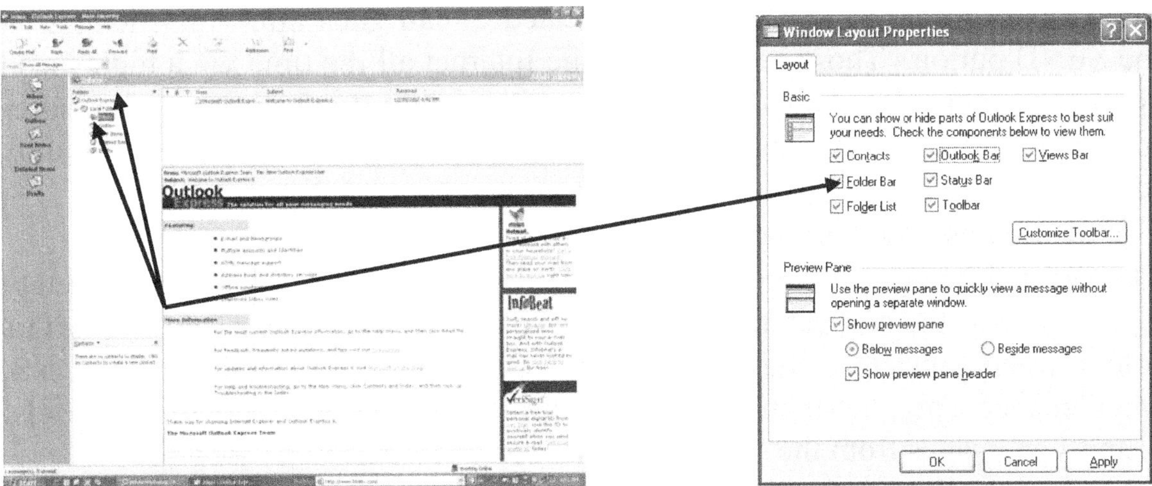

Figure 7 — Customizing your view.

Folder Bar

This option when active displays the name of the folder that is highlighted in the folder list.

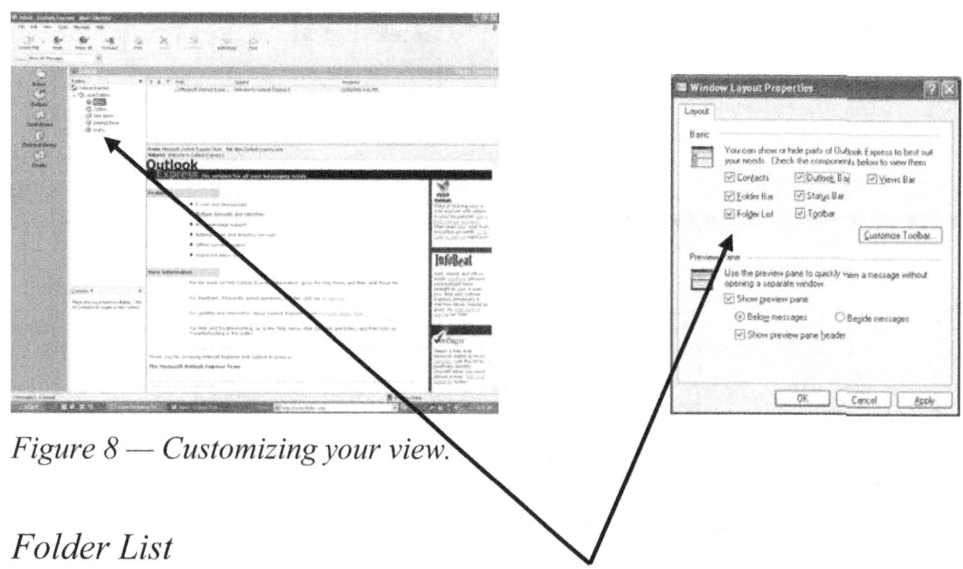

Figure 8 — Customizing your view.

Folder List

Viewing the folder list is invaluable. Crucial folders already created for you are the Inbox, Outbox, Sent Items, Deleted Items, and Drafts.

- The Inbox folder is where all your incoming e-mail goes by default (designed by the programmers of Outlook Express). You can change this but we recommend that you leave these five main folders as they are.
- The Outbox folder is where all your created e-mail goes after left clicking on the SEND button. Those connected to the Internet all the time via a high speed connection otherwise known as *broadband* probably don't notice outbound e-mail entering the Outbox folder because it goes in and out of the Outbox immediately.
- The Sent Items folder is a record of all e-mail you have actually sent.
- The Deleted Items folder holds any e-mail you delete. This folder is completely different from the computer recycle bin. To set Outlook Express to empty this folder when you close the program, left click once on TOOLS, OPTIONS, Maintenance Tab, and then place a check mark in the box next to the words: "Empty messages from the 'deleted items' folder on exit.
- The Drafts folder holds copies of e-mails that you have started but have not yet sent.

You can create as many folders as you like in this list. Let's say you wanted a folder underneath the Inbox called "Family" to keep e-mails from family. You highlight the Inbox by left clicking it once. Then left click once on FILE, NEW, FOLDER (or ctrl ı shift ı E), type "Family" and then left click on OK. Your new folder called "Family" would appear indented, and below the Inbox.

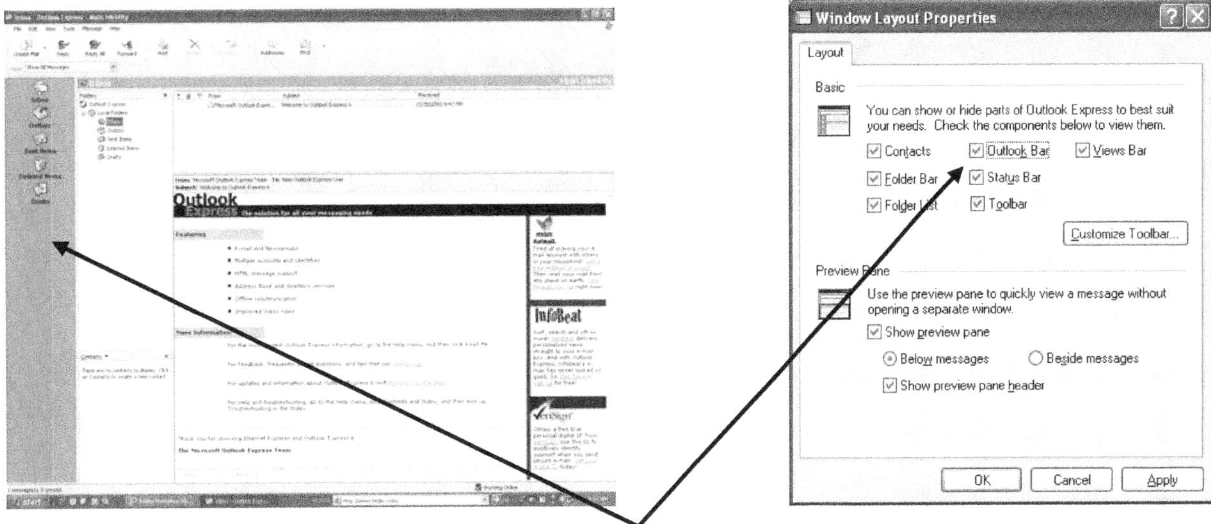

Figure 9 — Customizing your view.

Outlook Bar

The Outlook Bar largely displays those five crucial folders: Inbox, Outbox, Sent Items, Deleted Items, and Drafts.

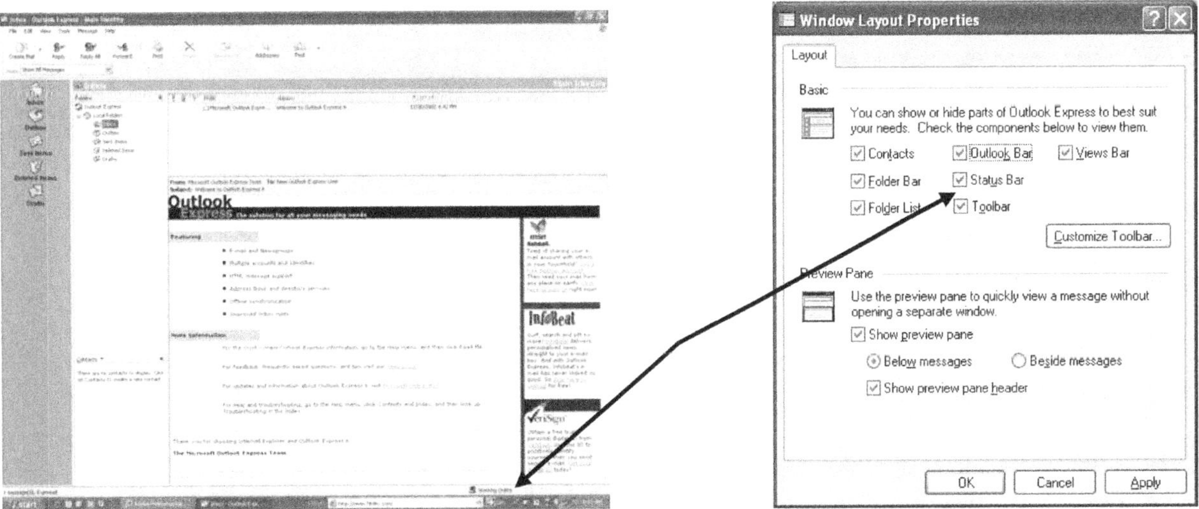

Figure 10 — Customizing your view.

Status Bar

The Status Bar lets you know if you are working on-line or not.

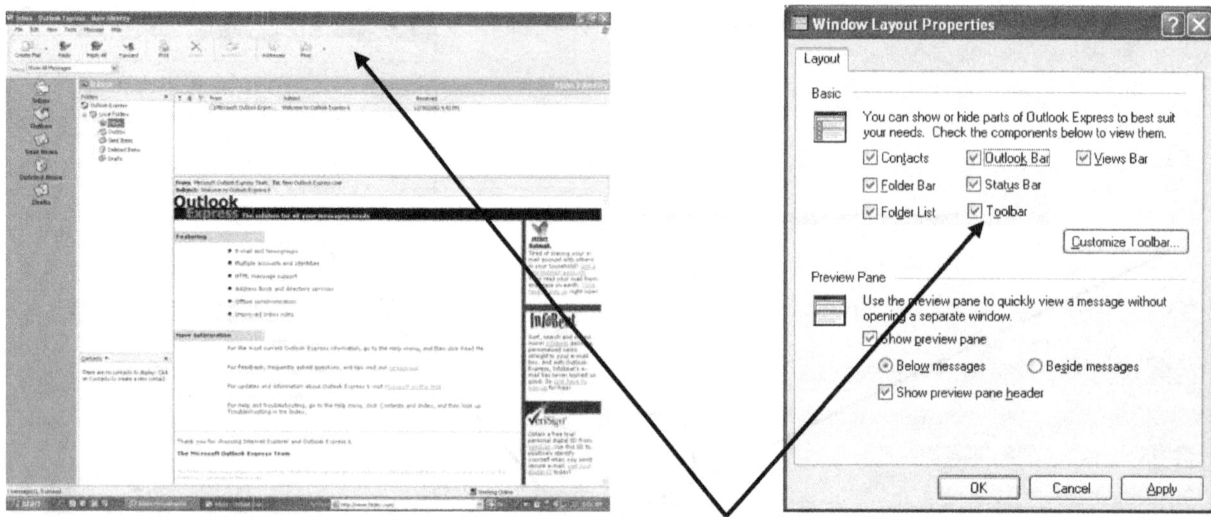

Figure 11 — Customizing your view.

Toolbar

The toolbar like the Folder List is crucial as it makes available all the necessary buttons for creating e-mail, sending/receiving, replying, forwarding, etc. You always want to be able to view the toolbar.

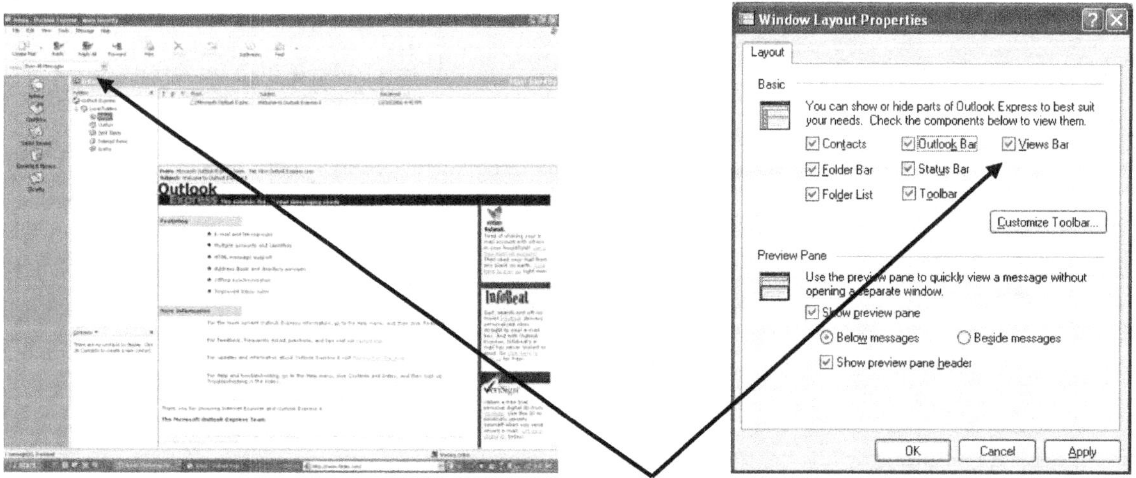

Figure 12 — Customizing your view.

Views Bar

The Views Bar when showing gives you the option of showing all messages, hiding read messages, or hiding read or ignored messages.

                                                    Use any and all information at your own risk.

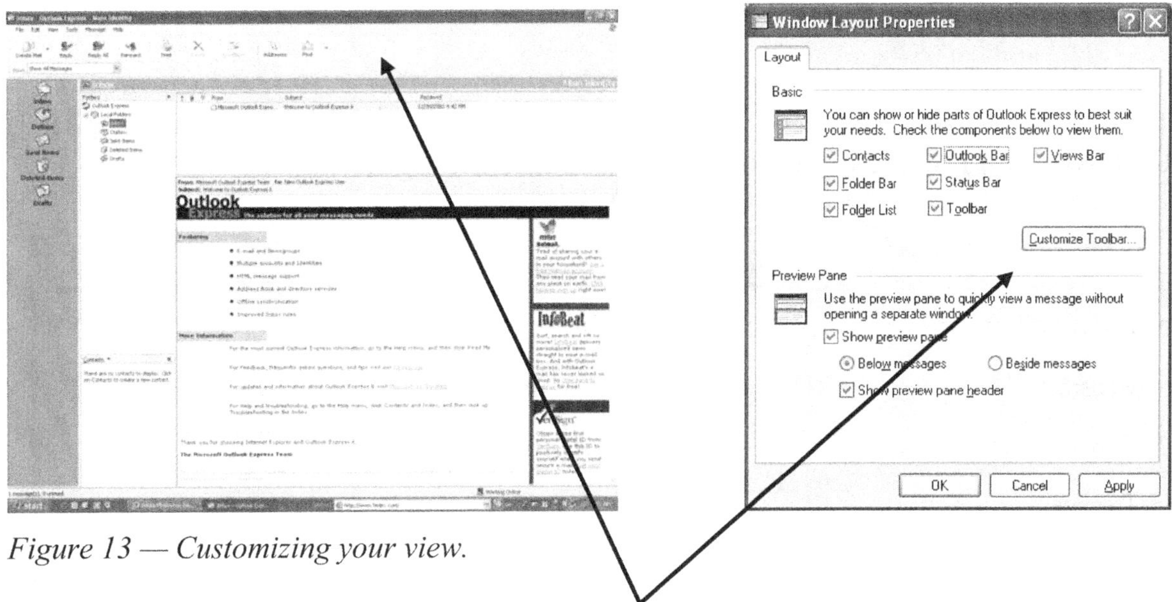

Figure 13 — Customizing your view.

Customize Toolbar

There are many options to customize the *main screen view* toolbar (discussed briefly on the next page) which work the same way as does customizing your *e-mail message view* which is discussed in great detail in Chapter 6.

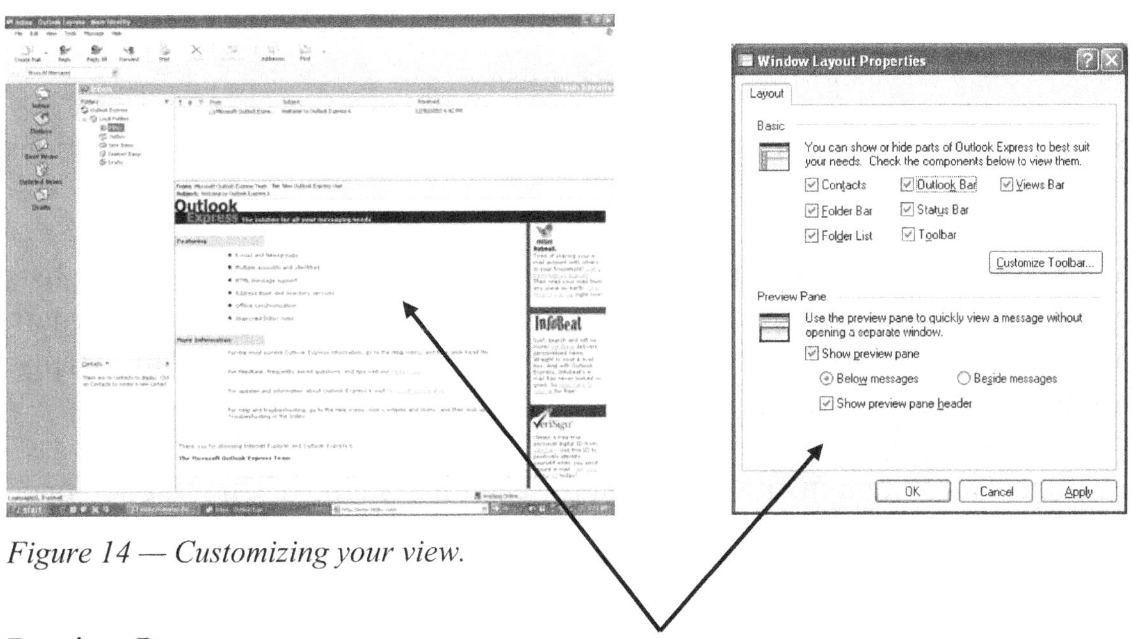

Figure 14 — Customizing your view.

Preview Pane

The Preview Pane is a nice feature because you can go through your e-mail very quickly to block and delete messages from unwanted senders.

Customize Main Screen Toolbar

When you left click once on VIEW, LAYOUT, and then on CUSTOMIZE TOOLBAR, you receive a window that looks like the figure below.

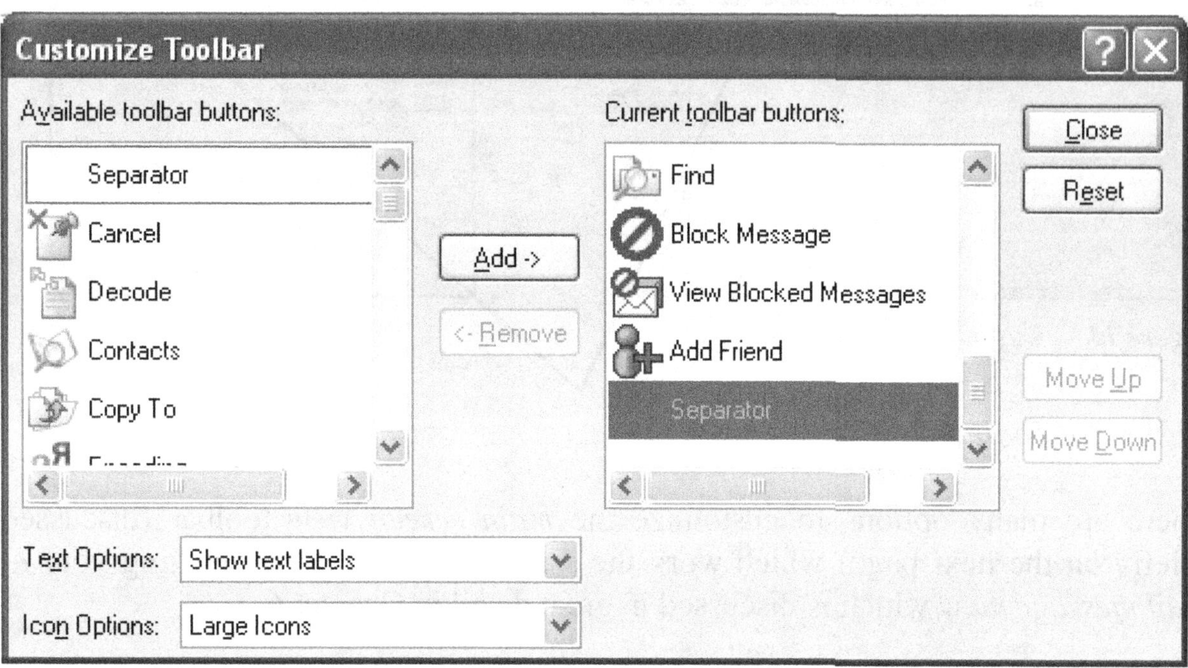

Figure 15 — Customize main screen toolbar.

For text options we recommend you choose "Show text labels." For icon options we recommend you choose "Large icons."

The column on the left lists available toolbar buttons. The column on the right lists the *current* toolbar buttons showing in *your* view. We recommend at a minimum that you have the following toolbar buttons showing: Create Mail, Reply, Forward, Print, Delete, Send/Recv, Addresses, Block Message, and Save As.

Left click once on an item in either column to select that item. Then left click once on either Add or Remove as you desire. You can also use the Move Up and Move Down buttons via left clicking for toolbar position placement.

This is exactly the same process as customizing your e-mail message screen view which is explained in Chapter 6.

                          Use any and all information at your own risk.

Chapter 3 — E-mail Accounts — Mail

Before you can send or receive e-mail, you must have at least one account with an Internet Service Provider (ISP). When using Outlook Express, this is a two-part process.

The first part is to initiate and setup an account with an ISP. The ISP to whom you pay money will provide you with at least one e-mail address and a connection to the Internet. You will either be assigned or be asked to choose an initial "User Name" and "Password." Your e-mail address will take the form of something like the example below:

UserName@ISP.whatever

In English, it will sound something like: Username at ISP dot whatever.

> When setting up an e-mail account with an ISP, it is in *your* best interest to pay monthly regardless of how wonderful paying quarterly or annually may sound from the sales person. Here is why. Let's say you use the service for a couple of weeks and don't like it. If you are paying on a monthly basis, you can switch with a clear conscience all the way around. Switching your provider, deciding whether you like the new service or not, and notifying all your contacts of your new e-mail address can take about a month. ISPs generally are not in any great hurry to issue refunds; that is assuming you can even find the correct person to ask for your money back. If an ISP happens to go out of business, your quarterly and/or annual payments may be lost forever.

The second part of the process is to setup the e-mail account(s) in Outlook Express. You have to tell Outlook Express your specific e-mail address, your user name, and your password. You also have to tell Outlook Express where to send your e-mail *to* and where to receive your e-mail *from*.

To begin the second part of this process, open Outlook Express with the main screen showing. Left click once on TOOLS, and then left click once on ACCOUNTS. That action will open a window that looks something like the figure on the next page.

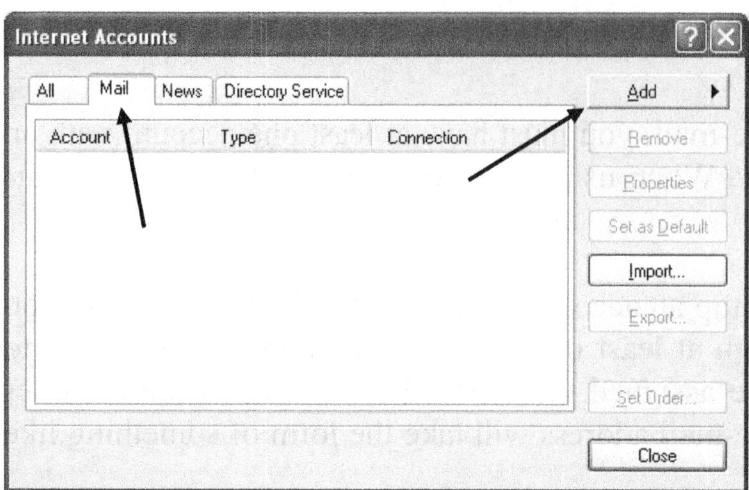

Figure 16 — Outlook Express Internet Accounts Window.

Left click once on the "Mail" tab to *select* it. Left click once on "Add." That last action brings up the figure below.

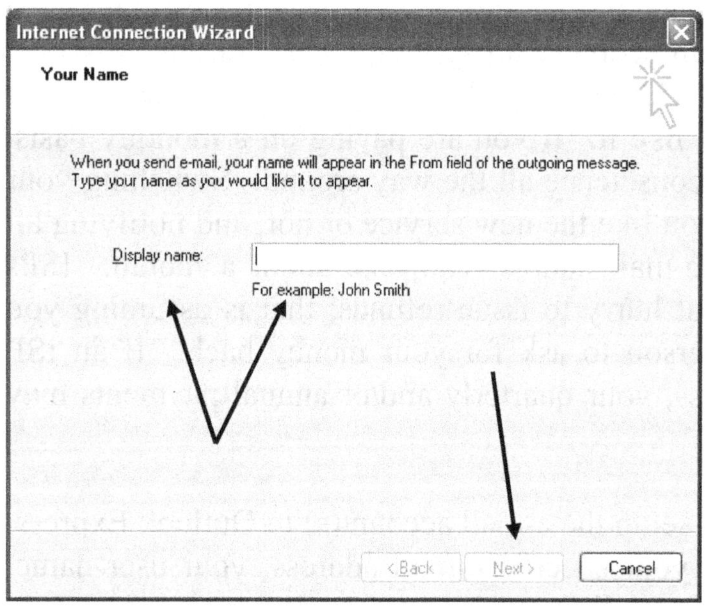

Figure 17 — Type your name as you would like the world to see.

Type in your real name, or whatever name you want to appear on e-mails you send in the box labeled "Display Name." This is *not* your e-mail address so feel free to use capitol letters as in "John Smith." As soon as you begin to type, the "Next" button will become active waiting for you to left click once on it when you finish typing your name. A window like the figure on the next page then appears.

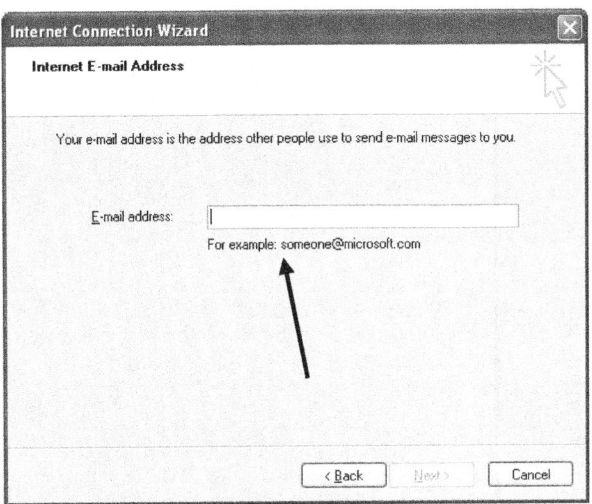

Figure 18 — E-mail address.

Now you type in your complete and *correct* e-mail address. Typing teachers of years ago wouldn't approve perhaps, but please *look at the keyboard* when typing in this information. As you begin typing your e-mail address, the NEXT button becomes active. When you are finished typing left click once on NEXT.

The figure below is where you must very carefully enter the information provided to you by your Internet Service Provider (ISP). Without this crucial information entered correctly, you cannot send or receive e-mail. If you do not know what to type in, this is when you call your ISP for some free technical support.

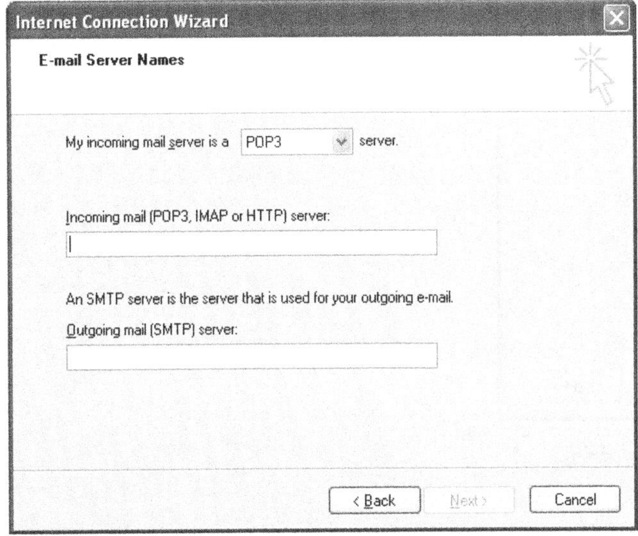

Figure 19 — Incoming and Outgoing E-mail server addresses.

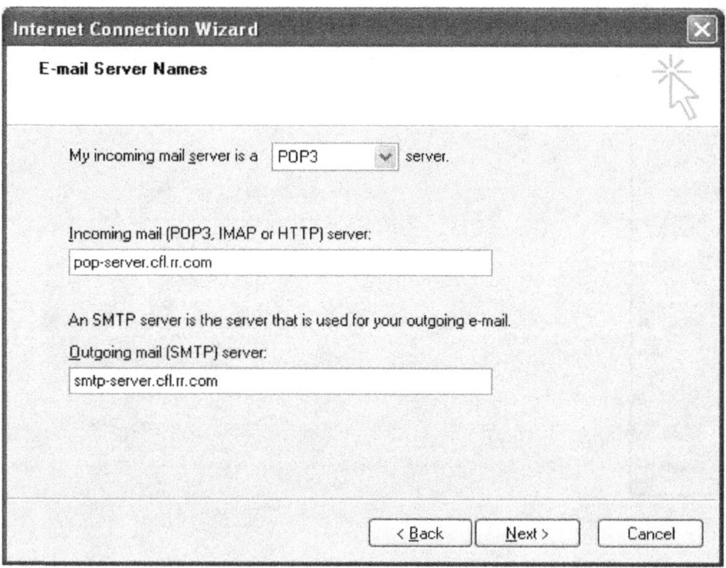

Figure 20 — E-mail servers.

The figure above gives is a mock demonstration. This information has to be absolutely correct. When you are finished typing, left click once on NEXT to bring up the figure below.

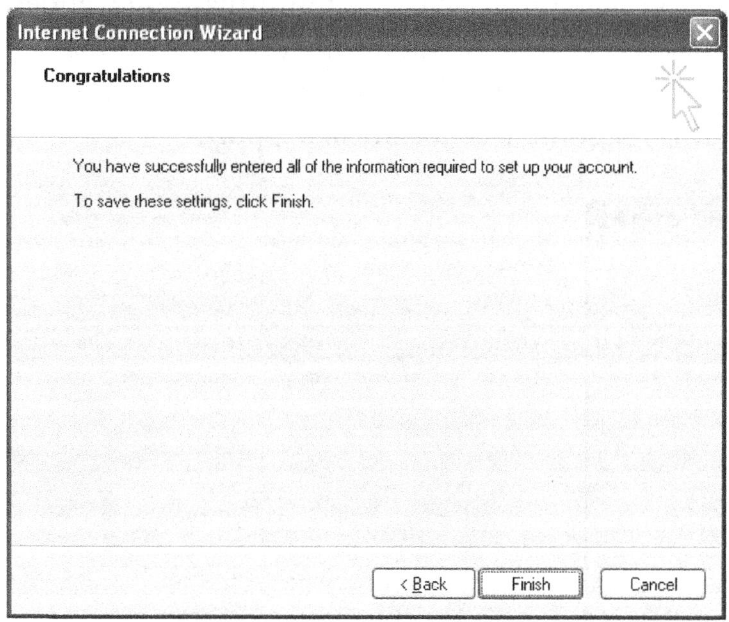

Figure 21 — E-mail account successfully completed.

Left click once on FINISH to complete an e-mail account set up.

Chapter 4 — Computer User Identities

Creating different identities is one way for more than one person to share Outlook Express and the Address Book on the same computer.

When you open Outlook Express and the "Folder Bar" is visible (see Chapter 2); the current user name or identity will be displayed in addition to the highlighted folder. In this example, the highlighted folder is the Inbox and the current user is "End The Clutter ETC."

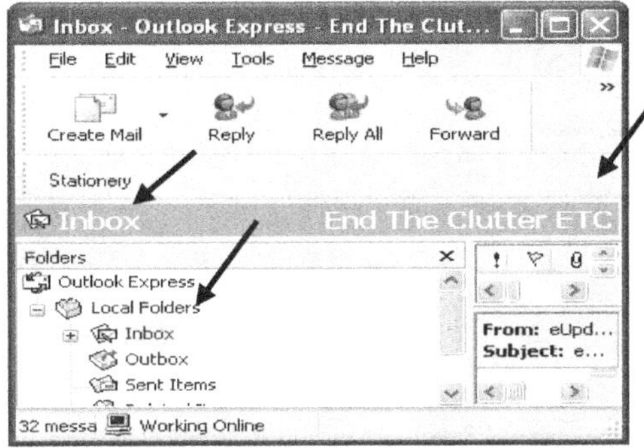

Figure 22 — View of the "Folder bar."

To manage identities within the Outlook Express program, left click once on FILE, then on IDENTITIES, and then on MANAGE IDENTITIES.

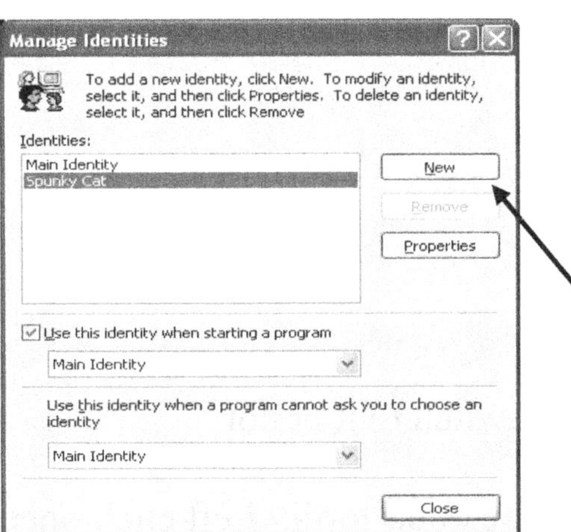

Figure 23 — Manage Identities window.

To create a new identity, left click once on NEW. That will bring up a window like the figure on the next page.

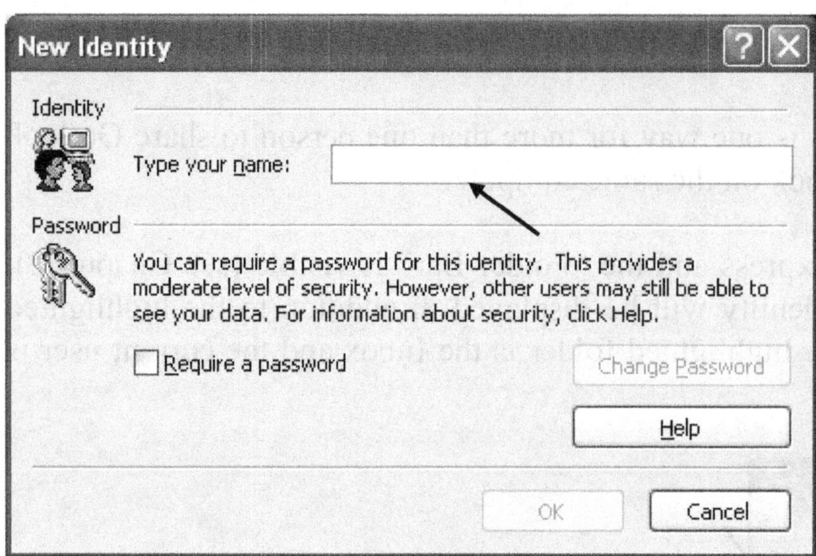

Figure 24 — Name of New Identity Window.

Type the name for the new identity.

Suggest you *do not* put a check in the "Require a password" box.

Let's say you decide to create a new identity called "Mike." As you type in "Mike," in the top figure example, the "OK" button becomes active. Left click once on OK. When you do, the figure below appears.

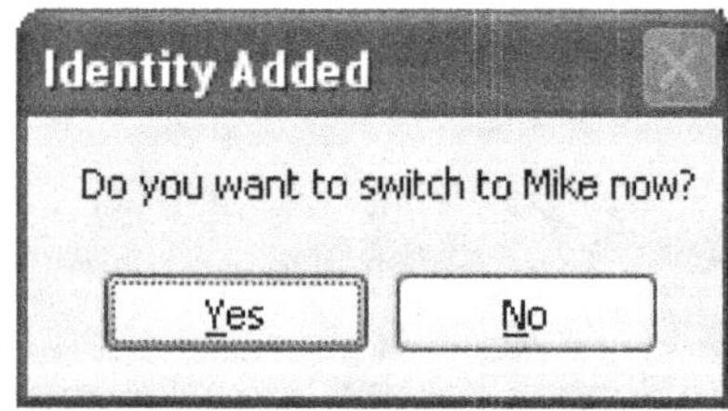

Figure 25 — Do You Want to Switch to the New Identity?

As the new identity is created, you have to option to switch to it or not.

After identities are created, here is how you switch back and forth: Left click once on FILE and then left click once on SWITCH IDENTITY. To keep things simple, create new identities *within* the Outlook Express program. Switch to a specific identity *before* trying to use that identity's address book.

                                                          Use any and all information at your own risk.

To delete an identity, left click once on FILE, left click once on IDENTITIES, and left click once on MANAGE IDENTITIES.

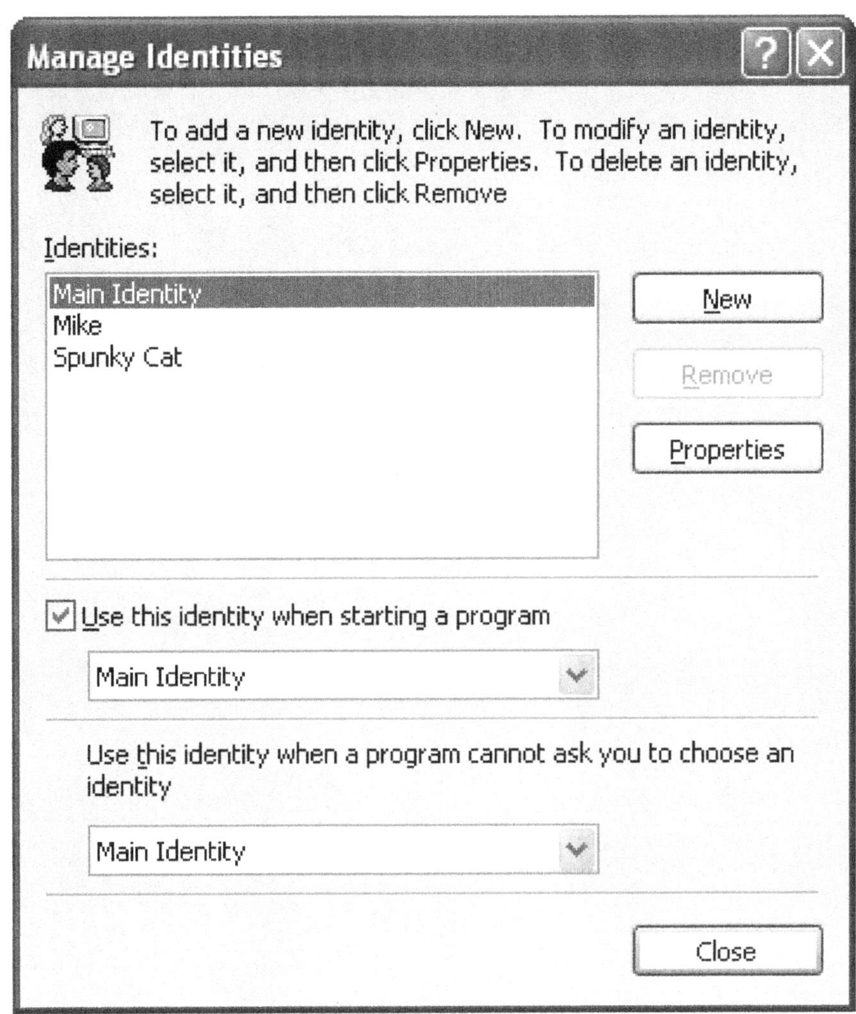

Figure 26 — Manage Identities window.

Select the identity you wish to remove by left clicking on it once to highlight it. As you perform that action the REMOVE button becomes active. Left click once on REMOVE. That action will bring up a warning message from the computer asking you if in fact you really want to remove that identity. If so, you will then left click once on DELETE and the identity will be deleted.

You cannot delete the current identity.

When in doubt, do not delete or create identities.

Chapter 5 — Address Book

It is easy to assume that the Address Book is part of Outlook Express. Technically it is separate from Outlook Express because you can open the Address Book without ever opening Outlook Express. For the purpose of this book, we will access the Address Book only through Outlook Express.

The Address Book keeps track of all your e-mail addresses as well as lots of other information available about your friends, relatives, colleagues, i.e. your "contacts." The Address Book takes the form of a database, which acts completely different from a word processing document or a spreadsheet program.

When you first open Outlook Express, hopefully you see a "view" something like the figure below. If you don't see a view similar to this, please go back to Chapter 2 for review and explanation of the main screen view.

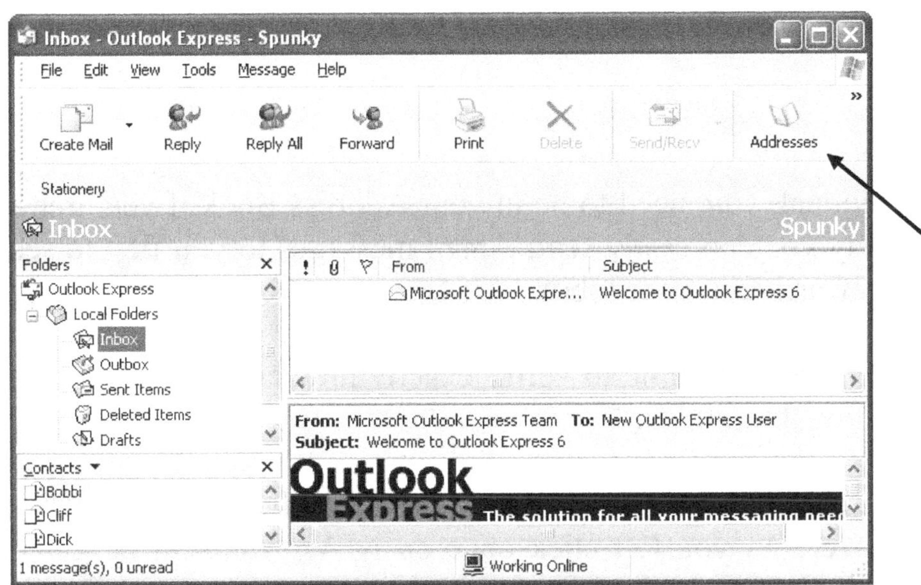

Figure 27 — Outlook Express main screen view.

You can also access the Address Book when composing an e-mail message (Chapter 6). However, getting to the Address Book via the Tool bar in the main Outlook Express screen allows you more control and additional options.

As you left click once on ADDRESSES, that action will bring up a window something like the figure on the next page.

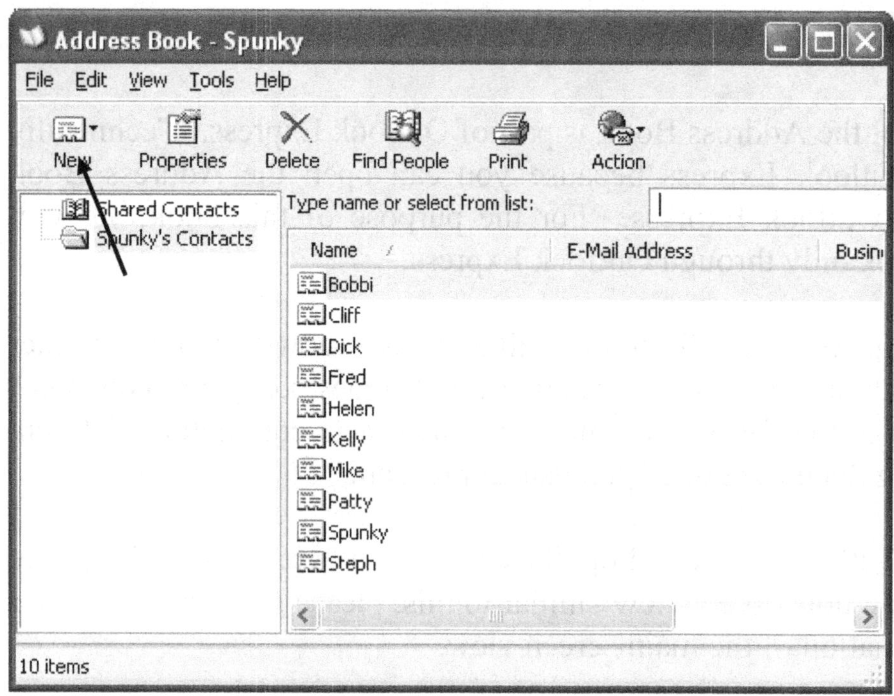

Figure 28 — The Address Book.

Adding a Contact

One very important individual, *you*, need to be in your Address Book if you aren't in there already. This way you can easily send e-mail messages to you first to see what they look like as they arrive in your inbox.

It is kind and respectful to take the time to verify exactly how an e-mail message will look — prior to sending it to others.

To add you, or any other individual to your address book, left click once on NEW. See the black arrow above. As you left click once on NEW, you will be given three choices:

1. New Contact
2. New Group
3. New Folder

Please choose NEW CONTACT by left clicking once. That will bring up something like the figure on the next page.

                                    Use any and all information at your own risk.

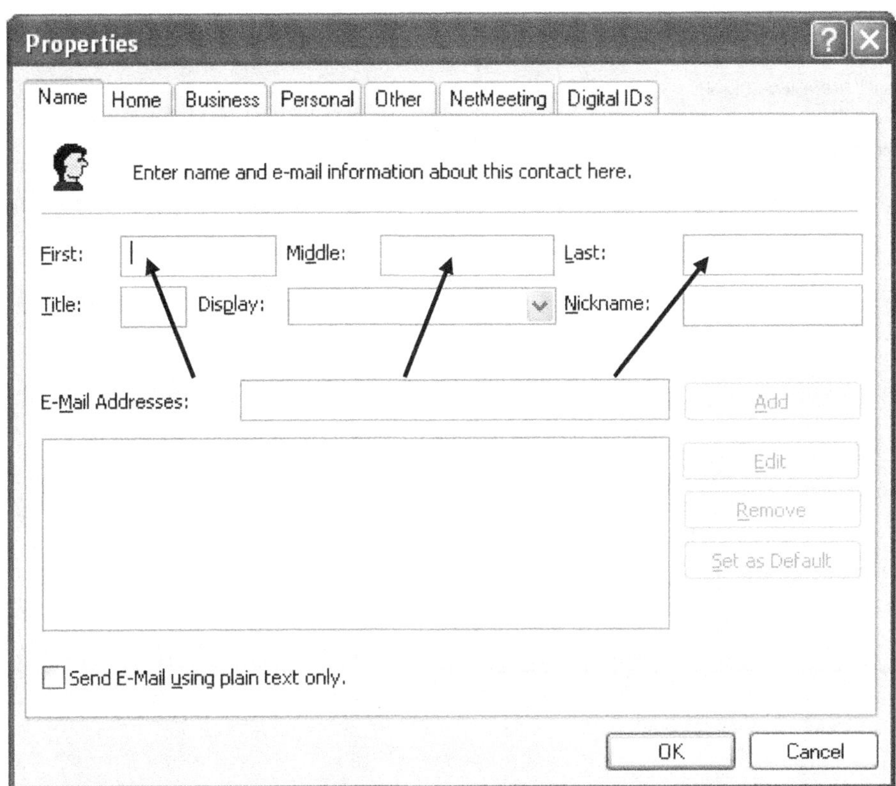

Figure 29 — "Name" tab window to enter a new contact.

Notice that there are 7 tabs (Name, Home, Business, Personal, Other, NetMeeting, and Digital IDs). These tabs each hold different "fields" of information. This is where you enter all sorts of information about the folks you know. This "Name" tab is where you enter the "real" names of people as well as their e-mail addresses.

As mentioned earlier, "The Address Book" is a database, and databases work differently from word processing or spreadsheet documents. The "TAB" key (upper middle left side of your keyboard) moves the cursor from field to field. A field is a place where specific information may be added to a database. In the figure above, the cursor is shown in the box labeled "FIRST" — the box where you enter an individual's real first name or the name they go by. The "field" immediately to the right is called "Middle" and the field to the right of that is named "Last." Pressing the TAB key slowly and gently moves you from field to field. Try this and become familiar with "tabbing" around a database window.

If you press and hold the SHIFT key down and press the TAB key, the cursor will move around the window in a backwards direction.

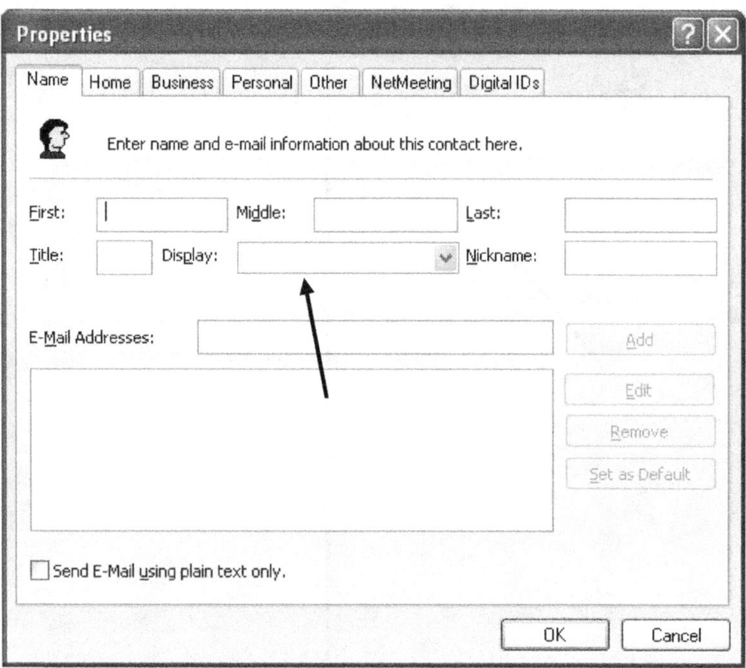

Figure 30 — "Name" tab.

As you type in the first name of the contact, the letters you type also show up in the "Display" field.

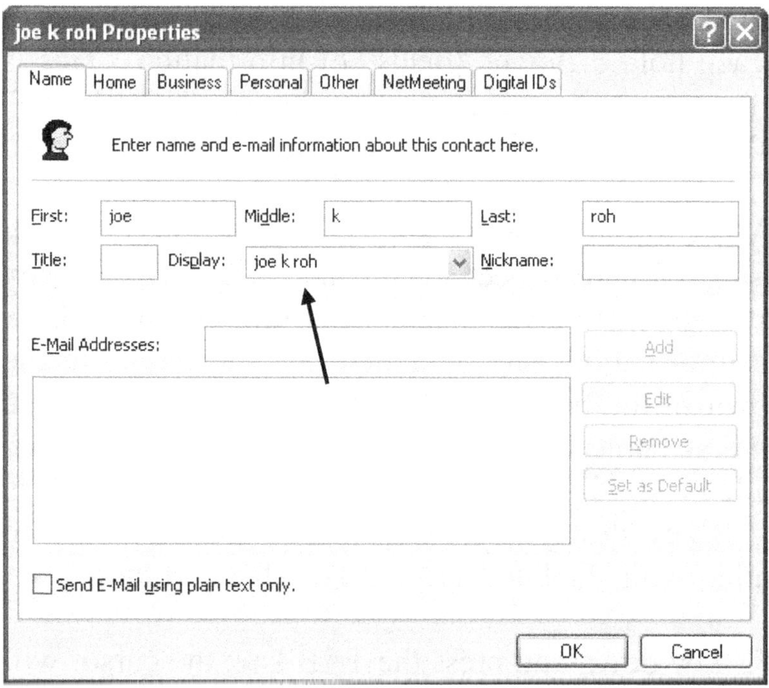

Figure 31 — Name fields also appear in the "Display" field.

Use any and all information at your own risk.

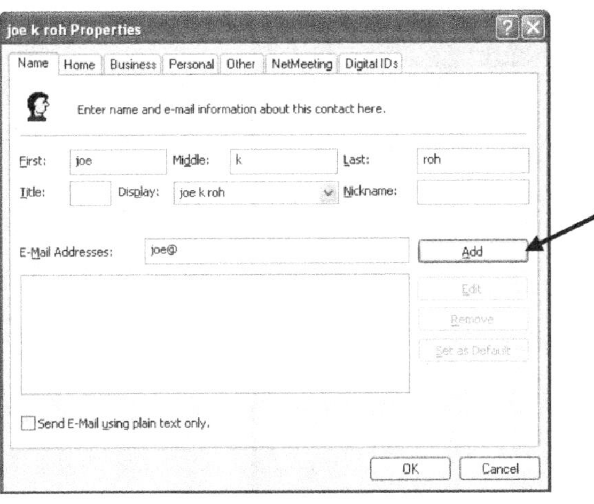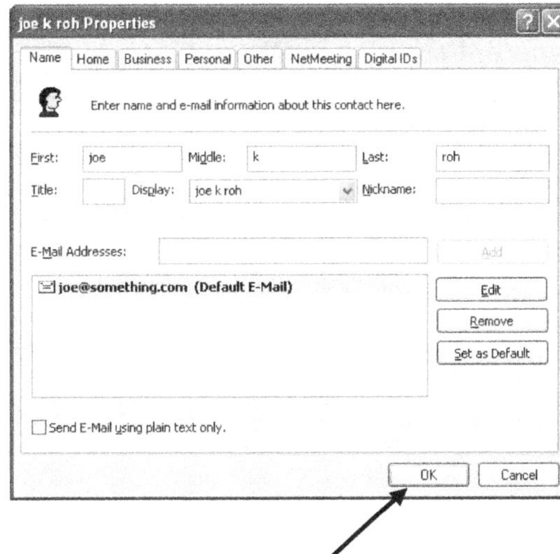

Figure 32 — "ADD" box.

After you type in the e-mail address, you must then left click once on the ADD button. That action brings up the top figure on the right.

You must then left click on OK for the information to be saved.

If you only enter one e-mail address for an individual, that e-mail address automatically is the "default" e-mail. If you enter two or more e-mail addresses for that person, you then have to decide which e-mail address you will use more frequently, and you make the one most often used the "default" e-mail address. This does not always suite everyone's desire however.

If you want for example to always send to two e-mail addresses for one person (like the home e-mail address and the work e-mail address), it is easier to create two different contacts for that one individual rather than to keep changing the "default" e-mail around every time you want to send an e-mail. For this scenario, the first contact entry for Joe might be Joe (home) and the second would be Joe (work) with the corresponding e-mail addresses.

The program is very flexible to suit your needs as a computer user.

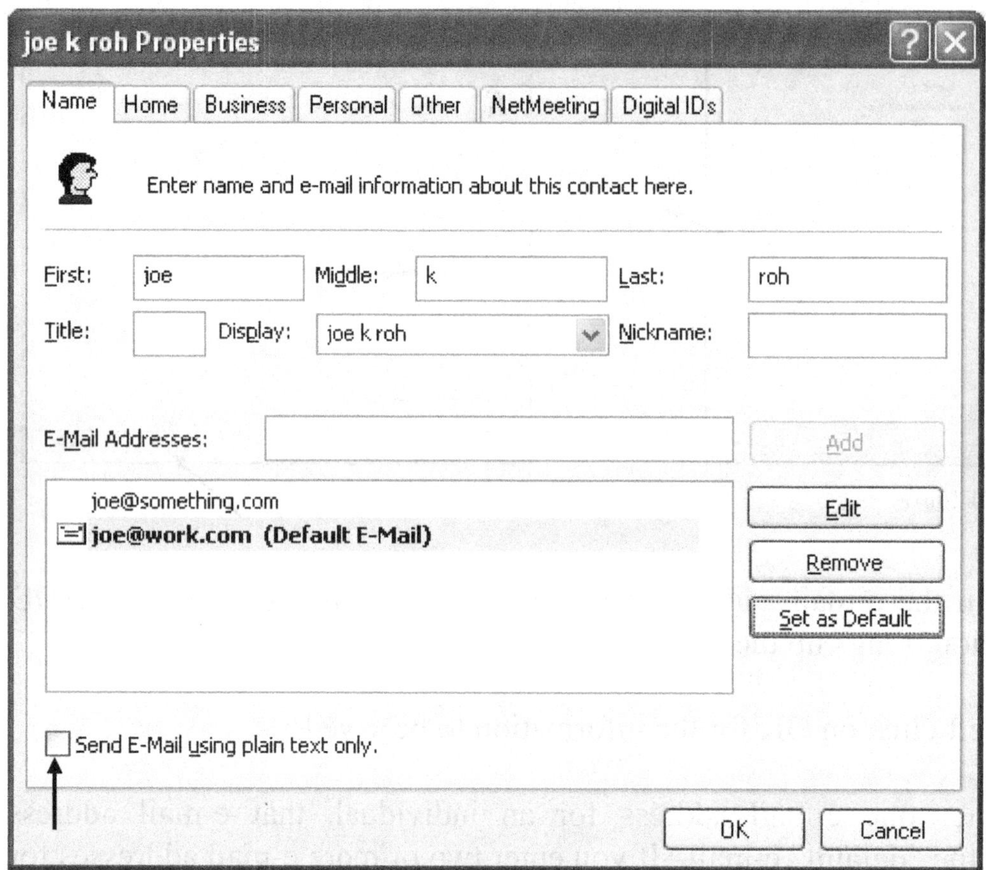

Figure 33 — E-mail address "Name tab" for a contact.

Please note the box in the lower left hand side of the figure above. If you place a check mark there by left clicking once, you will *always* send to this individual in "plain text." Unless you know this is specifically what you want to do with a particular individual, leave this box unchecked.

Before left clicking once on OK to enter the person into the address book, you may want to look at the other available tabs located at the top of the window. Beginners specifically may be interested in the Home, Business, Personal, and Other tabs.

Pictures of these other tabs follow.

                                        Use any and all information at your own risk.

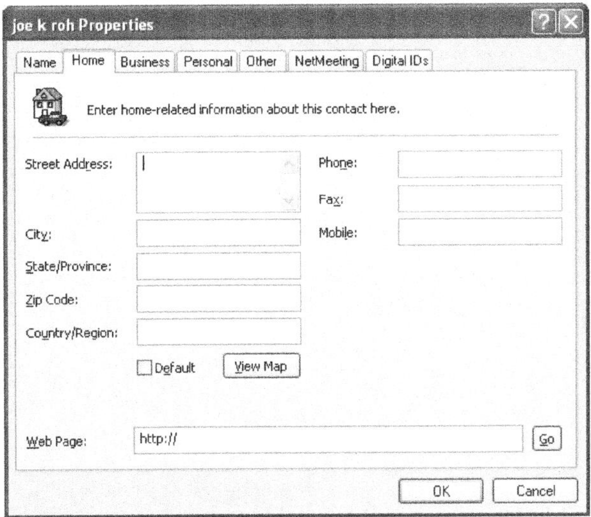

Figure 34 — "Home" tab.

This can be really useful for those of you who send out those yearly Holiday letters and cards. If you have all of your contacts and their snail-mail addresses entered into the Address Book, you can perform what is called a "mail merge" with a word processing software program allowing you to print labels or to print directly on envelopes. This is not exactly a beginner task although it is something you may aspire to learn how to do. As many do this task on an annual basis only, it is easy to forget what you learned how to do when the next mailing rolls around.

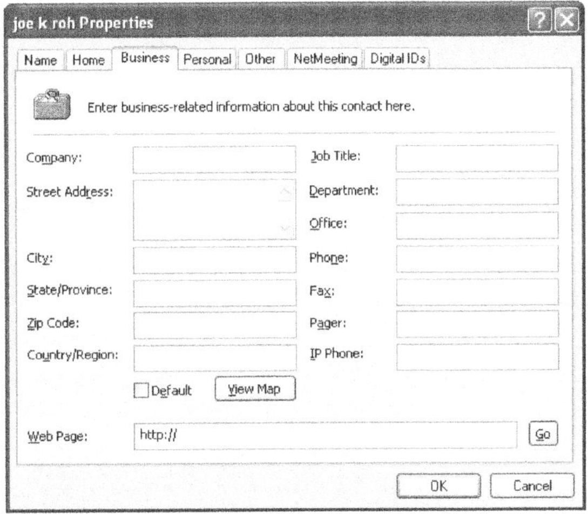

Figure 35 — "Business" tab.

This looks just like the "Home" tab, only this is for the individual's place of work and related information.

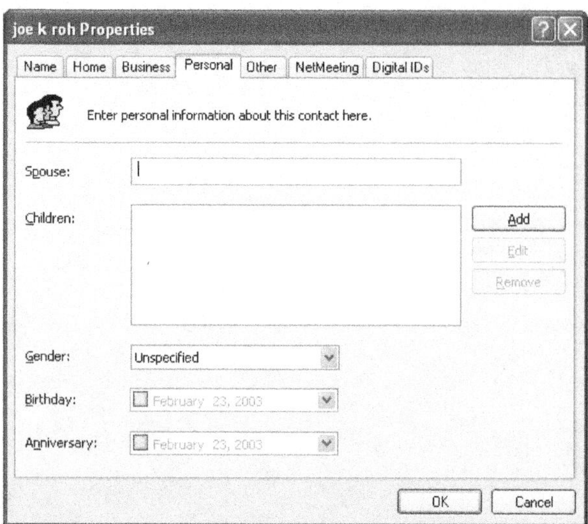

Figure 36 — "Personal" tab.

This is another wonderful feature of a database. Here is where you can put all that information that you have for family, friends, and colleagues, but maybe quite haven't decided how to organize it.

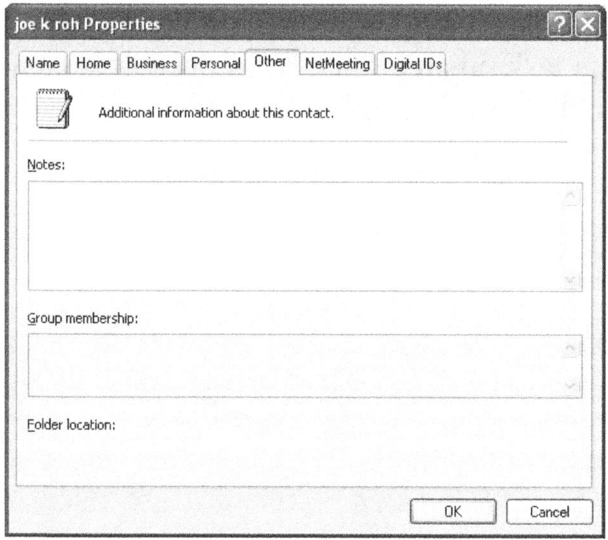

Figure 37 — "Other" tab.

Once again, just more room to put tidbits of information pertaining to an individual.

So when you are all done entering all your information on all the tabs, left click once on OK. Your contact is now entered.

                                   Use any and all information at your own risk.

Adding a Group

Earlier, as we began the process of entering a contact, there were three choices: a new contact, a new group, or a new folder.

Often times we like to send the same message to many people for many different reasons. This is when the "group" feature comes in handy. You might designate one group as your "Immediate Family." When something comes up that you want them all to know about, voila, you send one e-mail to many people — a *group* e-mail.

Here is how to create a group. First, open the address book from Outlook Express by left clicking on the Address Book icon in the tool bar.

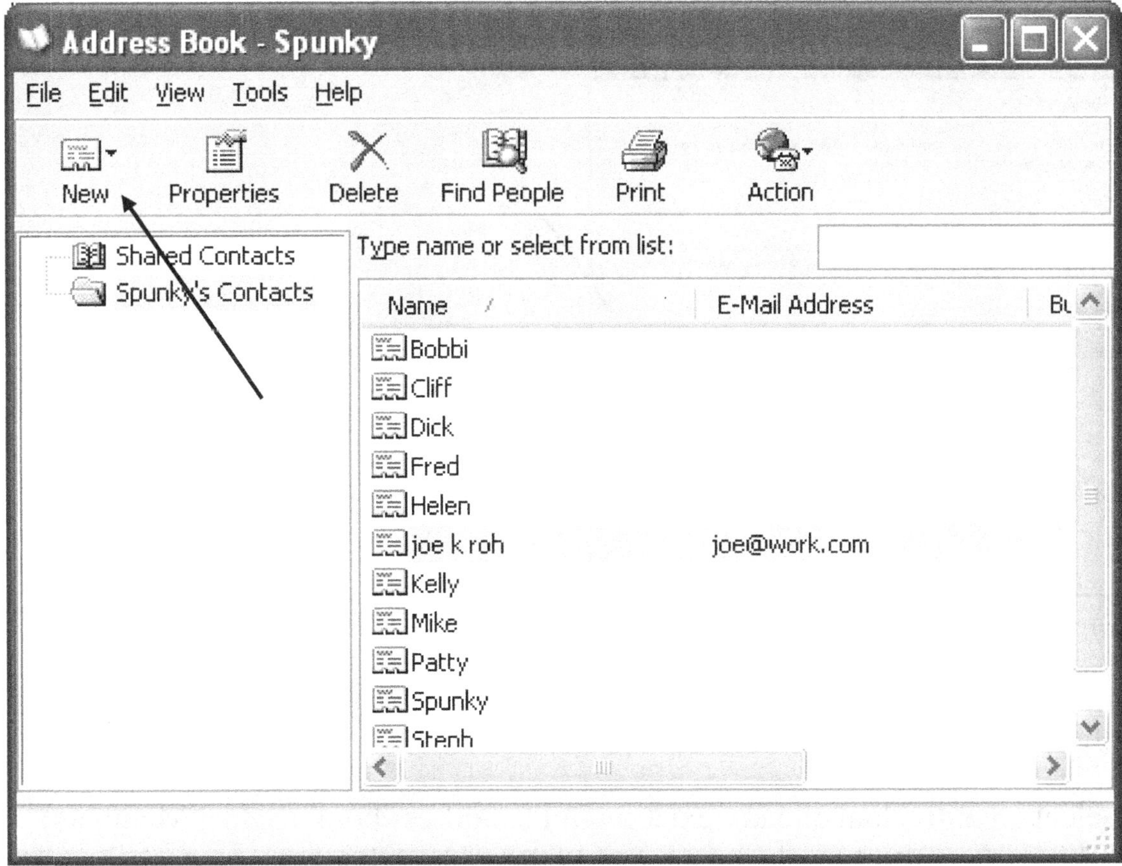

Figure 38 — Address Book.

Left click once on NEW. Left click once on NEW GROUP.

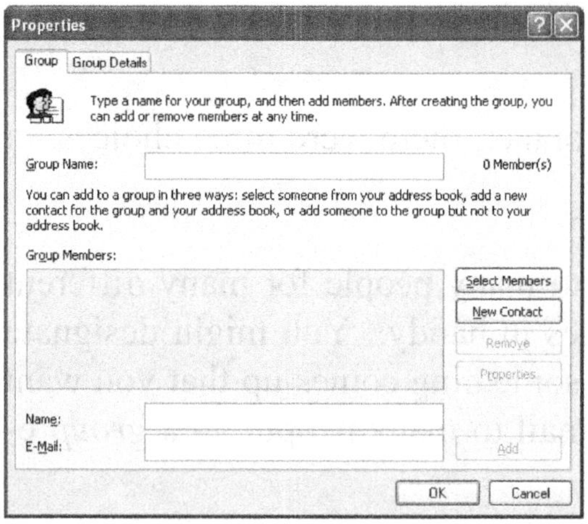

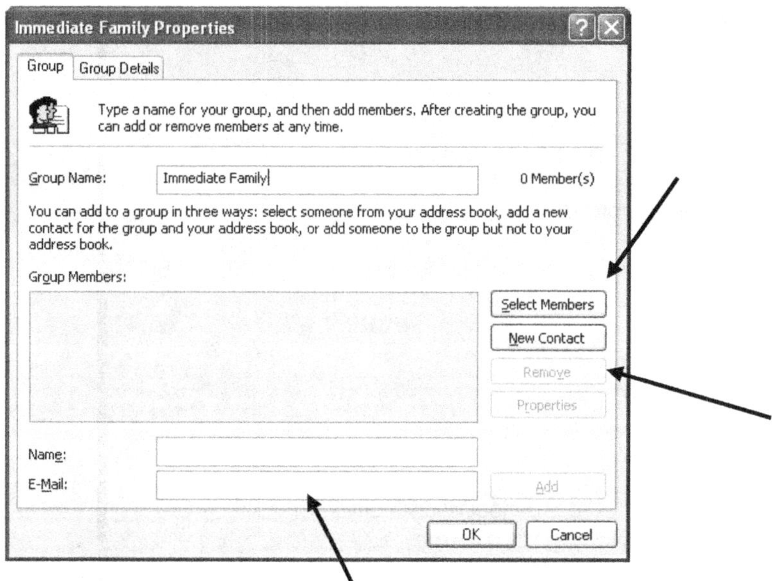

Figure 39 — A new group.

For our learning example, we call our new group "Immediate Family."

Figure 40 — Immediate Family Group.

You can add a contact to a group in 3 ways:

1. Select an individual already existing in the address book (Select Members).
2. Add a new contact for the group and to the address book.
3. Add an individual to the group and *not* to the address book.

For choice 1 left click once on "Select Members."

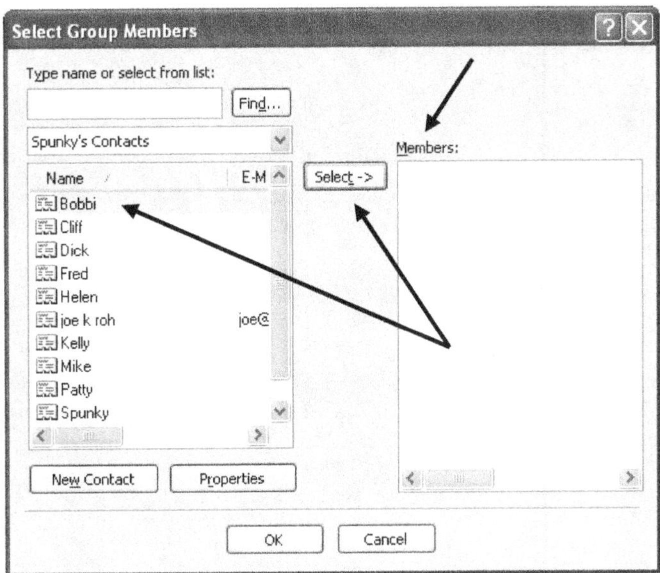

Figure 41 — Selection of group members directly from the address book.

Select an individual by left clicking the name once to highlight it. In this case we select "Bobbi." Then left click on the box entitled SELECT. That action will cause "Bobbi" to move to the right side of the window in the Member list.

- To select more than one contact at a time, select the first name you want to add to the group with one left click; then press and hold down the "CTRL" key (lower left side of the keyboard) as you left click once on the additional contacts you want to add to the group; then let go of the "CTRL" key. Then left click once on the box entitled SELECT. All the names that you have highlighted will move to the right side of the window.

- The "SHIFT" key works similarly. If you left click on the top name, then press and hold down the "SHIFT" key, and then left click once on the bottom name you will select or highlight all the names in between. You then left click on SELECT and all the names you have selected will move to the right side of the window.

The "Ctrl" key *controls* which names you select. The "Shift" key highlights all the names in between the top and bottom left clicks. When all the members you want to add to the group have been selected and are displayed in the right column, left click once on OK. That will bring up a window similar to the one on the next page.

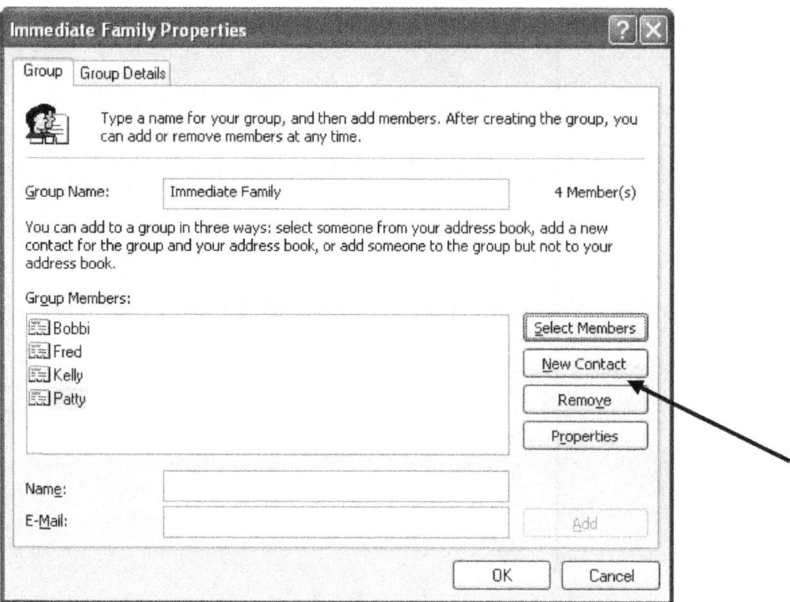

Figure 42 — Creation of a group.

To use the "New Contact" choice 2, left click once on the NEW CONTACT button. That action brings up a new contact properties window. After you enter all the information and left click once on OK, this contact is then entered into the Address Book and into the group.

Figure 43 — New contact properties window.

Here's how choice 3, entering an individual into the group only and not the Address Book works.

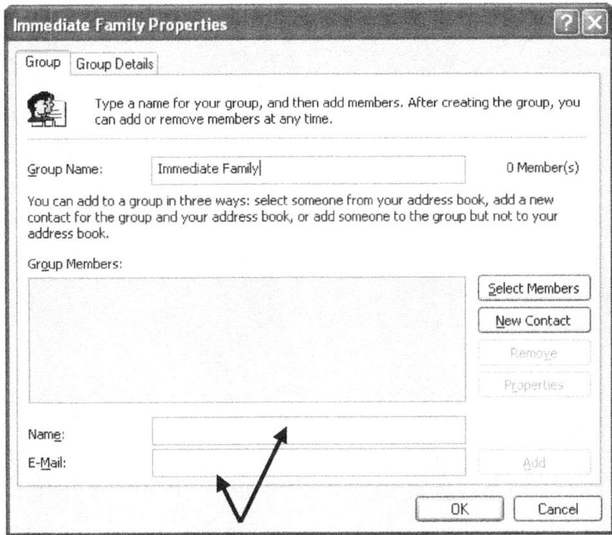

Figure 44 — Group properties window.

To enter an individual into the group and *not* the address book, you use the bottom two fields; the top one for their name and the bottom one for their e-mail address. You then left click once on OK and a figure similar to the one below appears. All the group members are listed.

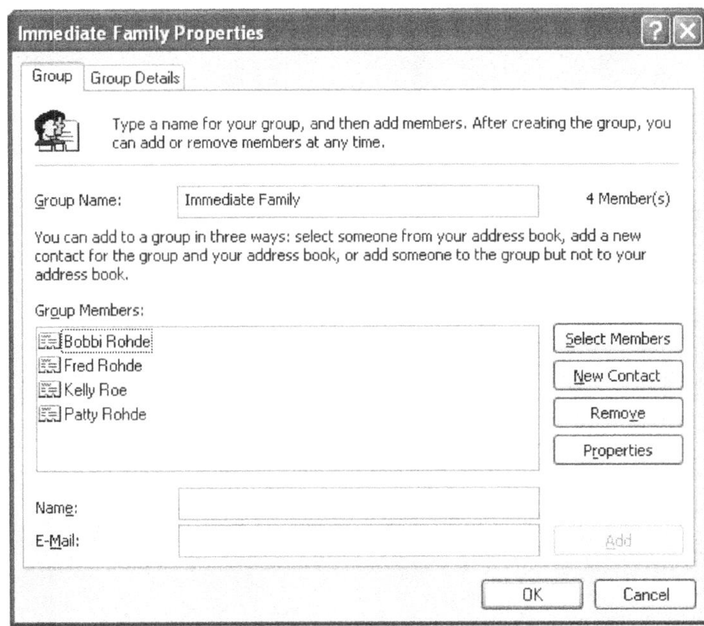

Figure 45 — Properties window for Immediate Family group.

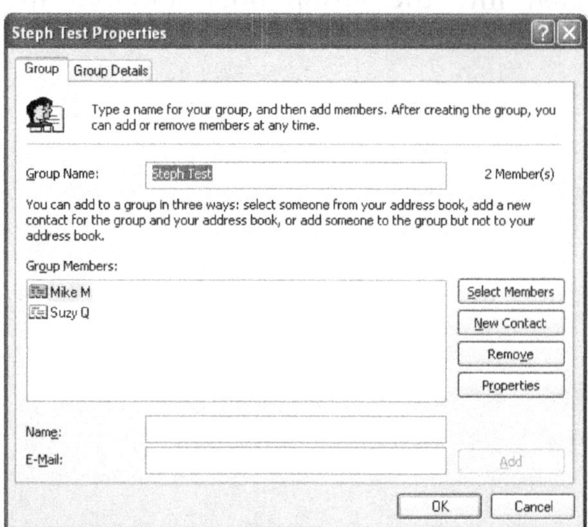

Figure 46 — Group Properties.

Choice 1 and Choice 2 group members are added as a green colored index card icon. Choice 3 group members are added as a blue colored index card icon; meaning they are part of the group and not part of the Address Book. This is difficult to visualize with black and white printing, however, if you enter individuals into groups using all three choices, you will see the difference in color on your computer screen. Left click once on OK.

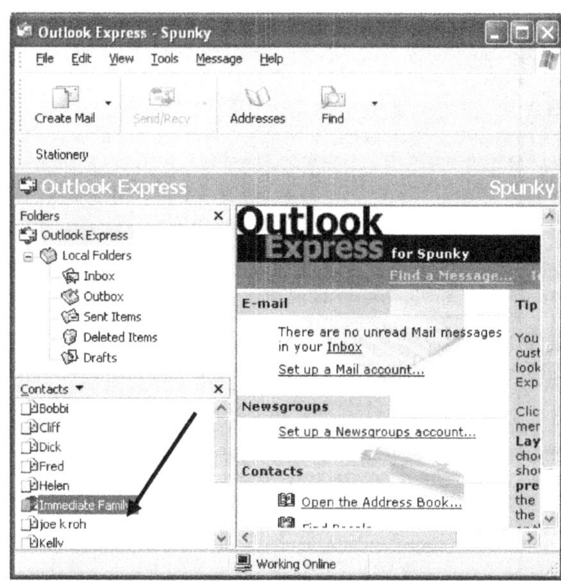

Figure 47 — Immediate Family group is in the address book.

The group is listed in the Address Book just as an individual would be.

                    Use any and all information at your own risk.

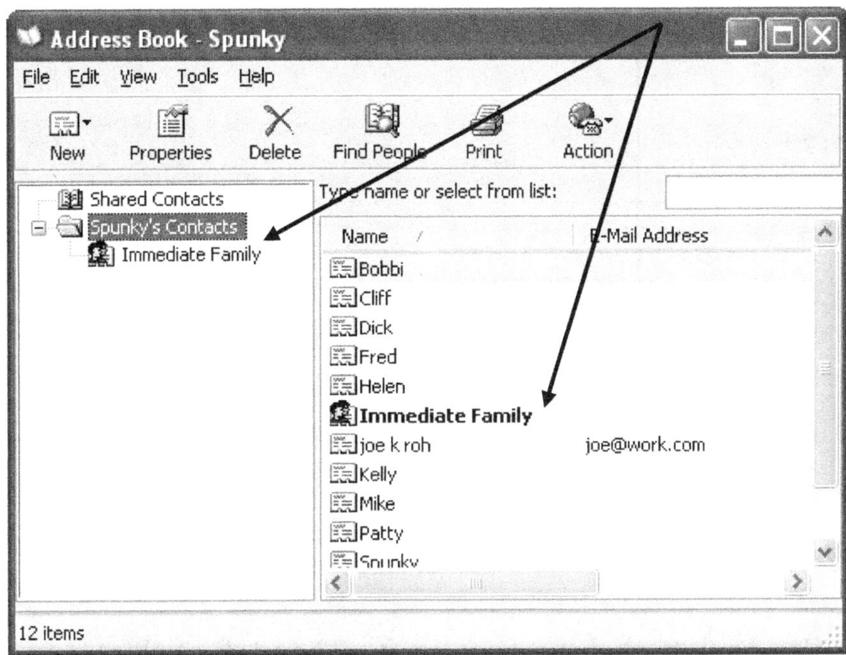

Figure 48 — Immediate Family group is in the Address Book.

To send an e-mail message to the new group Immediate Family, left click once on CREATE MAIL.

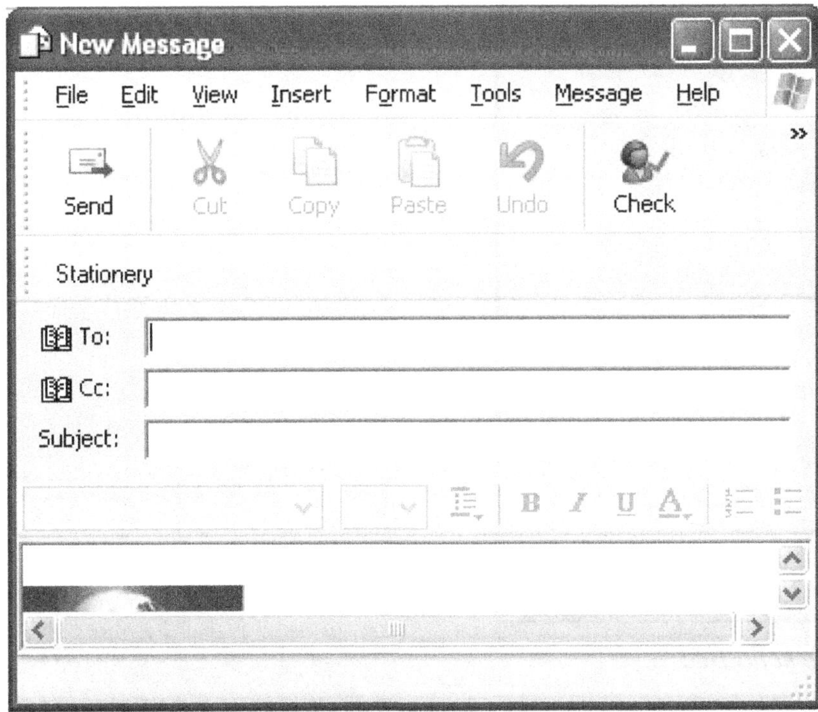

Figure 49 — New e-mail message.

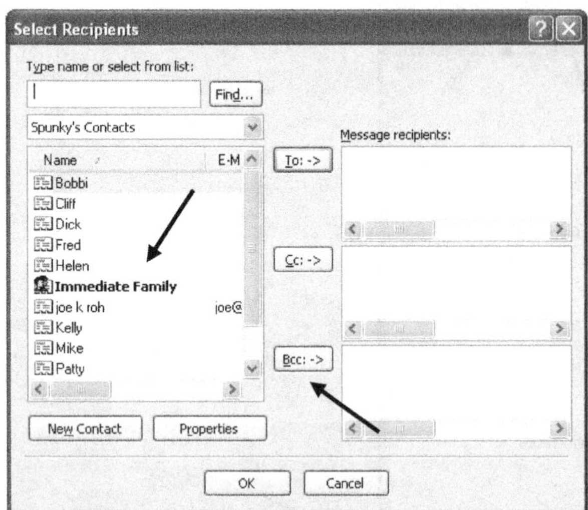

Figure 50 — Address Book from within a newly created e-mail message.

Select the "Immediate Family" by left clicking once on it. Then left click once on the "Bcc:" box. When sending to more than one person do not use "To:" or "Cc:" because when you do, all the e-mail addresses are out there for the world to see, capture, or harvest for telemarketing (Chapter 6). The safe and respectful field to use to send to more than one person is the "Bcc:" field.

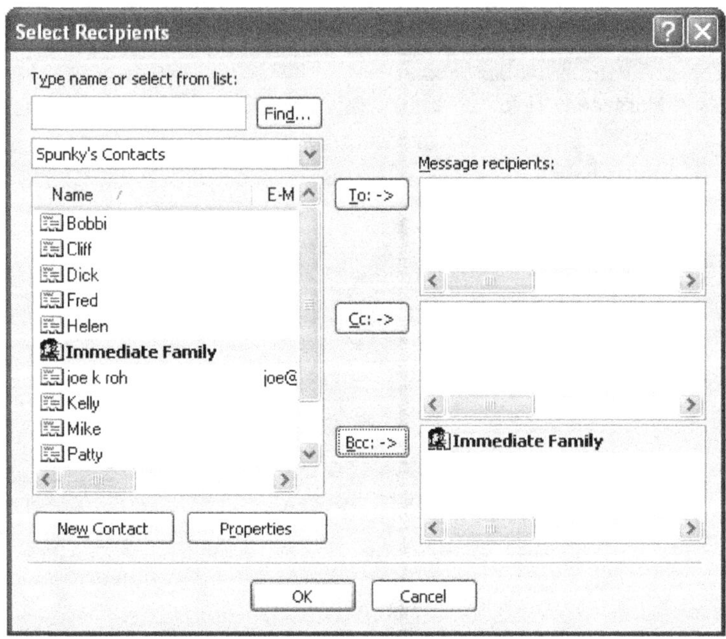

Figure 51 — Selecting a group to send Bcc.

Left click once on OK.

 Use any and all information at your own risk.

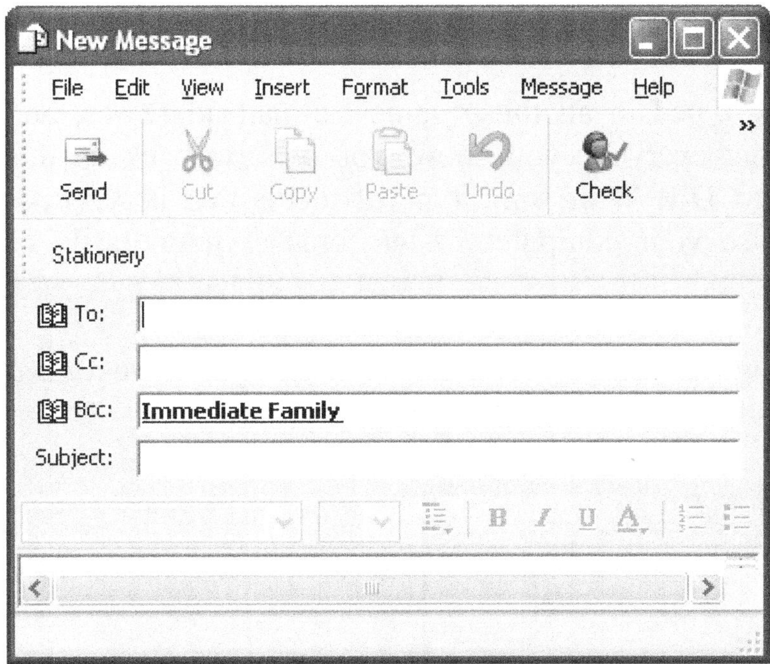

Figure 52 — Respectful e-mailing to more than one individual.

You send the message "To:" yourself and "Bcc:" everyone else for respectful e-mailing.

If the "Bcc:" field is not visible in your e-mail messages, open a new e-mail message. Left click once on VIEW, and then left click once on ALL HEADERS.

Backing Up

After you have conscientiously typed in all those names, e-mail addresses, and other pertinent information about everyone you know, you want to back up this information to a floppy disk, a CD-RW, or some type of media that is *separate from* your computer just in case your computer system crashes temporarily or permanently.

You might also consider printing out your entire address book so you have a *hard* copy. How to print the Address Book is covered later in this chapter.

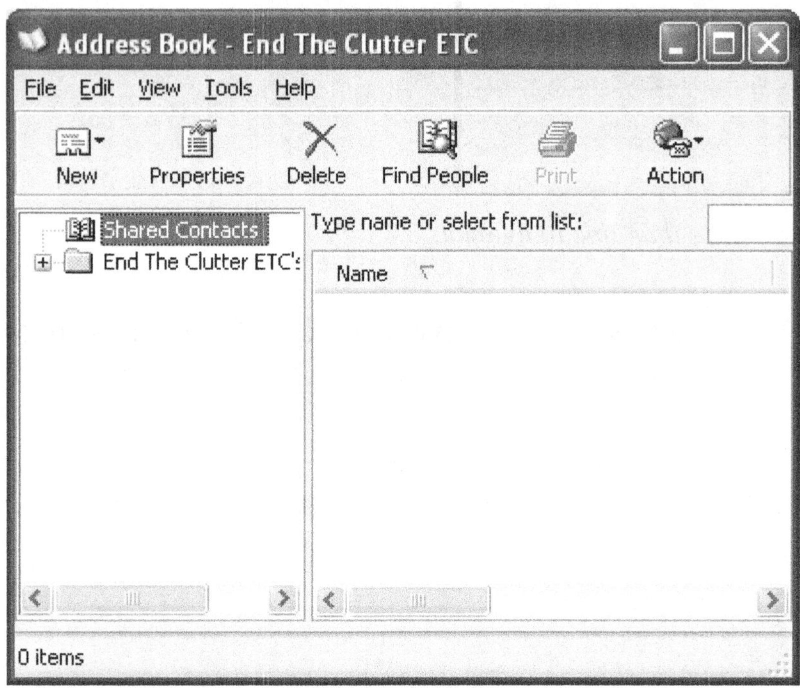

Figure 53 — Address Book.

Here is one way to back up the address book. Open the address book: Left click once on FILE; left click on EXPORT; left click on ADDRESS BOOK (WAB).

> Performing this action can be different on every computer. If at any time you do not feel comfortable in doing something, please do not do it. Ask someone who you believe to be qualified for assistance. The optimal situation is to have an individual in the room with you while you are in front of your computer. Assistance over the telephone is an option, but sometimes causes more confusion than help.

          Use any and all information at your own risk.

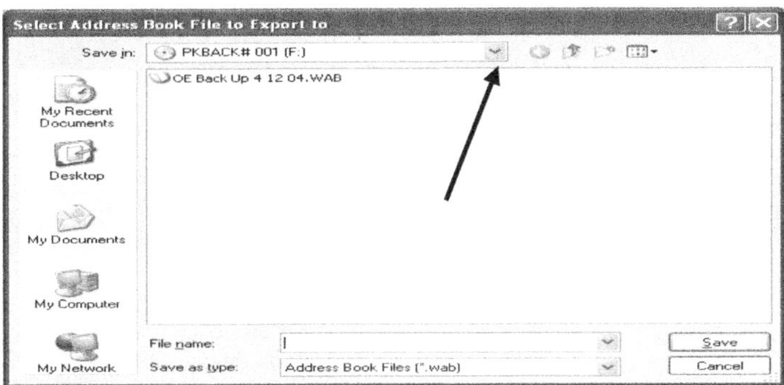

Figure 54 — Where you are exporting to.

Backing up the Address Book also means copying the Address Book and putting this copy somewhere else. When you tell the computer to "export" the Address Book, the computer asks you via something like the figure above "Where do you want to put the copy of the Address Book?" The above figure is the kind of window you are going to see under many circumstances, not just in this case of backing up the Address Book, so understanding what this means is very important.

The arrow above is pointing to a "directional down-arrow." When you left click once on that directional down-arrow, a sub-menu will appear. The sub-menu that appears is different on every computer because that sub-menu is a snapshot of your entire and unique computer system. In the example above, the "F:" drive is selected as the place the copy of the Address Book is going to go; and the "F:" drive happens to be a CD-RW drive on the computer writing this book. Recommend you back up anything and everything to a CD-RW disc if you have the capability to do so. If not, a CD-R disc, or floppy diskette will also suffice; but back up to something that can be removed from your computer in the unlikely event your computer malfunctions in some way.

The snapshot of your computer system lets you choose where you want this "backup" copy to go. In this example it is the "F:" drive. If you are backing up to a floppy disk, the drive may be the "A:" drive. For example sake, let's say we wanted to back up to a different drive than the one currently showing — like to the floppy "A:" drive. In that case you would left click once on the directional down-arrow and then left click on "A:" drive. If you want to save the backup to your Desktop just to see how the process works, left click on the directional down-arrow, then left click on "Desktop.: Often times the sub-menu that appears, has its own scroll bar and you may have to scroll up or down to find the choice you are looking for like "A:" drive or the Desktop.

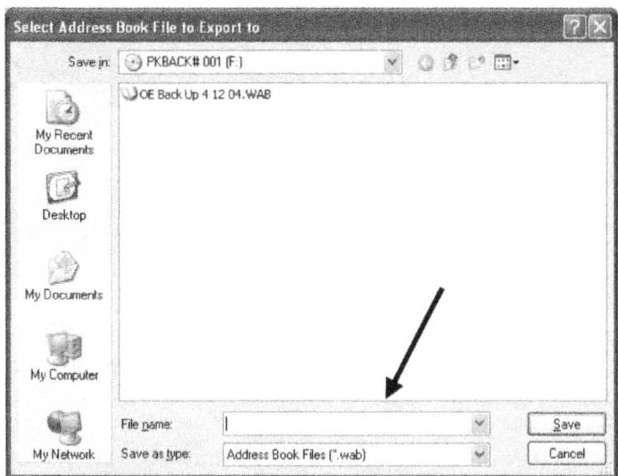

Figure 55 — What is the name of the backup?

After you decide *where* the backup is going, there are two other things to do. The first is to give this backup a file name — something like "Address Book Backup" is always an option. You can name the file just about anything you want; it just needs to make sense to you in the event you ever have to go looking for this file you hopefully will have an idea of what name you gave it. The computer is a bit finicky about certain characters or symbols used in file names so if you get a message telling you that you used an improper character or symbol, please change your file name to make the computer happy.

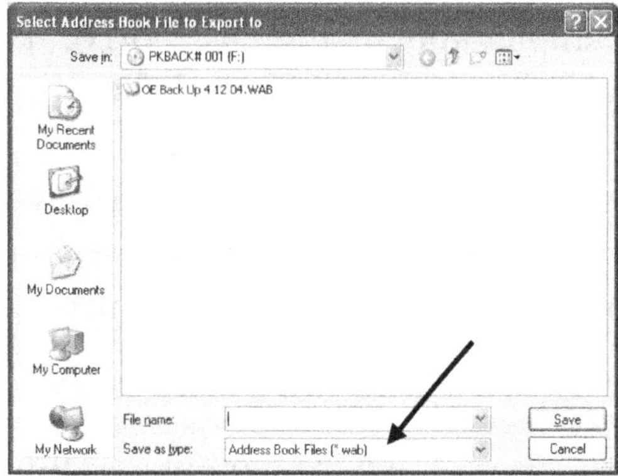

Figure 56 — What is the file extension?

The second thing is to check the file type or extension which in this example is ".wab" which Outlook Express uses for Address Book files. When you are ready left click once on SAVE.

You will be told by the computer that the address book has been backed up. Please note that this is just one way to back up the address book and these instructions may not work exactly the same on your computer.

                                           Use any and all information at your own risk.

Organizing

You can sort your contacts by name, e-mail address, home or business phone number.

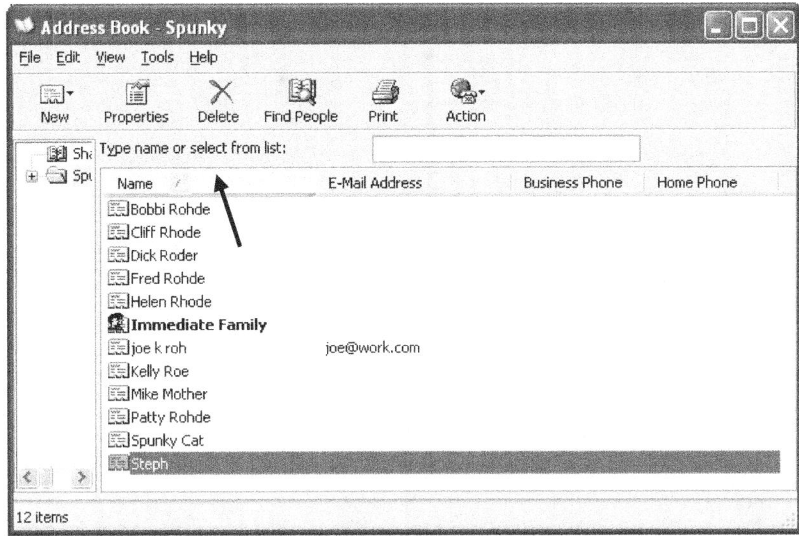

Figure 57 — Sorted by first name, ascending order.

By left clicking repeatedly on the column heading "Name," you will alternate the sorting process by first name, last name, and ascending or descending order. See the following three figures as well.

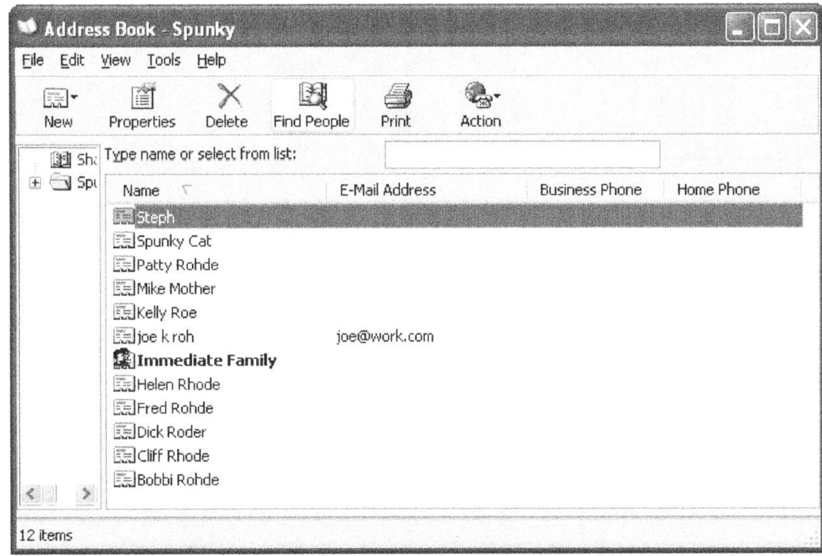

Figure 58 — Sorted first name descending order.

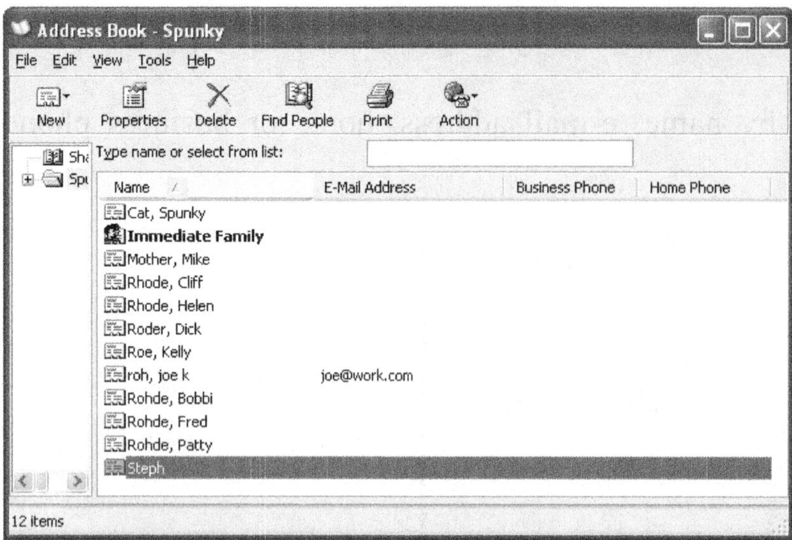

Figure 59 — Sorted last name ascending.

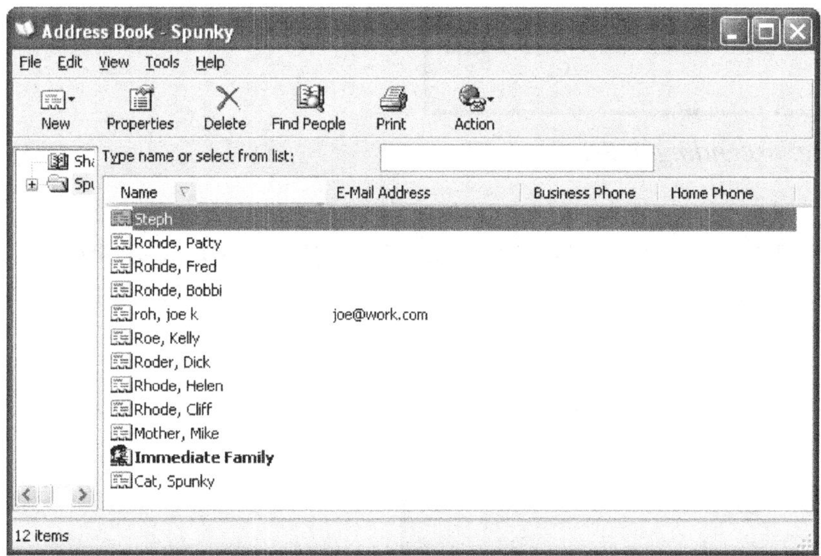

Figure 60 — Sorted last name descending.

Since the top entry "Steph" does not have a last name entered into the Address Book, it appears on top. This would be true of any other contacts entered without a "last name" field filled in.

To sort by e-mail address (ascending or descending), left click continually on the e-mail column heading.

The process works similarly to sort by the business or home phone numbers.

                                              Use any and all information at your own risk.

You can also change the order of the columns. Notice how in the figure below, the order of the columns is Name, E-mail Address, Business Phone, and Home Phone. Here is how to move the E-mail Address Column all the way to the left if you want.

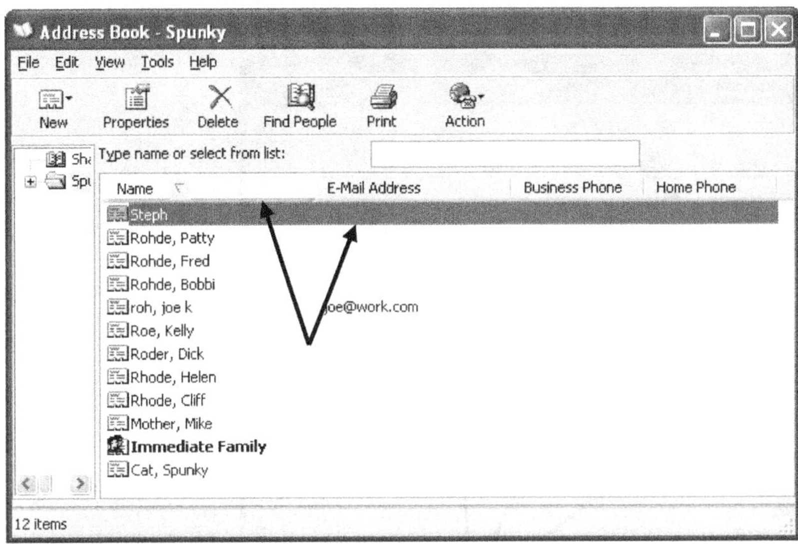

Figure 61 — "Name column all the way to the left.

To move the "E-mail" column all the way to the left, point the mouse to the middle of the column that says "E-mail Address." Once the mouse pointer is there, left click once, HOLD that click, and drag directly to the left. You will see the column move. Then let go of the click. This works similarly to move any column in the address book.

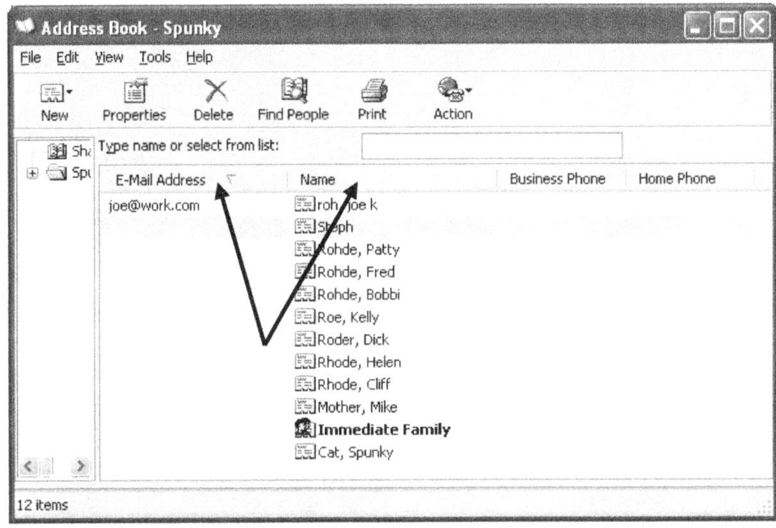

Figure 62 — "E-mail" column is now all the way to the left.

You can also change the width of the columns. Notice the dividing lines between the column headings. *Without* clicking move the mouse pointer towards one column dividing line. As the pointer gets near to a dividing line, it will turn into a double-edged arrow. At that point left click once, HOLD the click and slowly move the mouse to the left or right to make the column wider or narrower.

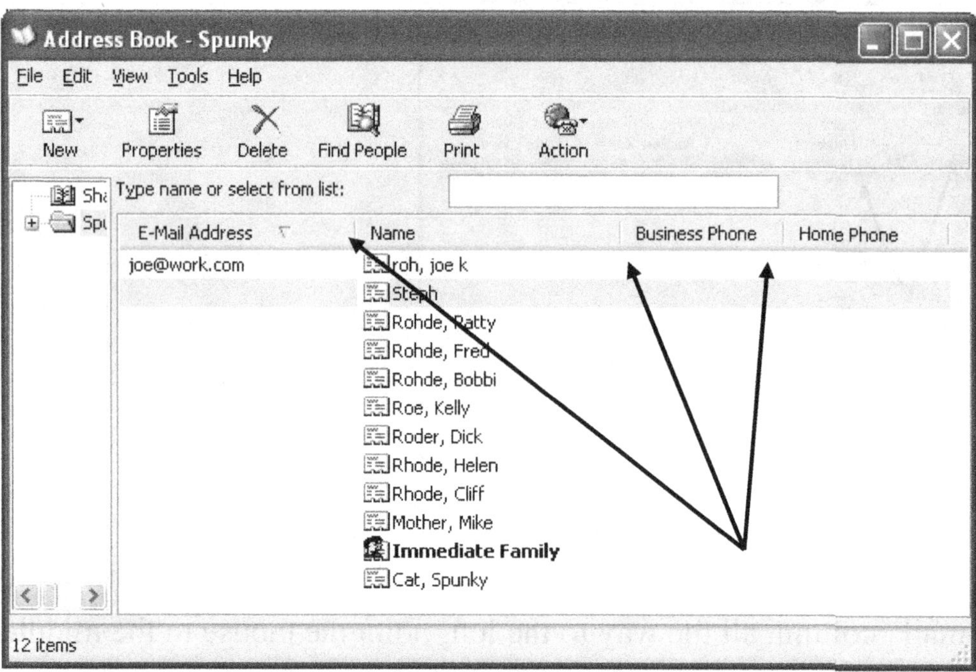

Figure 63 — Changing the width of the columns.

Printing

It's always a good idea to have a "hard" copy backup of the Address Book. Open the Address Book through Outlook Express and then left click once on ADDRESSES.

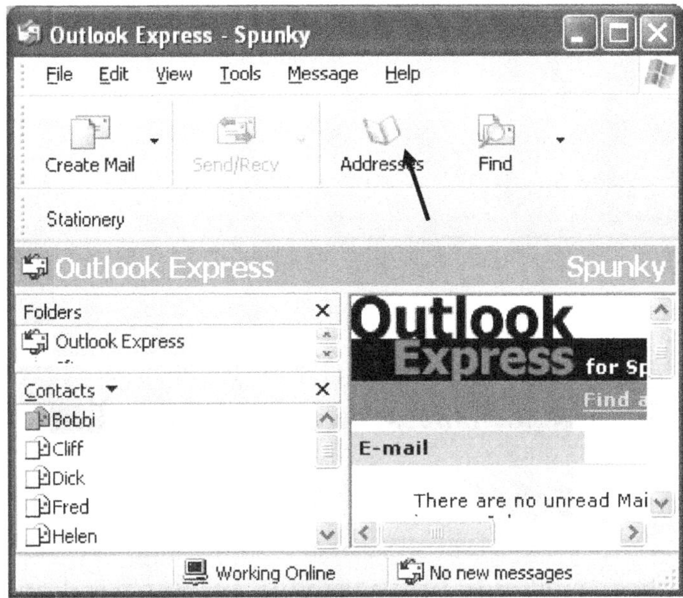

Figure 64 — Outlook Express main screen "view."

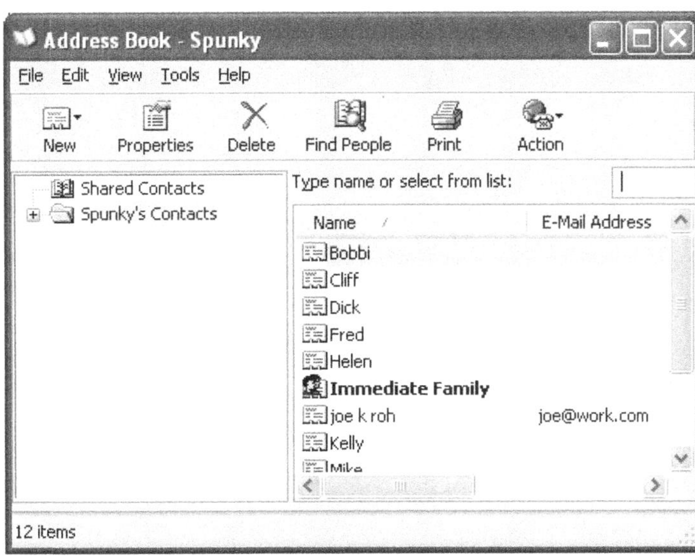

Figure 65 — Address Book.

There are several ways to get to the "print" window to print the Address Book.

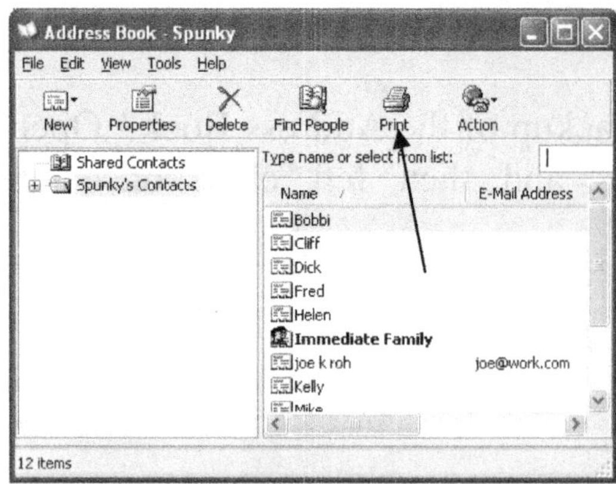

Figure 66 — Address Book.

Here are three ways:

1. Left click once on FILE and then left click once on PRINT.
2. Press down and hold the CTRL key and then press the letter "P" and then let go of both keys.
3. Left click once on the Print Icon.

On most computers any of the above choices *should* bring up your printer window. Please note that on some computers left clicking the Printer Icon may automatically begin printing without bringing up a printer window like the one below.

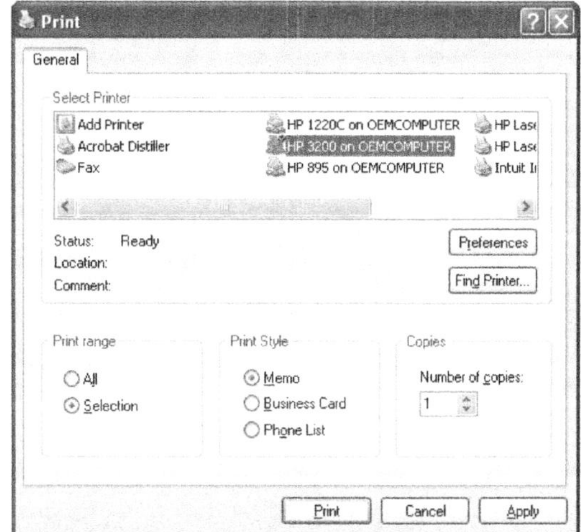

Figure 67 — Print window.

The print window is completely different with every computer system and printer.

                    Use any and all information at your own risk.

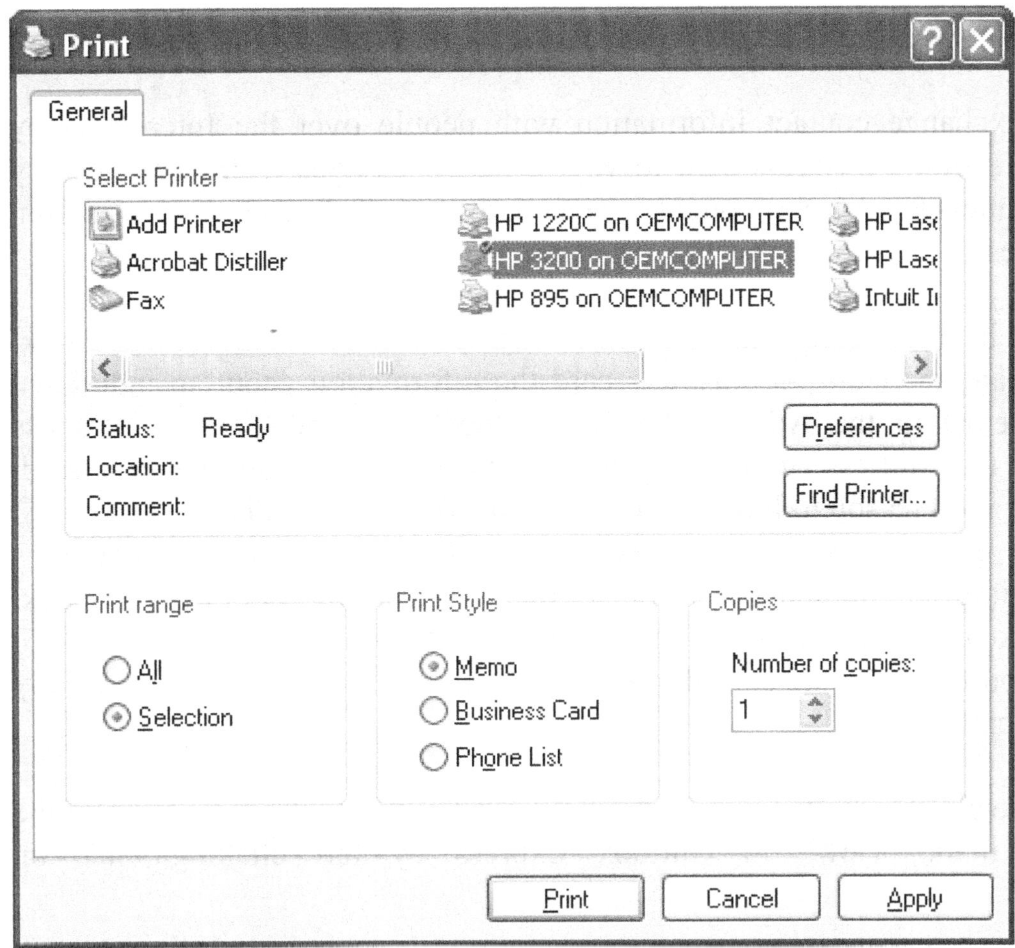

Figure 68 — Print window.

The "Print range" section tells the computer to print *all* of the contacts or just a selected few — those you have selected or highlighted prior to executing the print command. You can select more than one individual by holding down the "CTRL" key as you left click once on each contact name that you wish to select.

The "Print Style" section allows you three specific options:

1. Memo — prints all available information about the contacts.
2. Business Card — prints business related information only.
3. Phone List — prints a list of phones numbers.

After you tell the computer how many copies you want of the Address Book, left click once on PRINT.

Electronic Business Cards

One way to exchange contact information with people over the Internet is by attaching an electronic business card to your e-mail messages. This can be very helpful for businesses. An electronic business card is actually contact information from the Address Book stored in what is called a "vCard" format.

The electronic business card feature is initialized from within the Address Book. In order to create an electronic business card the information about an individual must already exist in the Address Book. Without your personal or business information in the Address Book, you cannot send your electronic business card; hence, another good reason to have *you* entered into your Address Book.

You can send information about any contact that you have in your Address Book; not just *your* contact information. So please remember it is helpful to send e-mail messages to you first to make sure that what you think you are sending is actually what you are sending.

To initialize the electronic business card function, open the Address Book from the Tool bar in main "view" in Outlook Express by left clicking once on ADDRESSES.

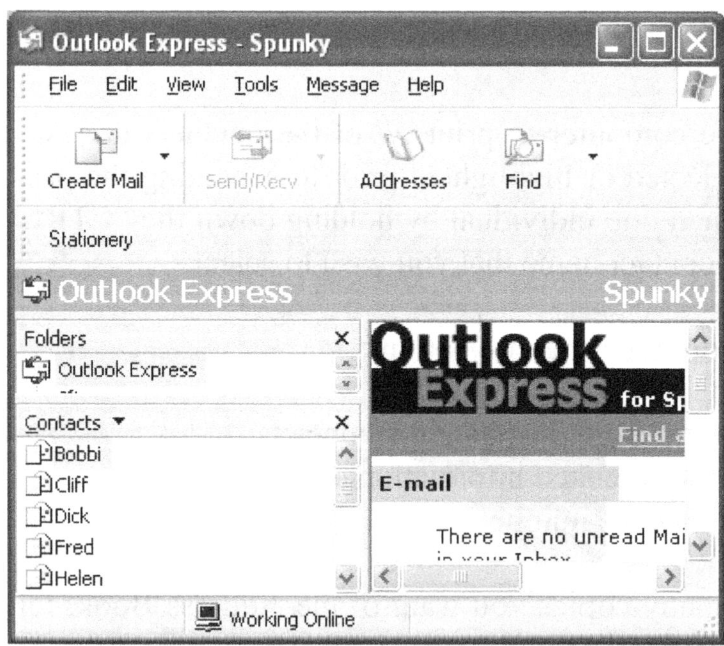

Figure 69 — Outlook Express main screen "view."

                    Use any and all information at your own risk.

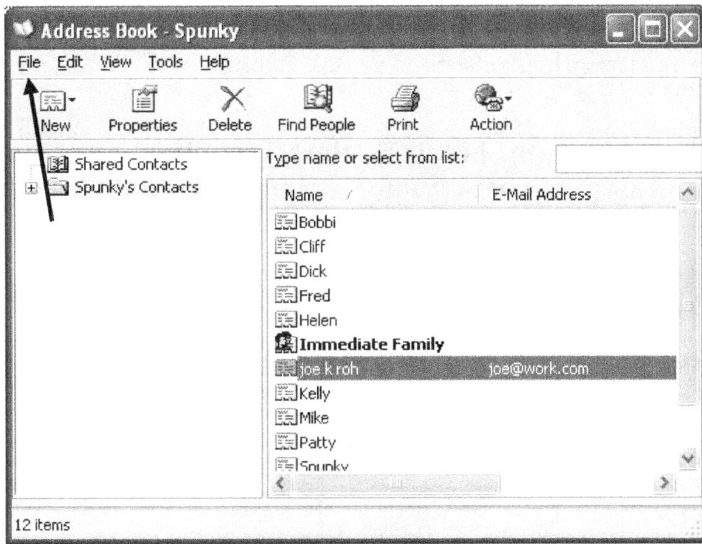

Figure 70 — Address Book.

For this example, we select "joe k roh" as our contact. In your address book, select your name with one left click. Then left click once on FILE (black arrow above), left click once on EXPORT, and left click once on BUSINESS CARD (vCard). A figure similar to the one below appears.

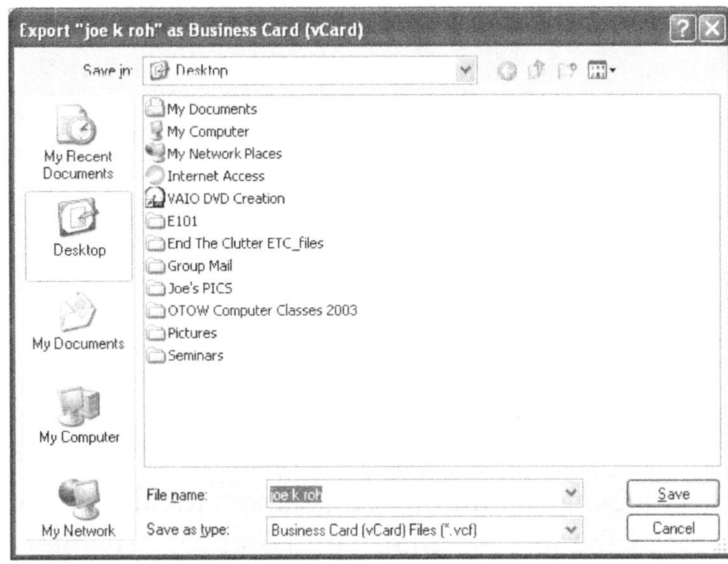

Figure 71 — Saving business card files.

When in doubt save to the "desktop." You can always move it later. Once you have left clicked on SAVE, the electronic business card function exists and is active.

You have the option of an electronic business card going with every e-mail you send or not. You can send an electronic business card for you or for any contact in your Address Book once this feature is turned on.

From the main screen view, left click once on TOOLS, then left click once on OPTIONS, and then left click once on the COMPOSE tab.

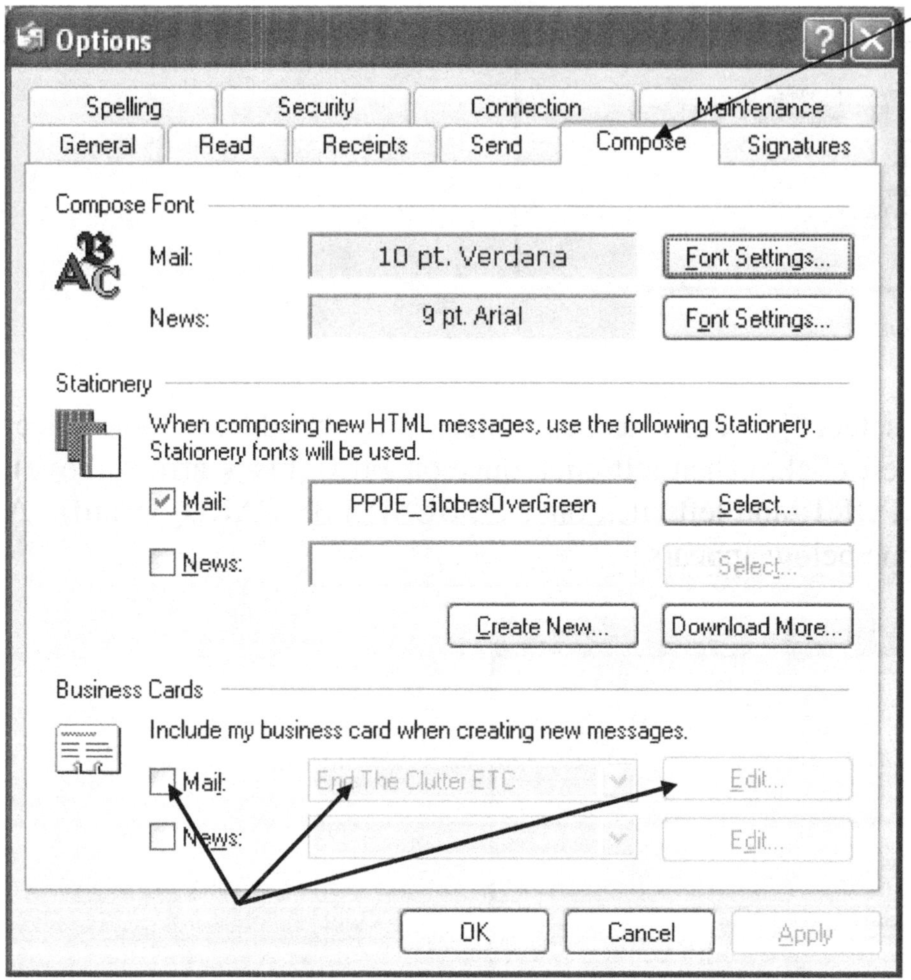

Figure 72 — "Compose" tab.

If you want your business card sent with every e-mail message automatically, place a check mark in the box immediately to the left of "Mail" in the lower "Business Cards" section. That action makes the next two fields active and not dimmed. If you left click once one the EDIT button, it opens up that particular contact for any modification.

The figure on the next page shows those two fields as active.

                    Use any and all information at your own risk.

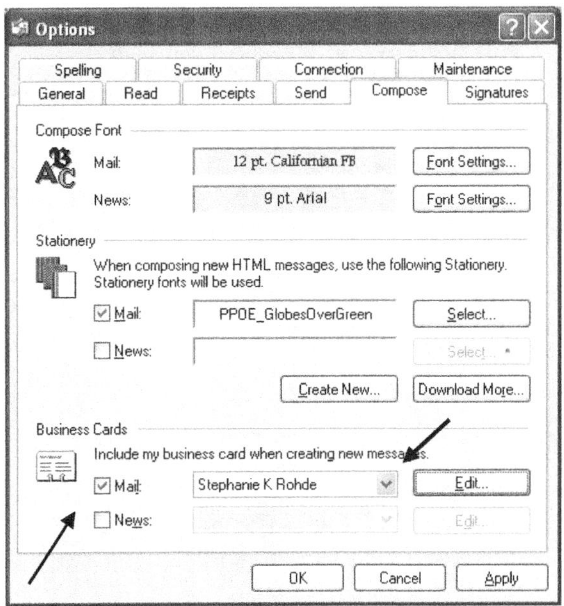

Figure 73 — "Compose" tab.

Notice the directional down-arrow. Left clicking on that arrow displays every one of your contacts. Whatever contact name is selected here is the one that is sent along with your e-mails when there is a check mark in the box immediately to the left of "Mail." Make sure you have the contact you want displayed.

Please refer to Chapter 6 for further clarification on sending electronic business cards with your e-mail.

Chapter 6 — Sending E-mail

Replying to and/or *forwarding* e-mail you have received are just another form of sending e-mail and are discussed in Chapter 7. This chapter teaches the absolute basics of sending e-mail with Outlook Express; specifically e-mail that you create from scratch. Everything discussed in this chapter applies to *replies* and *forwards* as well.

E-mail Message Screen View & Layout

In Chapter 2, the main screen view of Outlook Express was explained. Here we discuss the e-mail screen view.

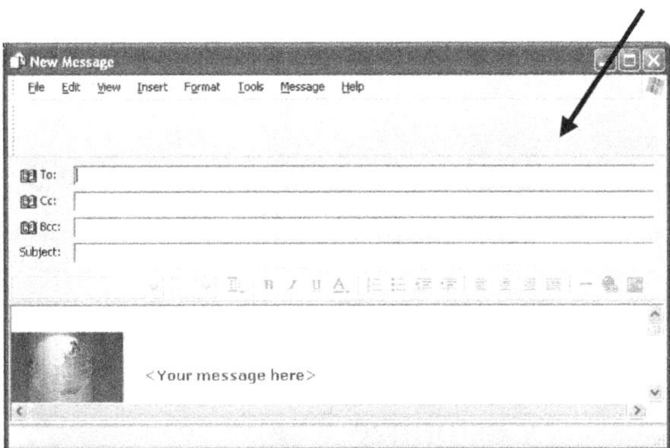

Figure 74 — E-mail message screen without toolbar showing.

The black arrow above is pointing to the space where items of the toolbar are displayed when the e-mail message toolbar feature is showing. You don't have to have the e-mail message toolbar showing; you can use the menu bar for e-mail functions. See arrow below pointing at the menu bar.

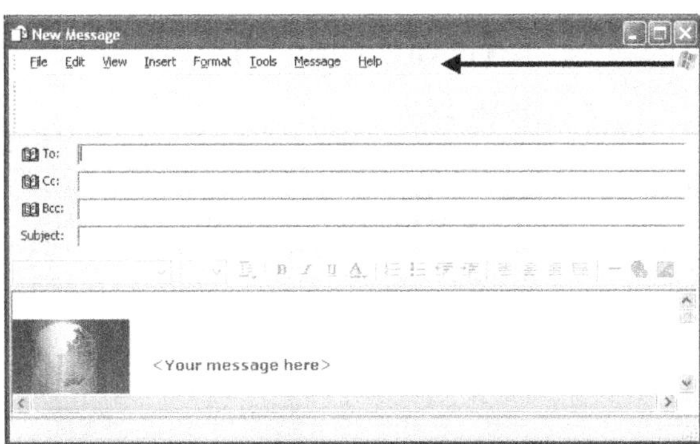

Figure 75 — E-mail message screen.

Many however, find the e-mail toolbar function helpful as well as convenient. If you *right* click once in the e-mail message toolbar area, there are two possible selections about the toolbar for you to choose:

1. Toolbar
2. Customize

When you right click, and there is a check mark to the left of the word "Toolbar," that means the Toolbar is currently visible in your e-mail messages. Absence of the check mark means the Toolbar is not currently visible in your e-mail messages.

If you want the Toolbar to be visible in your e-mail messages when it currently is not, following the right click, left click once on TOOLBAR. See figure below.

To customize the Toolbar for your needs, after the right click, left click once on CUSTOMIZE.

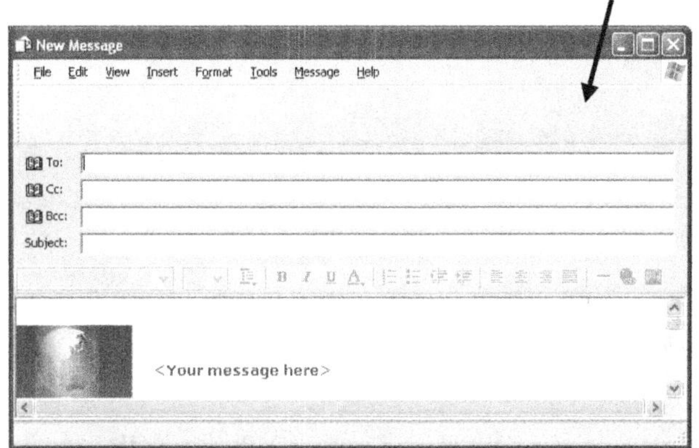

Figure 76 — E-mail message screen.

Right click once to reveal your choices of:

Toolbar

Customize

Ignore "Views Bar" option.

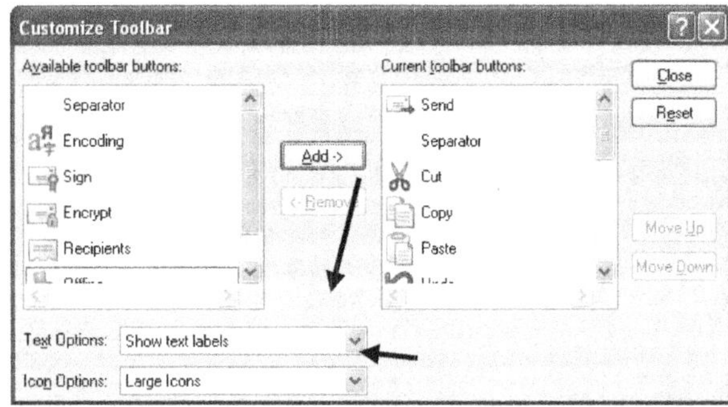

Figure 77 — Customize Toolbar window.

Display options are to show text labels, selective text on right or no text labels.

The display icons may be large or small.

When you left click on CUSTOMIZE, a window like the figure above is displayed.

      Use any and all information at your own risk.

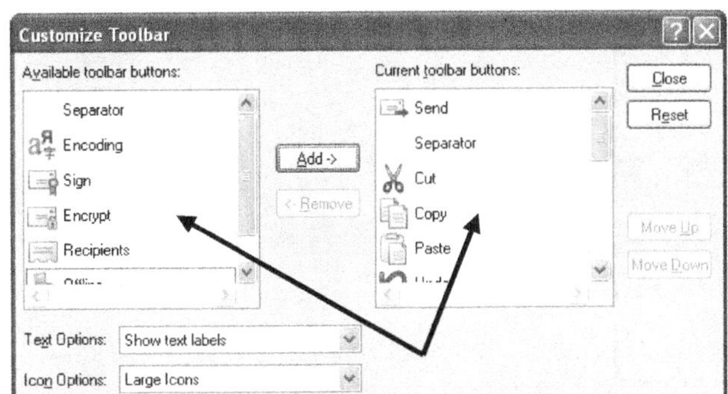

Figure 78 — Customize Toolbar window.

Customizing the e-mail message tool bar is extremely similar to how you can customize your main screen view toolbar introduced back in Chapter 2.

The left side of the figure above lists all the possible options that you can have displayed on your e-mail message screen tool bar when you have this toolbar showing in your e-mail message screen view. The right side lists the choices that were placed there by you or were set initially by Outlook Express programmers. You can completely customize what options you want and how you want them placed on this toolbar.

Customize E-mail Screen Toolbar

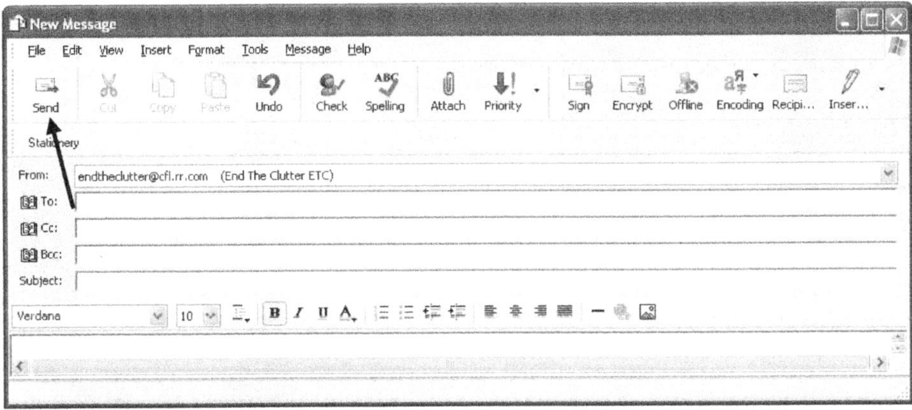

Figure 79 — New e-mail message.

Send

When you are ready to send your e-mail message, this is the button that you left click on once. If the send button is not showing, you can left click once on FILE, and then left click on "SEND MESSAGE" or press and hold down the ALT key and then press the "S" key.

Figure 80 — New e-mail message.

Cut, Copy, and Paste

Please refer to Appendix D for further explanation of blocking text, as well as cut, copy, and paste. The cut, copy, and paste icons displayed above to the right of the "Send" button are not active in this example. They will not be active on your computer either unless you have something selected, highlighted, or blocked in the "Text" portion of an e-mail message.

Figure 81 — New e-mail message.

Undo

This command is really handy in any program that makes it available. If you do something within an e-mail message that you don't like, one left click on this button will take you back to immediately where you were before. In your e-mail message, you can undo many times, often back to the very beginning of your message. Try this command and get familiar with it. You can also left click on EDIT, and then left click on UNDO or press and hold the CTRL key while you press the "Z" key.

Be very conscious and go slowly so you can see the changes via the command.

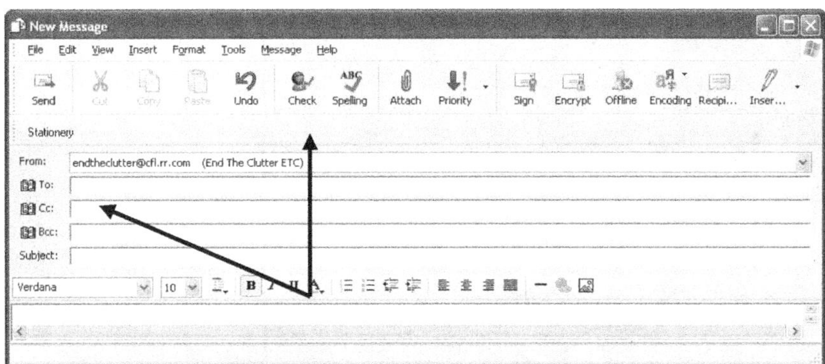

Figure 82 — New e-mail message.

Check

If you begin to type an e-mail address and can only remember part of it, by left clicking once on the "Check" button, the program will confirm if that address exists in your address book and if so will fill in the rest of the e-mail address for you. It is optimal *not* to type in e-mail addresses. Get used to using your address book for this task.

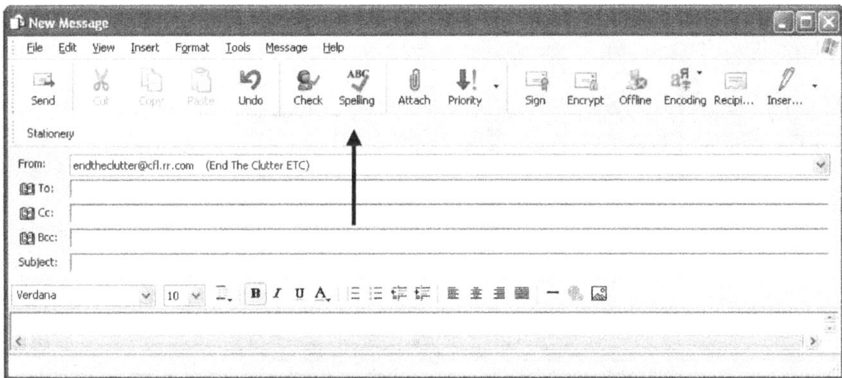

Figure 83 — New e-mail message.

Spelling

Outlook Express does not have its own "built in" spelling checker and therefore this option may not be available to you on your computer unless you have Microsoft Word, Excel, or PowerPoint installed. To customize the spell checker if available, in the main screen view (not an e-mail message window) left click once on TOOLS, then left click once on OPTIONS, and then left click once on the "Spelling" tab.

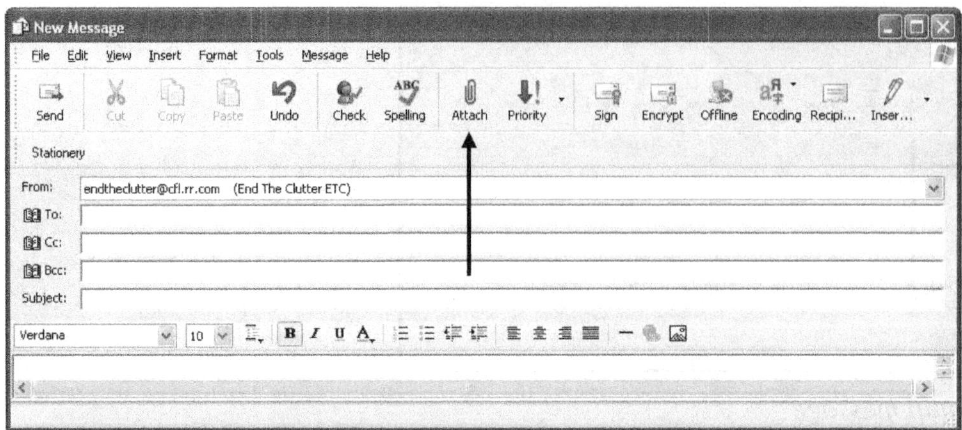

Figure 84 — New e-mail message.

Attach

This is one button to become intimately familiar with. This is one way to attach all those pictures and files to send to family and friends.

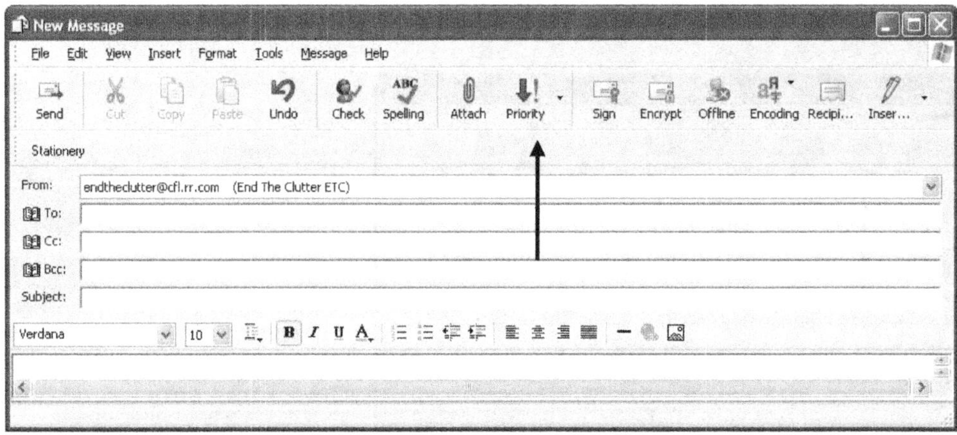

Figure 85 — New e-mail message.

Priority

This button allows you to determine the priority of the e-mail message you are sending. Your options are low, normal, and high. The program is automatically set on "normal" priority.

Left click on the directional down arrow to the left of where it says "Priority" to make your selection of low, normal, or high.

                                             Use any and all information at your own risk.

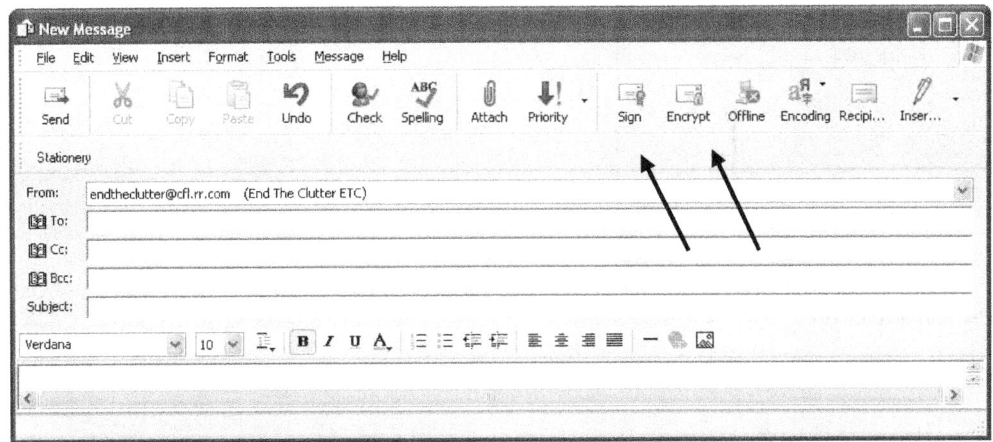

Figure 86 — New e-mail message.

Sign

This button allows you to digitally sign an e-mail message and is beyond the scope of this book.

Encrypt

This button allows you to encrypt an e-mail message and is beyond the scope of this book.

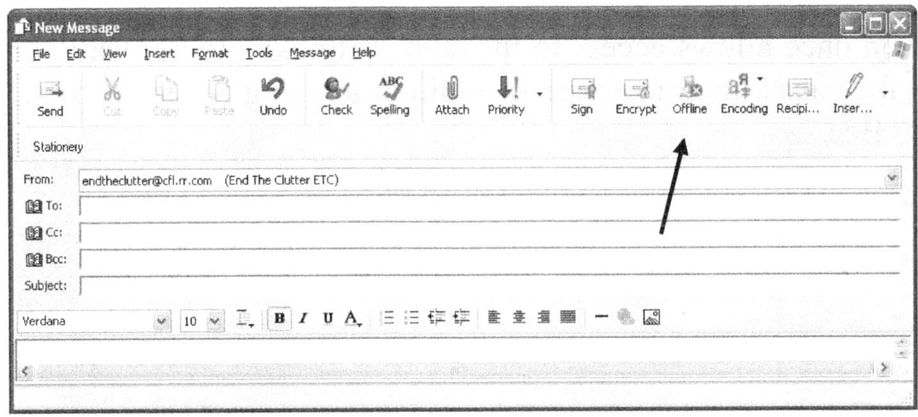

Figure 87 — New e-mail message.

Offline

If you are not connected 24/7, you can work offline.

Figure 88 — New e-mail message.

Encoding

This has to do with the language; sending a message typed in German rather than English and is beyond the scope of this book.

Figure 89 — New e-mail message.

Recipient

Left clicking this button once allows access to the address book; another way you may select recipients for your e-mail message in addition to using the icons to the left of "To:" "Cc:" or "Bcc.".

Figure 90 — New e-mail message.

Insert

This button quickly inserts your e-mail signature; creating an e-mail signature is covered later in this chapter.

                    Use any and all information at your own risk.

Now that you know your options, you can customize your e-mail message screen view exactly the way you want it.

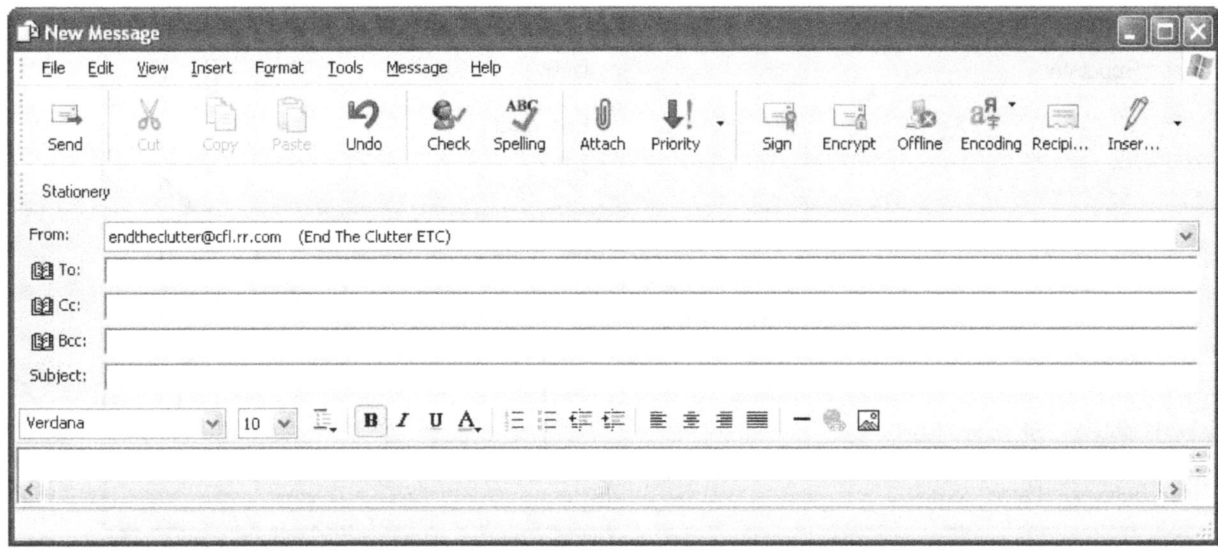

Figure 91 — Customize the message tool bar.

To customize the e-mail message tool bar, right click once in an unoccupied spot in the toolbar and then left click once on CUSTOMIZE.

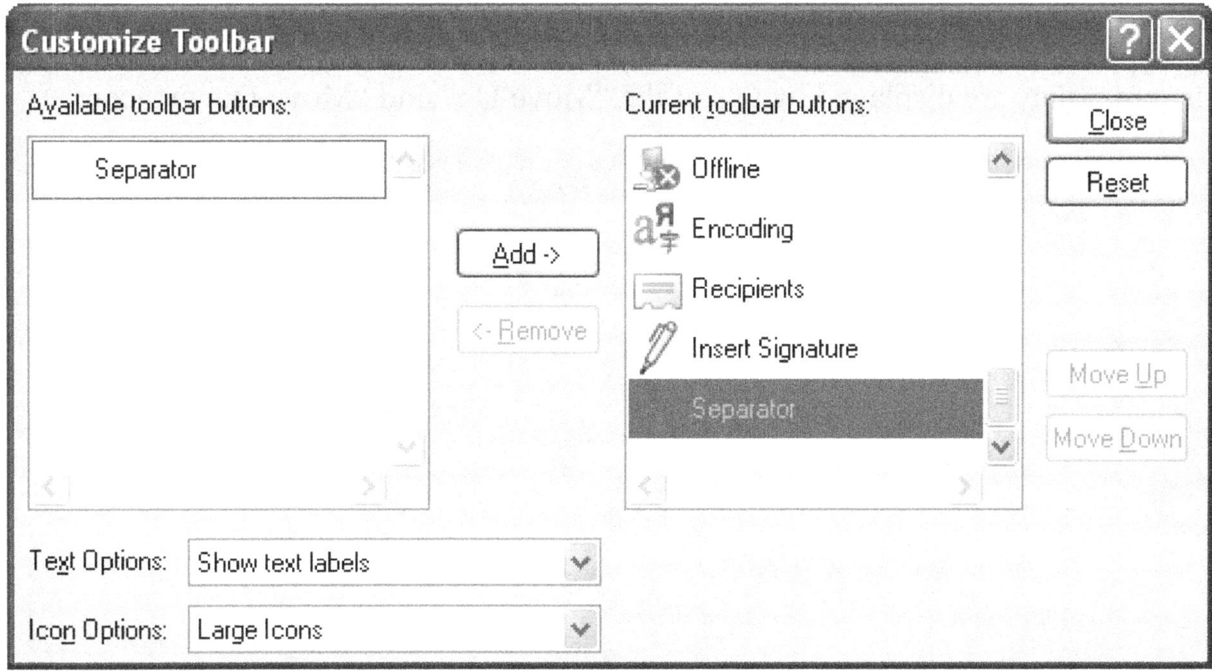

Figure 92 — Window to add or remove toolbar icons..

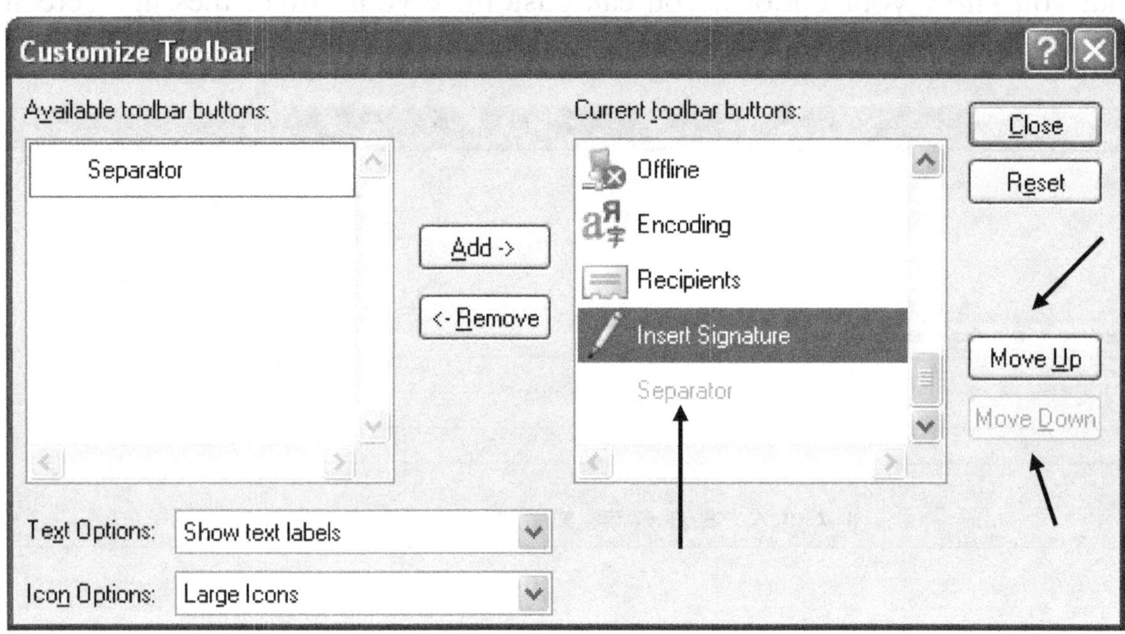

Figure 93 — "Insert Signature" is highlighted.

In this example, all of the available toolbar buttons are listed on the right hand side column because they are all displayed in the "New Message" window below. Like in Chapter 2 when discussing the main screen view, here for the e-mail screen view, recommend that you add them all to see how they look and then remove the ones you don't want after you are sure you don't want them. You can customize the order they are displayed by use of the "Move Up" and "Move Down" icons.

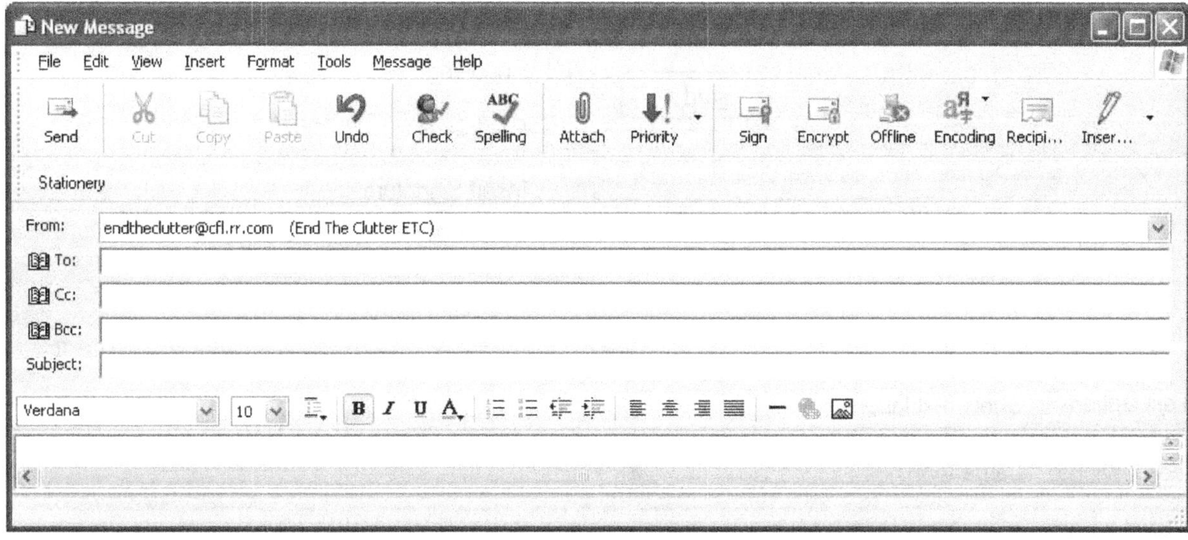

Figure 94 — E-mail message screen.

Use any and all information at your own risk.

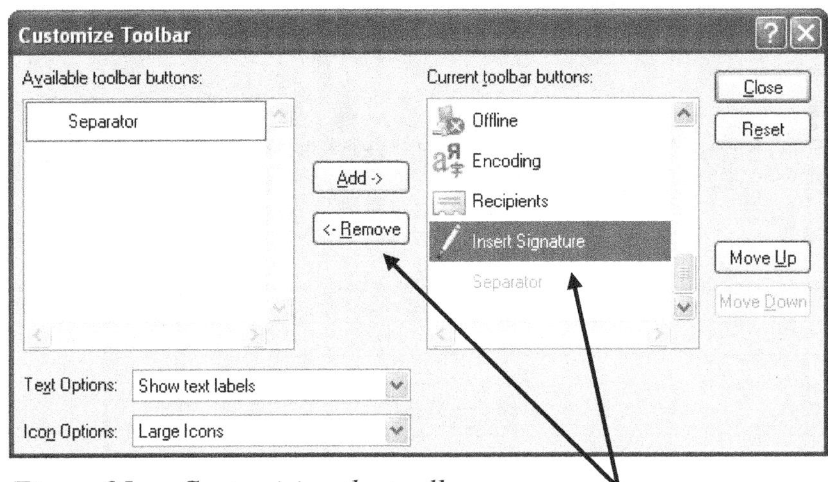

Figure 95 — Customizing the toolbar.

If you wish to remove a particular button from showing up in a newly created e-mail message, you highlight it by left clicking on it once. Let's for this example remove the "Insert Signature."

Highlight by left clicking once on "Insert Signature." Once the button you wish to remove is highlighted (in this example "Insert Signature") the REMOVE button becomes active. Left click once on REMOVE, and "Insert Signature" moves to the left hand side like the figure below.

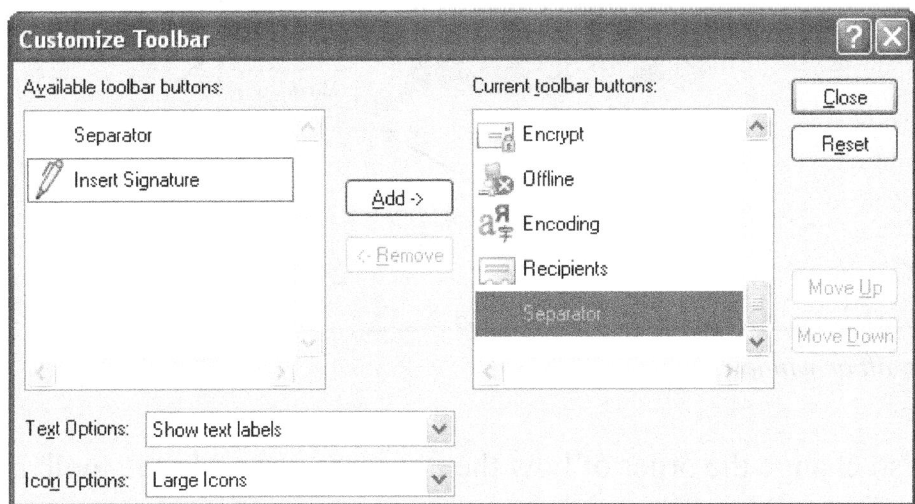

Figure 96 — Removing "Insert Signature" icon from the message toolbar.

At this point on your computer, you would remove any other buttons in the same manner. When complete, left click once on the CLOSE box.

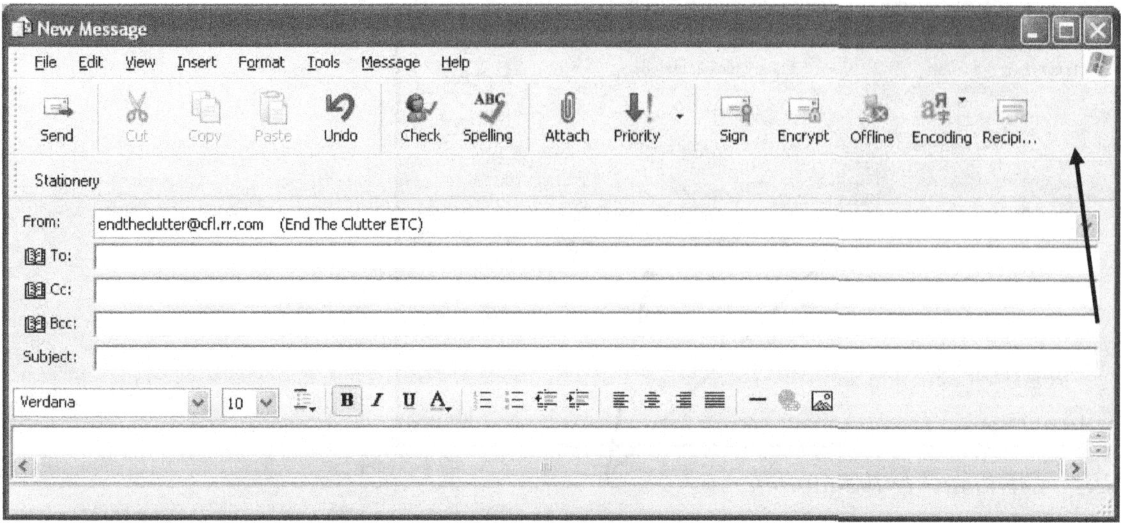

Figure 97 — New message window without the "Insert Signature" icon.

The "Insert Signature" was removed so it is no longer in the tool bar.

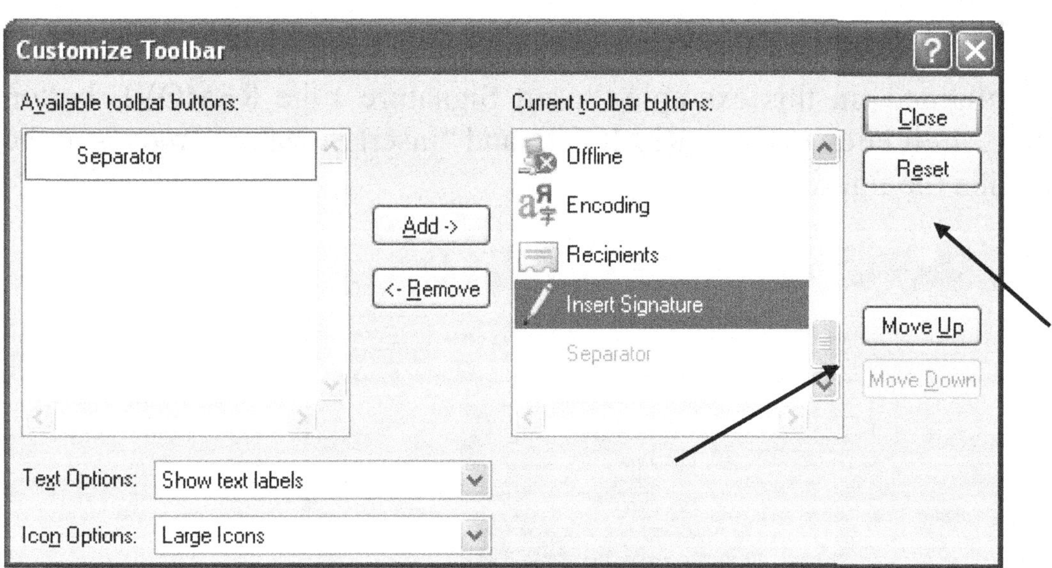

Figure 98 — Customize toolbar window.

Remember you can also change the order of how the items are placed in the toolbar by using the "Move Up" and "Move Down" buttons.

If things get totally out of control you can always left click once on the "Reset" button and that will place everything as it was originally set by the Outlook Express programmers.

     Use any and all information at your own risk.

Creating E-mail

Left click once on CREATE MAIL — located on the Outlook Express main screen Toolbar. A window like the one below "should" appear exactly as you have customized it.

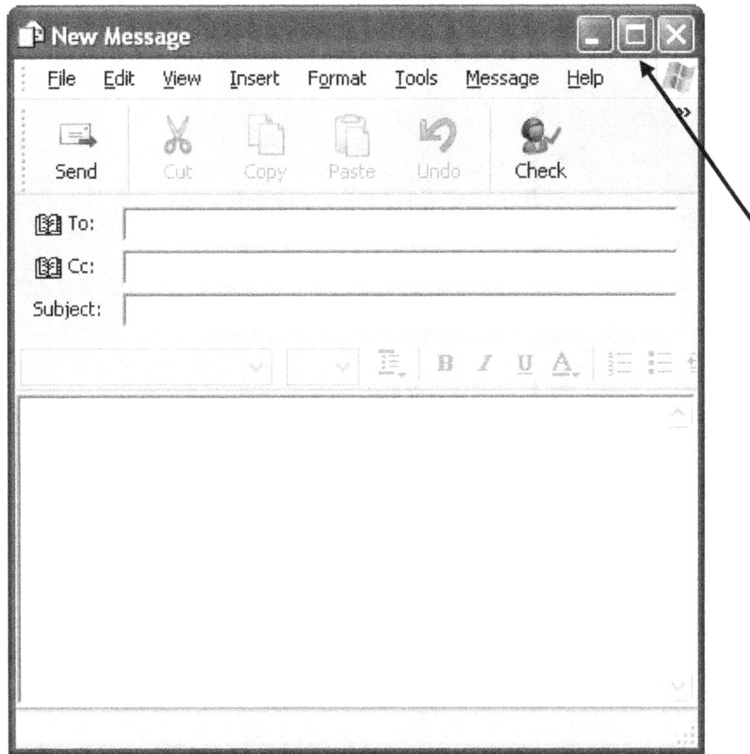

Figure 99 — New E-Mail Message

The new message window that you will see is now the active window. It sits on top of the main Outlook Express main screen window. If you can, ignore everything else except this "active" window. If you get distracted, you can make this window nice and large (full screen) by left clicking once in the middle box located at the top right hand corner of the message window.

The box with an X to the right of the black arrow, if left clicked by mistake once will close this new e-mail message window.

The box to the left of the black arrow pointer will minimize this message window. For more information about minimizing, maximizing, and closing please see Appendix C.

If you don't want to make an e-mail window full screen but you want to move it, here is how.

Without clicking, slowly move the mouse pointer inside the top of the active window somewhere in the area to the right of where it says: "New Message." When the mouse is positioned correctly, hold the mouse steady; left click once, HOLD the click, and move the mouse up, down, left or right. The window will move in the direction of your choice.

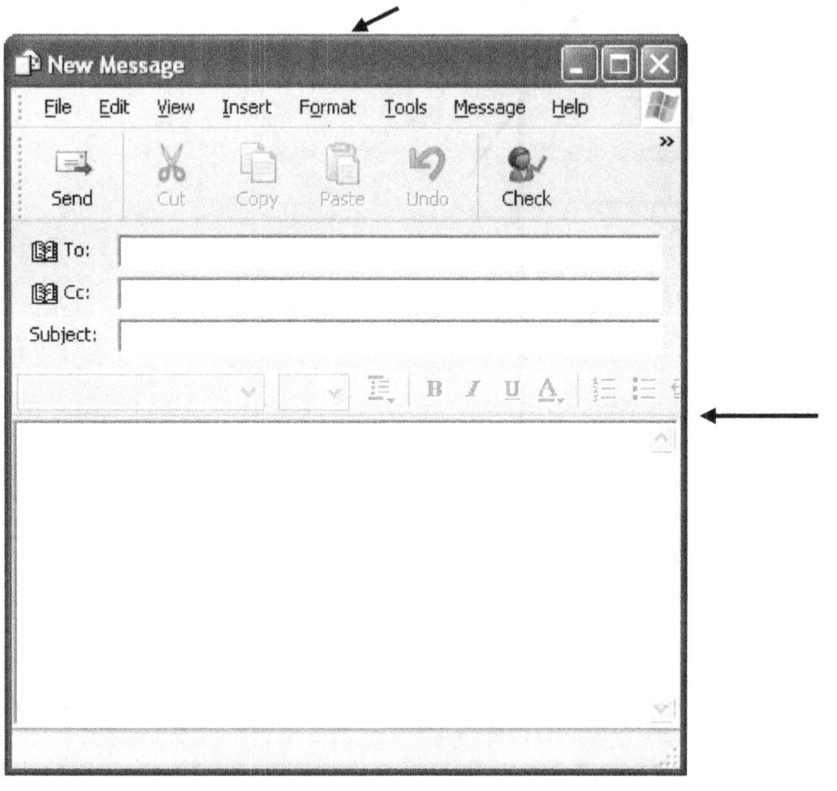

Figure 100 — E-mail Message Window

You can resize this window by slowly moving the mouse pointer without clicking to one of the borders (top, bottom, left, or right). As the pointer comes close to the edge, it will turn into two directional arrows; the arrows will be horizontal for the left and right sides; the arrows will be vertical for the up and down borders. When the arrows appear, left click once, HOLD the click, and drag which ever way you are going (up, down, left, or right).

You may also resize the e-mail message window on any of the four diagonal corners. To keep proportionality, resize via the diagonals. This is especially important when resizing pictures.

                    Use any and all information at your own risk.

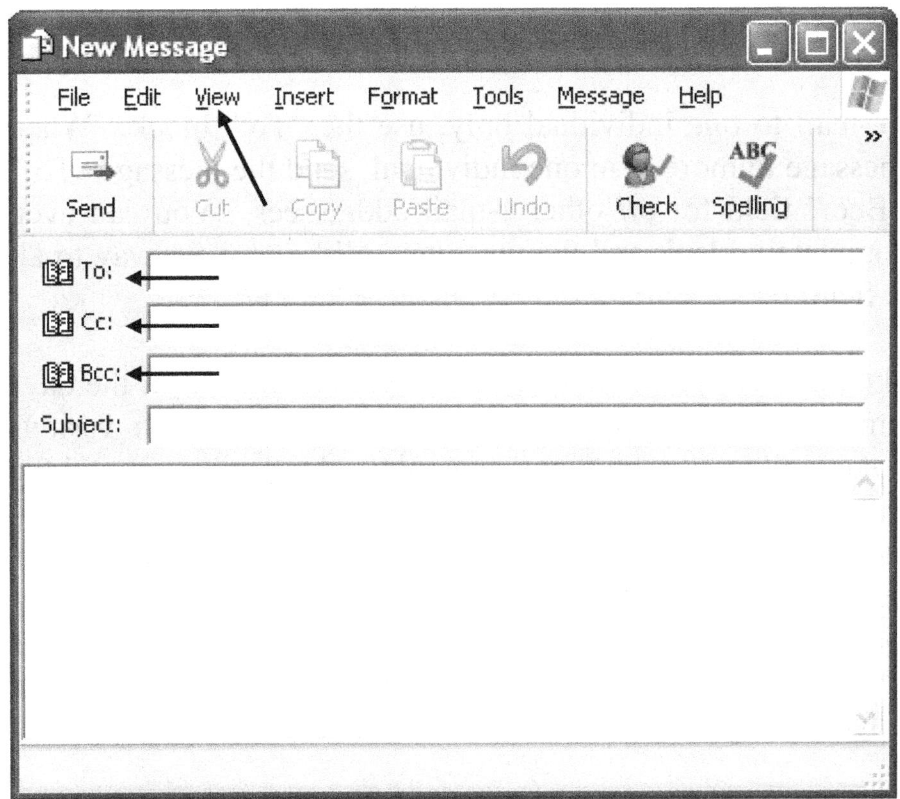

Figure 101 — New e-mail message window.

Outlook Express needs to know the e-mail address of the individual(s) you want to send your message to. You can type the e-mail address(s) into the "Bcc:" "Cc:" or "To:" block(s) or optimally you enter the addresses via the Address Book. If all three choices above are not showing up when you left click on "Create Mail," left click once on VIEW, and then left click once on SHOW ALL HEADERS.

If you choose to type in e-mail addresses, please look at the keyboard, so you have a high probability of typing the e-mail address correctly. Separate each e-mail address with a semi-colon. This really isn't the best method because there can be so much confusion in e-mail addresses that use the number "1," the letter "l," or the letter "i;" as well as the letter "o," or the number "0" — not to mention upper and lower case issues. Using the address book is optimal because hopefully the address book has the e-mail addresses entered correctly.

Additionally, please be advised that any and all e-mail addresses entered in the "To:" or "Cc:" fields are available for the world to see and can be used by *anyone* who wants them.

Respectful E-mailing

If you are sending an e-mail to *one* individual only, use the "To:" block. When you are sending your message to more than one individual, send the message "To:" yourself and use the "Bcc:" field for *all* other e-mail addressees. You can even leave the "To:" field completely blank and the message will be sent anyway to all addresses in the "Bcc:" field.

"Bcc:" stands for blind carbon copy; this has evolved electronically from the days of old when correspondence was actually typed on a typewriter with various carbon copies, a pink, or yellow, or blue for example. At the bottom of the correspondence, often we would type "cc:" and then to whom the copy was going. A *blind* carbon copy indeed went somewhere; however, to whom it was going was not found anywhere on the original, only on the copies. A small piece of paper was placed in the typewriter exactly where the keys would hit and "bcc:" was typed along with where the blind copy was headed. The individual(s) receiving the original had no knowledge that a blind carbon copy even existed.

Let's say you send an e-mail to 15 people. Any e-mail address placed in the "To:" or the "Cc:" fields shows up for everyone to see when the message is delivered to those 15 individuals. All the e-mail addresses, all 15 of them will appear on all the messages delivered. Using the "Bcc:" field prevents this from happening because when using the "Bcc:" field each individual receives your e-mail message with only their own e-mail address showing. No one has any idea who else received the same message. It looks like one e-mail was sent to one individual, when it could have been sent to hundreds of people.

Folks often wonder how "so-in-so" go his or her e-mail address. This is one very easy way to openly share e-mail addresses across the planet. When you *forward* e-mail to many e-mail addresses that already have a gazillion e-mail addresses showing, you are compounding an already frustrating problem.

Read on to find out how to become part of the solution.

                                   Use any and all information at your own risk.

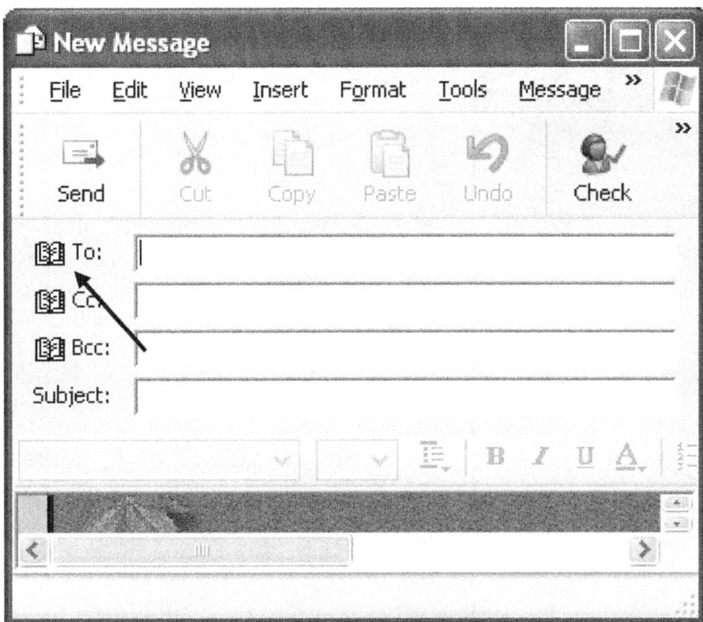

Figure 102 — New e-mail message window.

One easy and quick way to get to the "Bcc:" field is through the Address Book indirectly via an e-mail message screen.

In the figure above, immediately to the left of the "To:" "Cc:" or "Bcc:" are icons resembling an "address book." Left clicking once on any one of those address icons brings up a window similar to the figure below.

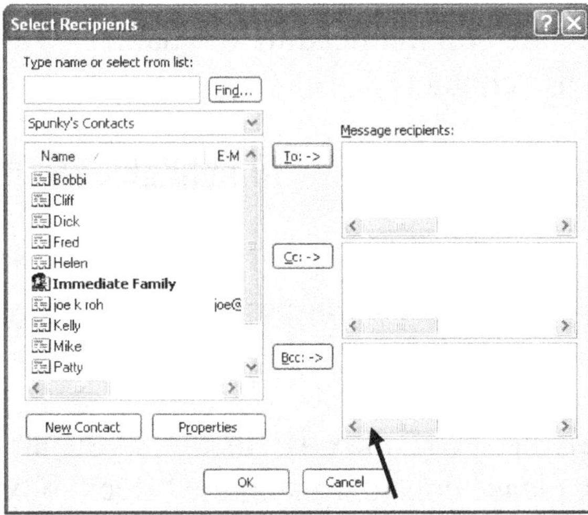

Figure 103 — Selecting e-mail recipients.

Left click once on any contact to highlight that contact. Then left click once on the "Bcc:" When in doubt use the "Bcc:" field for *all* e-mail addresses.

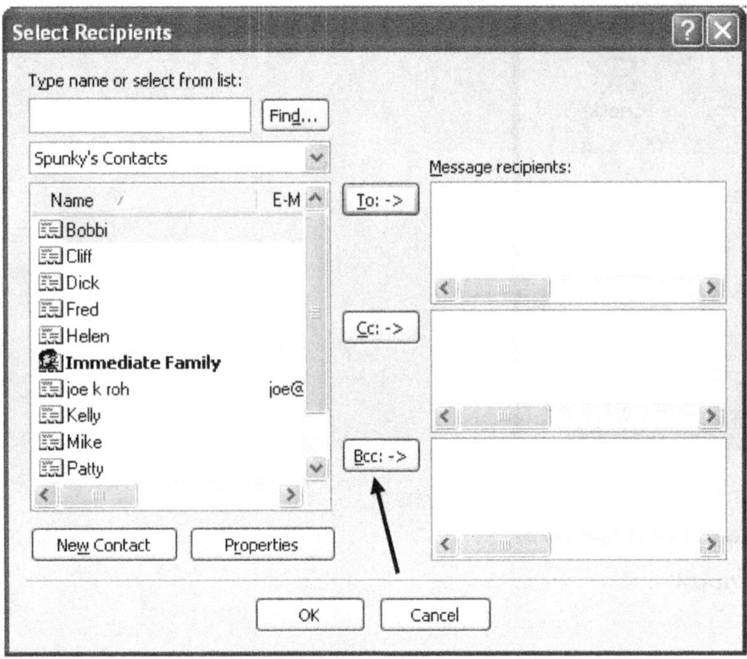

Figure 104 — Select Recipients window.

Again the above figure appears when you access the Address Book *indirectly* from a newly created e-mail message. This view of the Address Book is very different from the window you receive when you open the Address Book from the Outlook Express main screen view discussed in Chapter 5.

On the left hand side of the above figure under the column heading of "name," will be a list of your addressees; otherwise known as "contacts."

To select a contact left click once on the name. Once the name is highlighted, left click once on the "Bcc:" box.

You can use the CTRL key to select specific names. You can use the SHIFT key to select all names in between two selections via left clicks.

If the e-mail is going to just one individual the "To:" box is fine. If you are sending to more than one individual however, please consider using the "Bcc:" box to protect the e-mail addresses. When sending to more than one individual, use the "To:" block for *your* e-mail address only or leave it blank.

                    Use any and all information at your own risk.

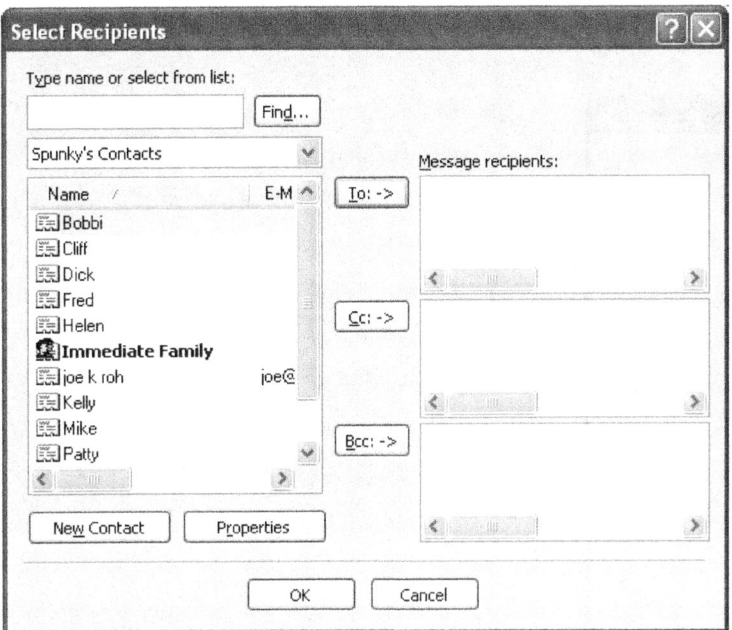

Figure 105 — Select Recipients window.

Let's review.

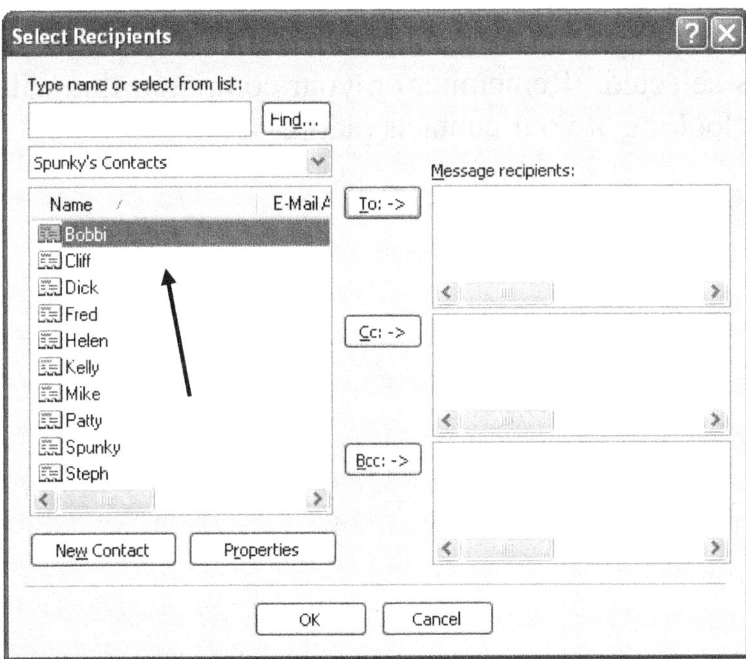

Figure 106 — E-mail addressee "Bobbi," is selected.

To select one addressee, you left click that addressee once.

To select more than one addressee, hold the CTRL key down as you left click once on each addressee that you wish to select.

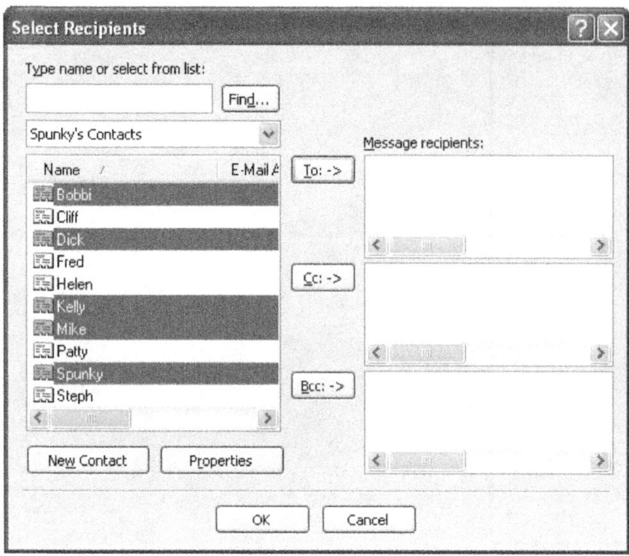

Figure 107 — Bobbi, Dick, Kelly, Mike, & Spunky are selected.

To select many addressees at once, select the top addressee. In the figure below, this would be "Bobbi." Hold down the SHIFT key, and left click once on the bottom addressee; in this example, "Steph." This action shows all the contacts in between "Bobbi" and "Steph" as selected. Remember on your computer, this will be different, because you will be looking at your contacts (addressees).

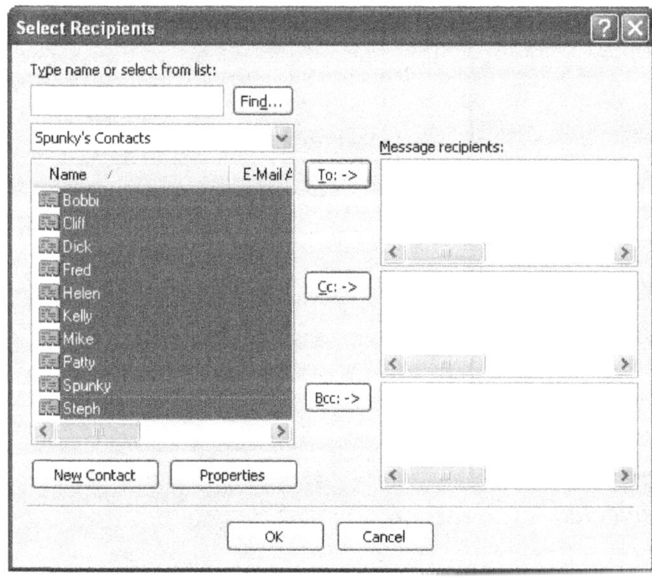

Figure 108 — Selection of several addressees.

Use any and all information at your own risk.

Let's say for example, you want to send an e-mail to Cliff, Mike, and Spunky.

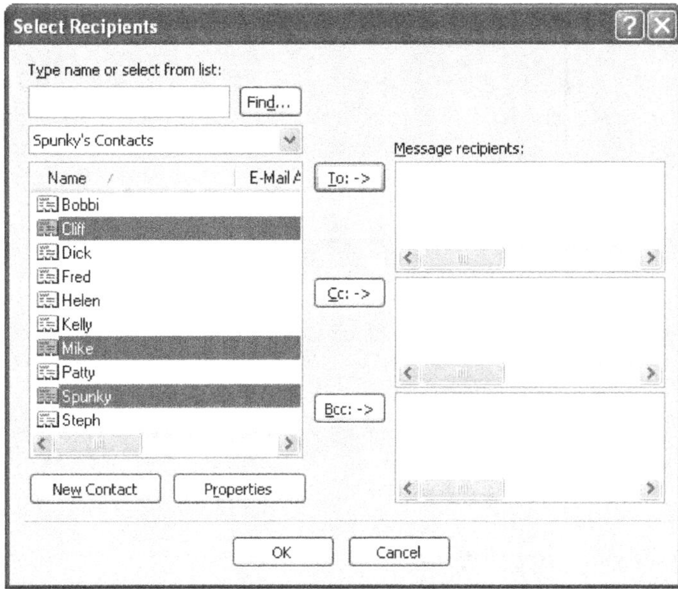

Figure 109 — Select Cliff, Mike, and Spunky by holding the CTRL key.

Now that Cliff, Mike, and Spunky are selected, you left click once on the "Bcc:" box.

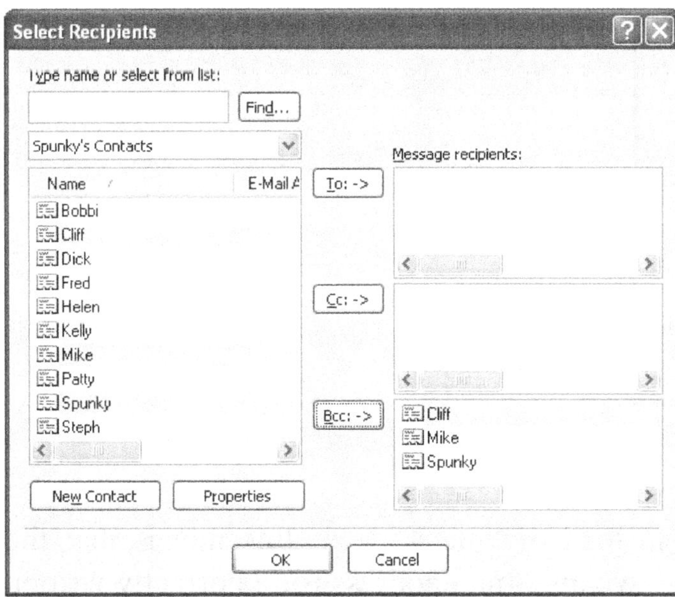

Figure 110 — Cliff, Mike, and Spunky are in the "Bcc:" box.

Let's say you are "Steph" for this example; you now select yourself and place your name in the "To:" box.

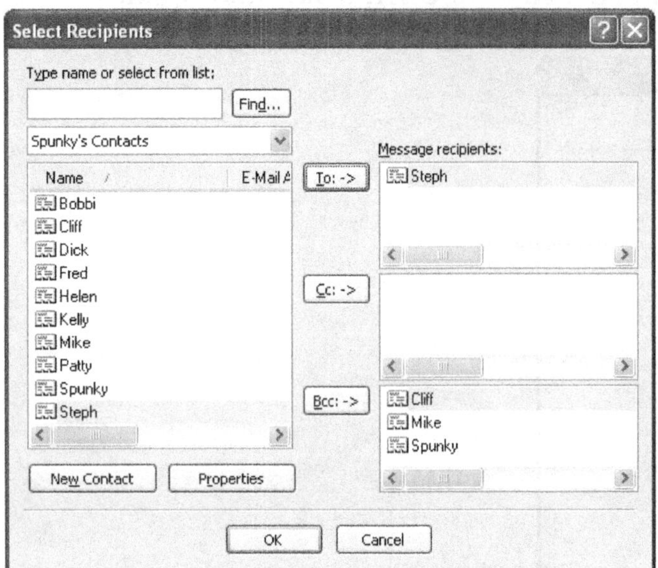

Figure 111 — Send to self with three addressees in "Bcc:" field.

Now, you left click once on OK.

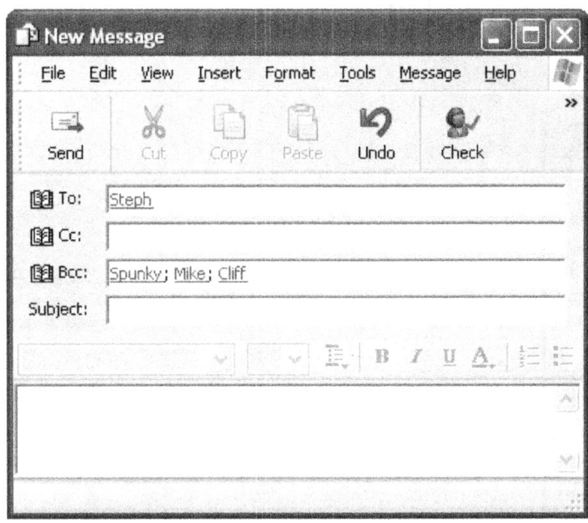

Figure 112 — E-mail using "Bcc:" field.

If the addressees are ever in "red" instead of "black" text, this means that the addressee you have selected does not have an e-mail address (or a correctly written e-mail address) in the Address Book.

Now you are ready to type in the subject and text of your e-mail.

   Use any and all information at your own risk.

To review if you would like to always see the "Bcc:" field displayed in all your e-mail messages, open a new e-mail by left clicking once on CREATE MAIL.

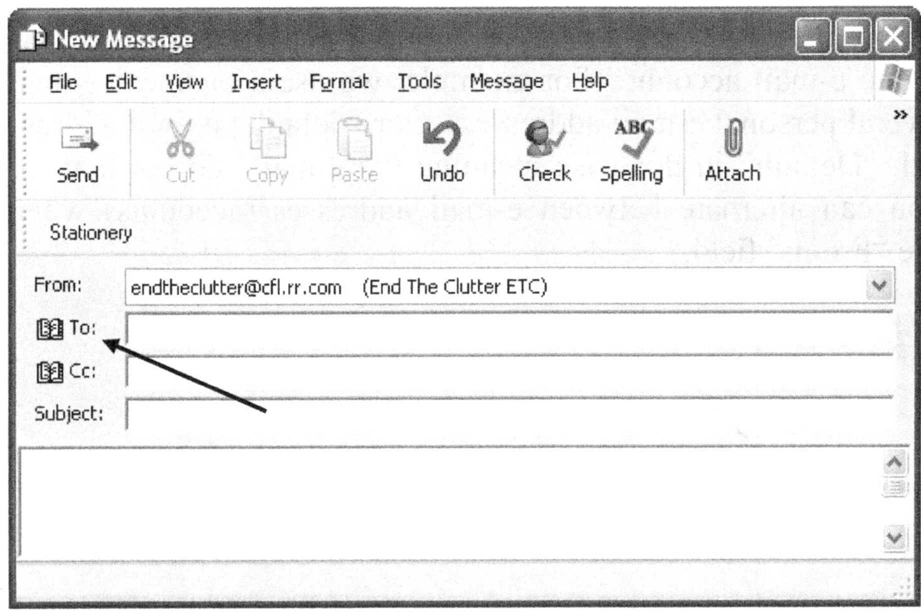

Figure 113 — New e-mail message without BCC field showing.

Left click once on VIEW, and then left click once on ALL HEADERS.

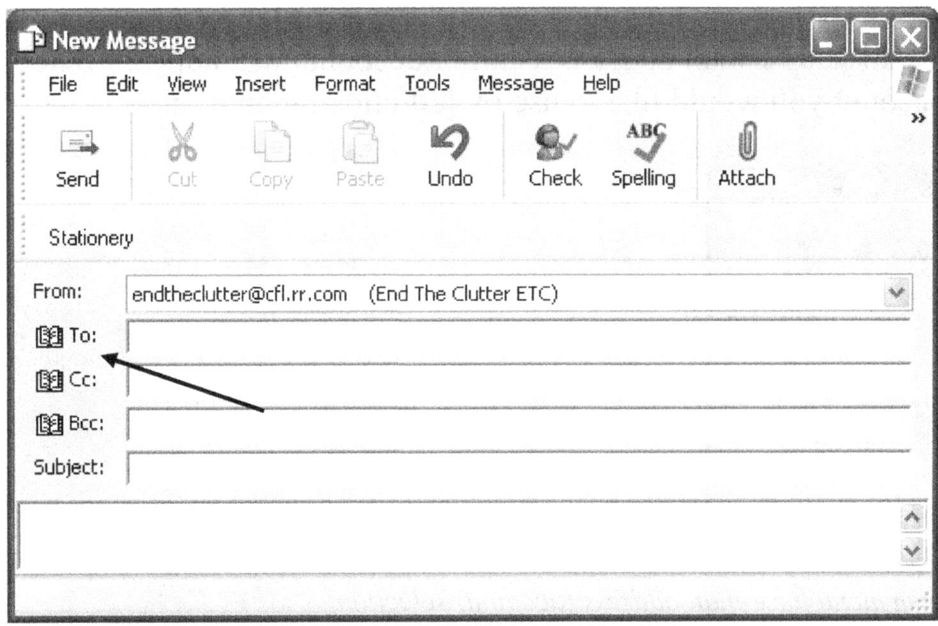

Figure 114 — New e-mail message with the BCC field showing.

The "From" Field

If you have and use more than one e-mail address, in Outlook Express that means you have more than one e-mail account. For example, we use a business e-mail address as well as several personal e-mail addresses. Our "default" e-mail address is the business e-mail. "Default" in this case meaning the e-mail address that we use most often. You can alternate between e-mail addresses (accounts) when creating e-mail via the "From:" field.

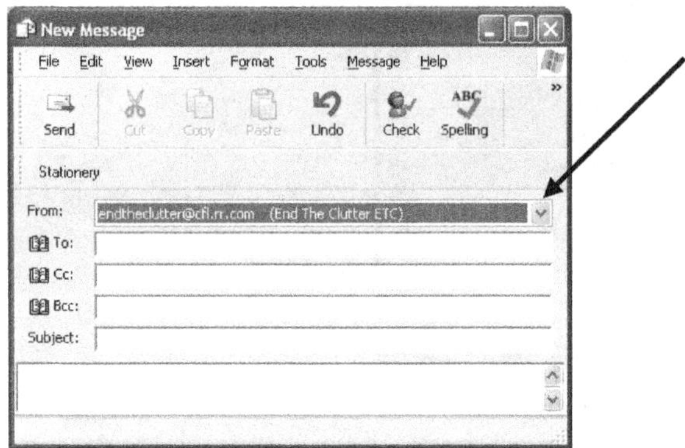

Figure 115 — Changing the "From" address.

See black arrow above. By left clicking once on that downward directional arrow, a drop down menu of all your e-mail addresses and/or accounts will appear. Select the e-mail address account you would like to use by left clicking on it once.

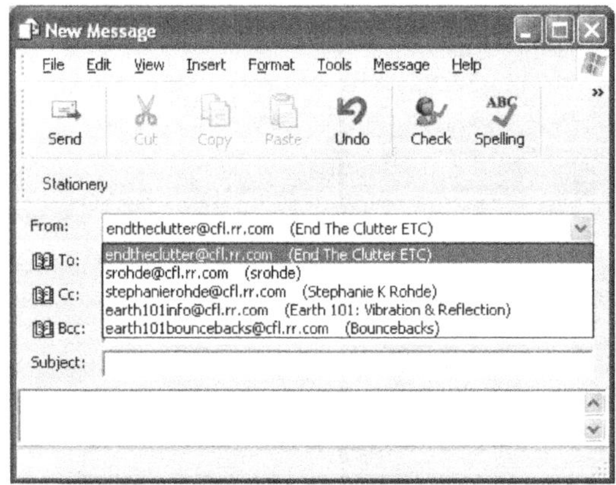

Figure 116 — Drop-down menu for e-mail address (account) selection.

This drop-down menu will look differently on each computer depending upon the number of e-mail addresses accounts there are.

                    Use any and all information at your own risk.

The "Drafts" Folder

Let's say you are in the middle of typing an e-mail message and something happens and you have to step away from the computer.

Close the e-mail message by left clicking once on the "X" in the box.

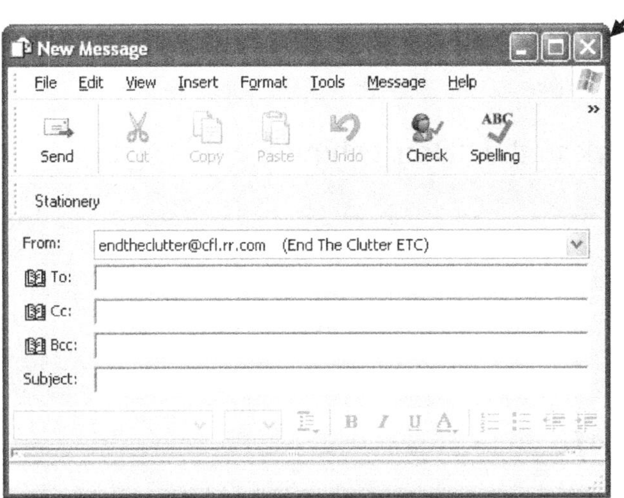

Figure 117 — New e-mail message.

Left clicking the "X" in the box brings up the following question from the computer:

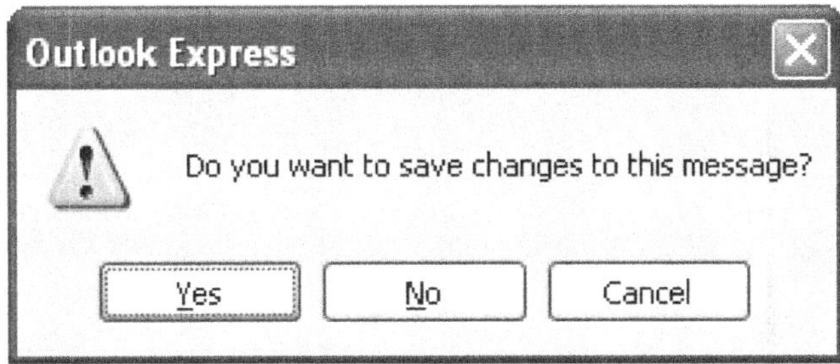

Figure 118 — Closing an e-mail prior to sending.

Left clicking once on YES saves a copy of the e-mail message in the "Drafts" folder. Left clicking once on NO does not save this e-mail message anywhere; the message is deleted. Left clicking once on CANCEL brings you back to your e-mail message.

Left clicking YES brings a message like the one on the next page.

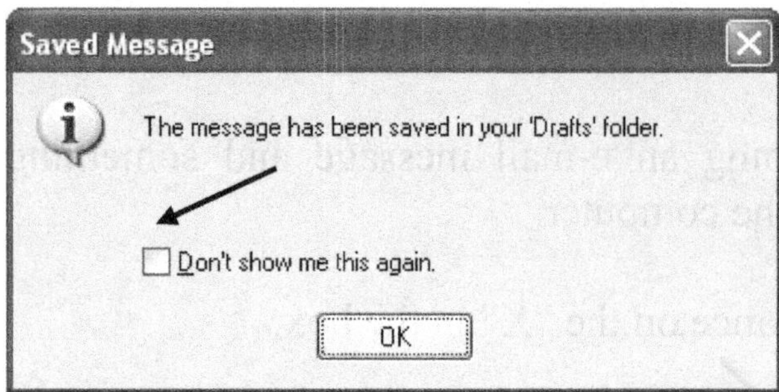

Figure 119 — After clicking YES to save a copy of the e-mail message.

Recommend you *do not* place a check mark in the "Don't show me this again" as a precautionary measure.

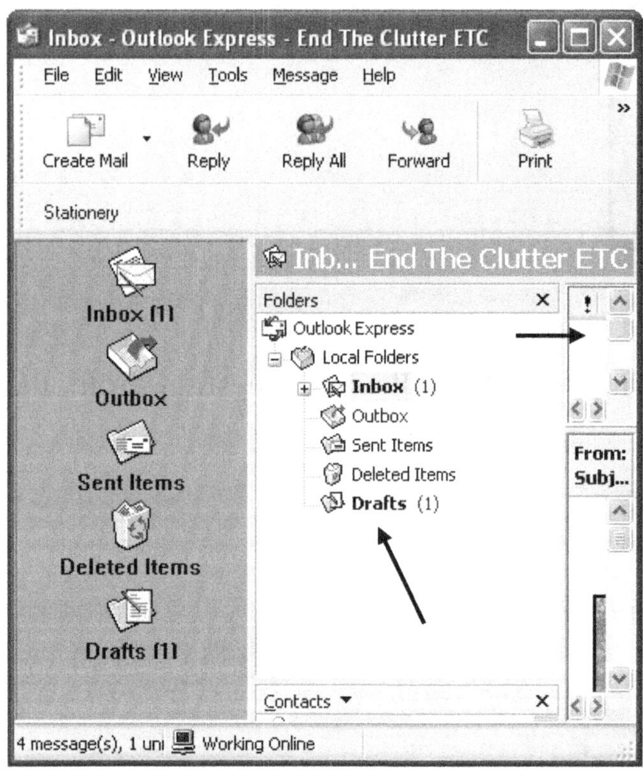

Figure 120 — One item placed into the "Drafts" folder.

When you return to your computer and open Outlook Express, your message is waiting for you in the "Drafts" folder. Left click once on this folder and all messages in this folder if there is more than one, will be displayed to the right. You may also save your e-mail message to external media like a floppy diskette or to a CD-R or RW disc.

                                  Use any and all information at your own risk.

The "Outbox"

If you are not connected to the Internet, and you create an e-mail message, and left click once on SEND, the message goes into your "Outbox" until you have a connection to the Internet once again.

When you are connected to the Internet and you left click once on the SEND button, the message goes in the "Outbox" and is sent as per the way the program is set up. From the main Outlook Express screen, left click on TOOLS, and then OPTIONS, Send tab.

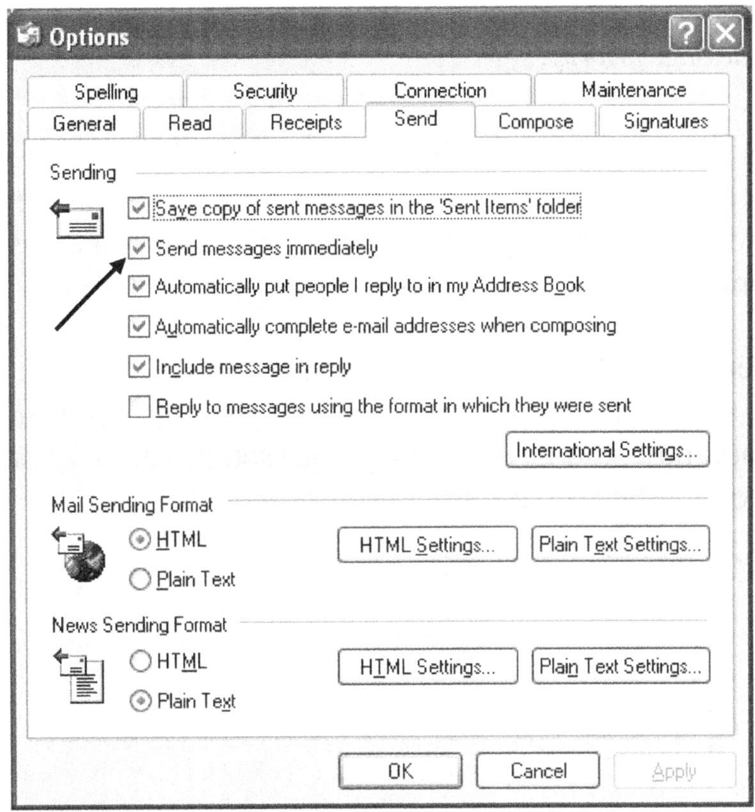

Figure 121 — Tools, Options, Send tab.

In order for your e-mails to be sent immediately as you left click on the SEND button, you must have a check mark placed in the "Send messages immediately" box.

The higher your connection speed, the faster your e-mail leaves your outbox. Sometimes it goes so fast you don't even see it in the Outbox.

Message Priority

You may send your e-mail with a low, normal, or high priority.

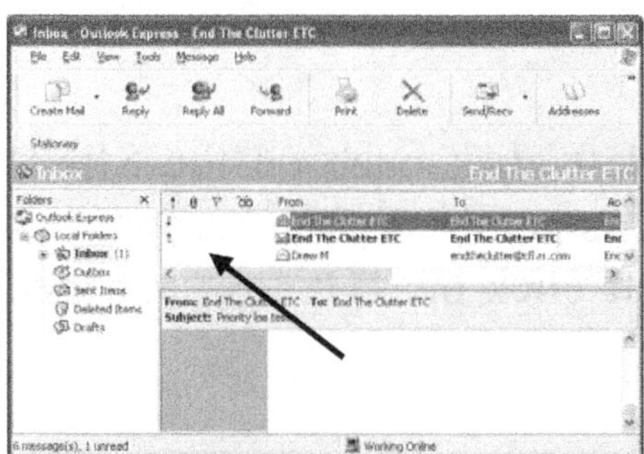

Figure 122 — Low, high and normal message priority.

There are three e-mail messages showing above. The top one has a down facing arrow usually blue indicating a low priority. The middle message has an exclamation point usually red indicating a high priority. The bottom message has no blue down arrow or red exclamation point as it was sent with normal priority.

The priority of the message is determined by the individual who sent the message. To see how this works, create a new e-mail message by left clicking once on CREATE MAIL. Depending upon how you have your tool bar setup, you may or may not have a button showing to left click on to set the priority.

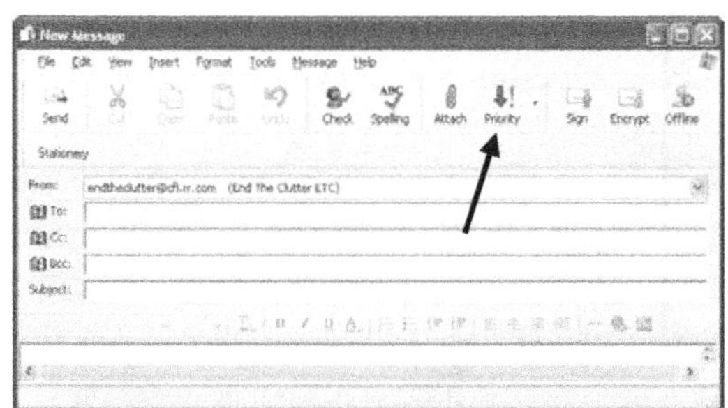

Figure 123 — Setting message priority.

In the above example there is a button showing to select the priority of the message about to be sent. If the button is showing, left click once on the down arrow immediately to the right of the word "priority" and you will receive three choices. Choose low, normal, or high. If the button is not showing, you may left click once on MESSAGE, SET PRIORITY, and chose one of the three available choices.

     Use any and all information at your own risk.

If the priority button is not showing and you would like it to be showing, the e-mail screen view needs to be adjusted. The message "view" screen can be adjusted from within a new message. Right click once in an unoccupied spot in the message toolbar

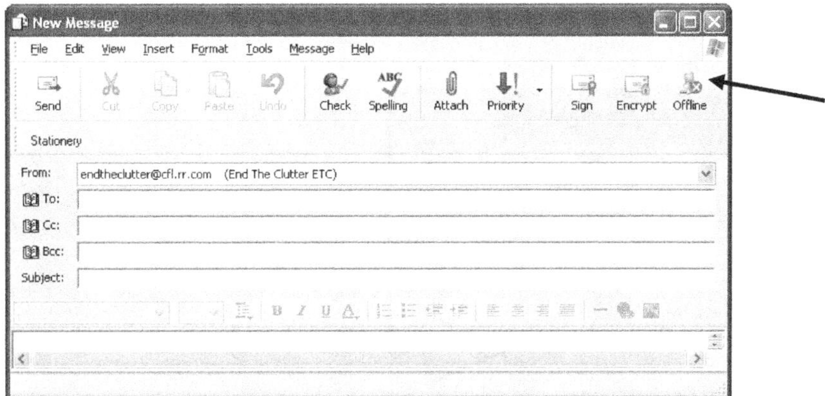

Figure 124 — E-mail message.

By right clicking the message toolbar, the figure below appears.

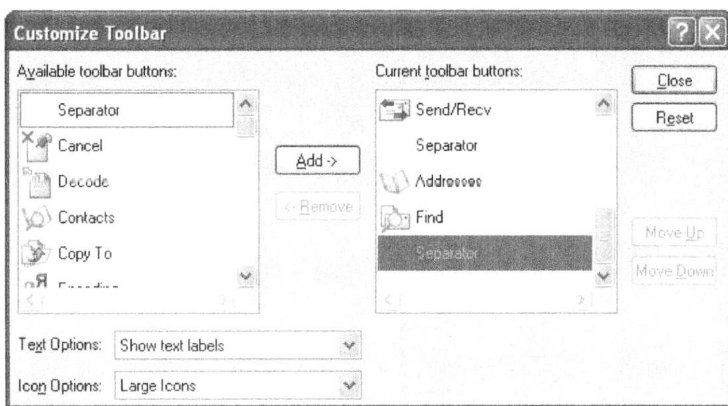

Figure 125 — Customize the e-mail message toolbar.

The "Priority" button will be located in the left column if it is not currently showing up in your newly created messages.

Select any item one at a time on either side and then left click once on ADD or REMOVE, which ever is the appropriate action.

When you are finished, left click once on CLOSE.

Please refer if need be back to the section in this chapter called Toolbar Options.

The "Sent Items" Folder

Outlook Express will keep a copy of every e-mail you send if you like. This is a really good option for beginners. Left click once on TOOLS, then left click once on OPTIONS, and then left click once on the SEND tab.

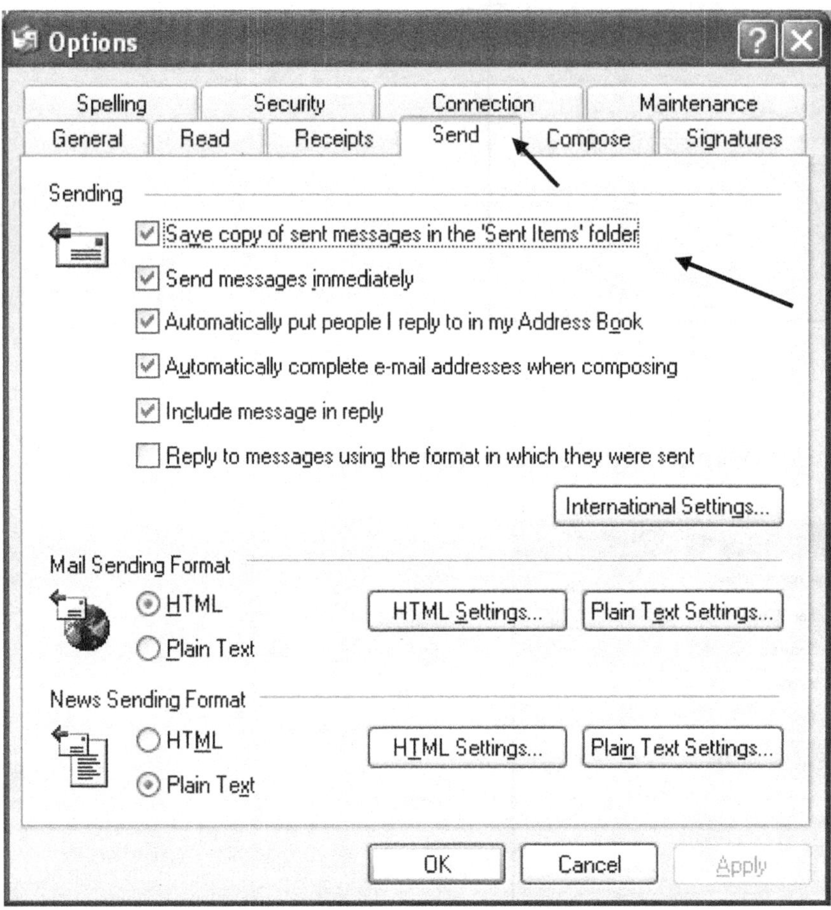

Figure 126 — Sent messages in the "Sent Items" folder.

Make sure there is a check mark in the box immediately to the left of "Save copy of sent messages in 'Sent Items' folder."

If you left click on the "Sent Items" folder in the folder list in the main screen view, all the e-mails you have sent are listed on the right. To see who the addressees were in any e-mail, right click once on the message, then left click once on PROPERTIES, and then left click on the Details tab. This displays all the folks you sent to via the "Bcc:" that are not listed if you were to open the message.

                    Use any and all information at your own risk.

Plain Text, Rich Text, & HTML

Plain Text

Plain text is sometimes called clear text and it means pretty much what it says. There are no graphics and no formatting. It is the most portable format to send information from one computer to another because just about every software application can read plain text, on nearly every operating system. Plain text is extremely limited however; there is nothing fancy about it at all.

When the term is used in conjunction with "encryption," plain text can also mean "not encrypted."

Rich Text

Rich text in the general sense is a step up from plain text as this allows for page formatting including fonts, borders, underlining, italicizing, and color, to name a few. This form is used in many word processing programs. A document created with rich text in one program can look slightly different in another. Rich text can also be referred to as Rich Text Format (RTF).

HTML

This is the fun stuff. HTML stands for Hyper Text Markup Language. It is what Web pages are made of. You can create e-mail messages in this format in Outlook Express. This is the next step after Rich Text in many programs. HTML tells a Web browser (like Internet Explorer) how to display the Web pages it receives.

When you use HTML formatting in your e-mail message and the recipient's e-mail program does not understand HTML, your message appears to them in plain text with an HTML file attached. Only e-mail programs that support Multipurpose Internet Mail Extensions (MIME) can read HTML formatting.

To format *all* of your outgoing messages in Outlook Express using HTML, left click once on the TOOLS menu, then left click once on OPTIONS, and then left click once on the SEND tab.

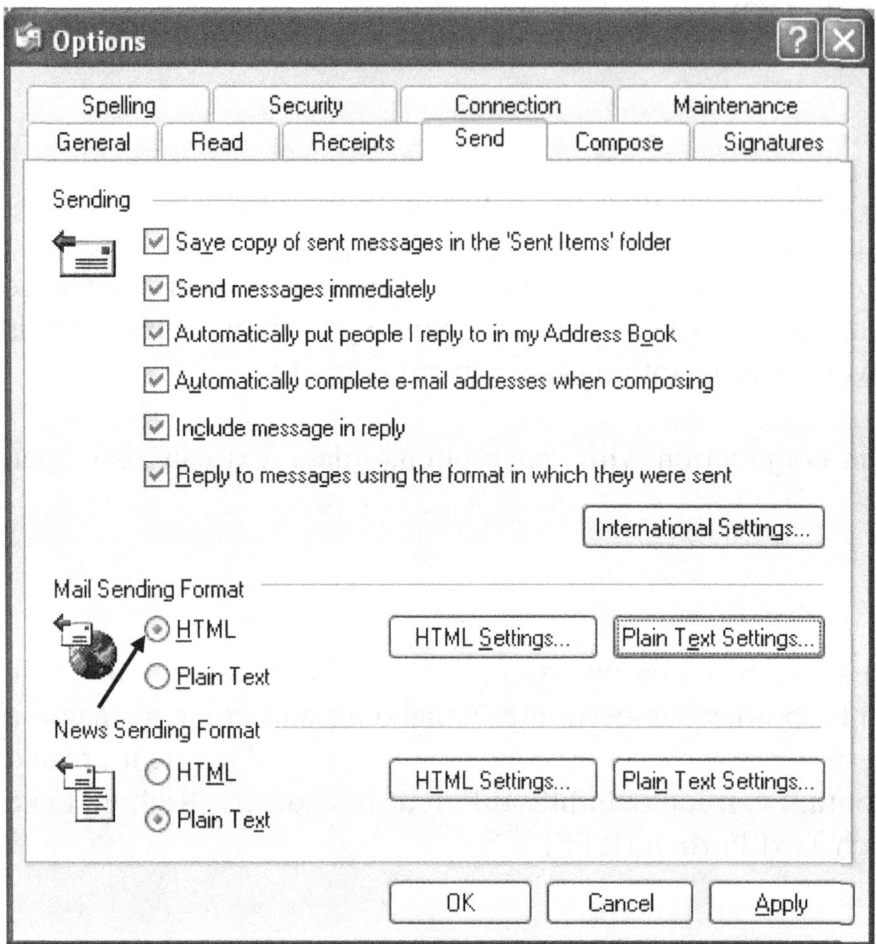

Figure 127 — Tools, Options Window, Send Tab.

In the Mail Sending Format section, left click once in the little circle to the left of where it says "HTML" if there is not already a dot showing. Selecting this option will create all your outgoing e-mail messages in HTML format.

If this option is not selected on your computer like it is in the figure above and you want to format just one individual e-mail message in HTML, open a new e-mail message by left clicking once on CREATE MAIL. At the top of the e-mail message left click once on FORMAT. In the drop-down menu, a black dot will appear to the left of Rich Text HTML if HTML is already selected. If there is no black dot visible next to Rich Text HTML, left click once on Rich Text HTML to select HTML for that message only. In Outlook Express, Rich Text and HTML happen to mean the same thing. This is not true in every e-mail management program however.

                    Use any and all information at your own risk.

The "Send" Tab

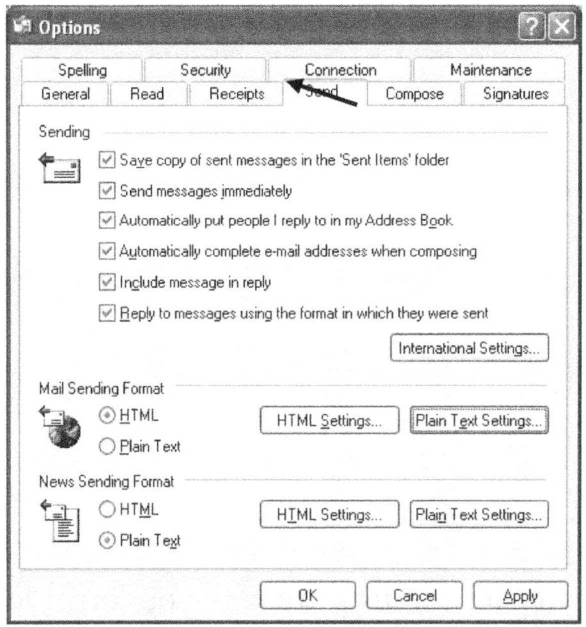

Figure 128 — "Send" tab.

Save copy of sent messages in the 'Sent Items' folder

As discussed earlier this is a good option to check because sometimes you want to refer back to a message you sent. You can always delete these messages in the future. While you are learning about your computer and about Outlook Express please keep copies of the e-mails you send. Remember you can also backup "Sent Items" to a floppy diskette or to a CD-RW disc. This of course is the user's choice with regard to the importance of the e-mails sent.

Send messages immediately

When you left click once on the SEND button, and you are connected to the Internet, and this box is checked, your message is on its way immediately. It actually stops in the "Outbox" for a split second before being sent. If you blink you may miss it as it enters and exits the "Outbox."

If you are not connected to the Internet and you left click once on the SEND button, your message is sent to the "Outbox" where you can clearly see it. Your message resides in the Outbox until you have an Internet connection once again.

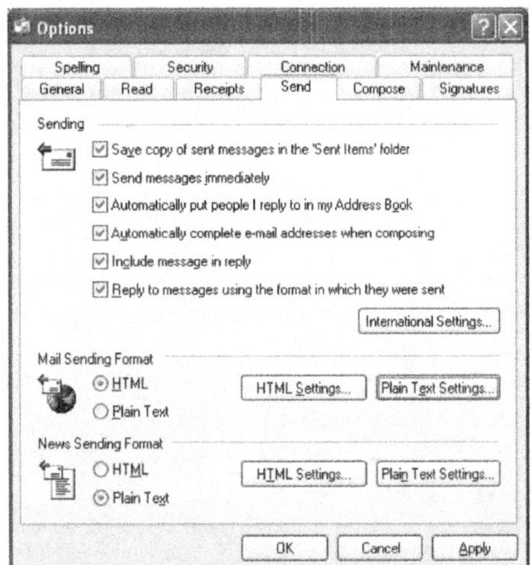

Figure 129 — "Send" tab.

Automatically put people I reply to in my Address Book

This is a very good feature especially when you are learning. In case you forget to add an e-mail address from a message that you just received from a friend you haven't heard from in years, the computer will automatically save the address for you in the Address Book as long as you send them a reply.

Automatically complete e-mail addresses when composing

For those of you who do not want to use the Address Book to enter the e-mail address(s), the program tries to help you get the correct e-mail address into the message. If an e-mail address that you begin to type is in your Address Book, the computer will automatically finish the e-mail address for you.

Include message in the reply

When you left click once on the REPLY button (to an e-mail you have received), you have the option of having the original message included in your reply or not.

Reply to messages using the format in which they were sent

You can set up Outlook Express so that your replies to individual's e-mail messages are sent back to them in a known readable format. This way you are assured they will be able to read your response.

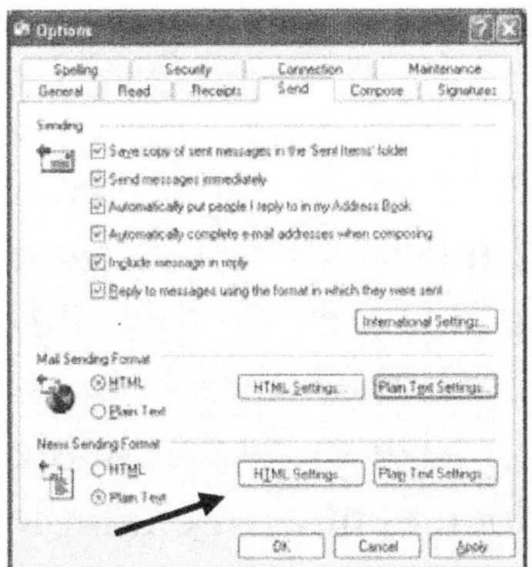

Figure 130 — "Send" tab.

International Settings Button

Beginners please leave this default pre-defined setting as it is.

Mail Sending Format

This section allows you to choose how your e-mail messages are created. Let's take a look at the HTML Settings button.

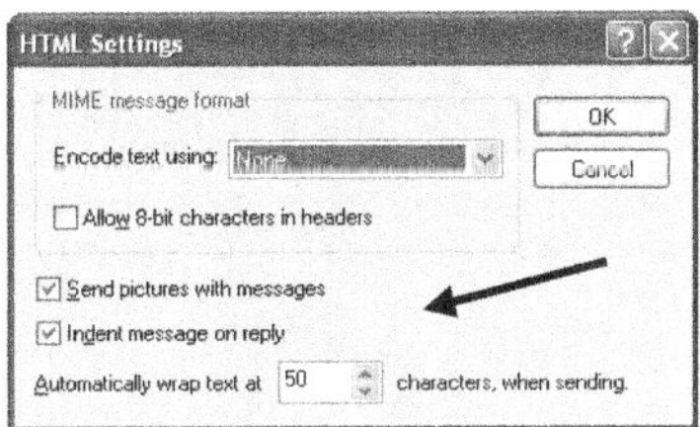

Figure 131 — Automatic HTML Settings.

Beginners please leave the MIME message format box however it is on your computer.

Sending pictures with messages is good, because it allows for more options for the receiver. Place a check mark here if it is not already there.

Indenting the message on reply is a nice touch, so the receiver can see the original message that they sent to you.

Beginners please leave the Plain Text Settings as they are as well as the News Sending Format section. Left click OK to close the Send tab window.

Fonts, Styles, Size, Effects, & Color

Fonts, styles, and size of text work similarly. You can set them up for all your messages, and you still have the option to change individual messages to suit your mood at the moment. The font is the kind of type you are using; for example, this book is written with the "Times New Roman" font. Style on the other hand is something you do with the font; **bold** or *italics* for example. Size means how big or small the particular font is you are using in your current document. An example of an "effect" in Outlook Express is the "Underline."

To change the font, style, size, effect, or color of text in your e-mails, it's back to left clicking once on TOOLS; and then left clicking once on OPTIONS. This time however, you left click once on the COMPOSE tab, and then left click once on FONT SETTINGS.

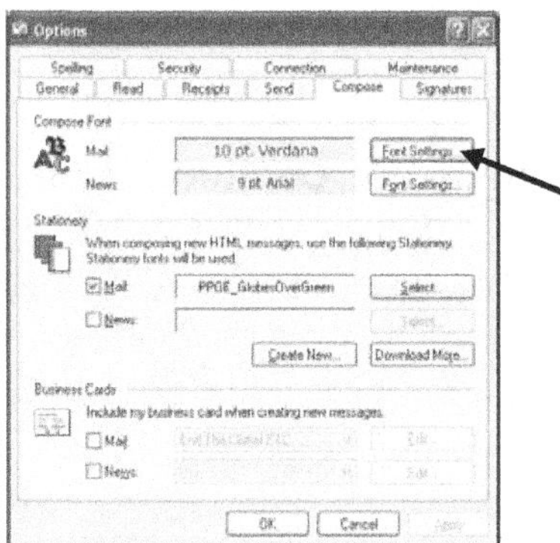

Figure 132 — Tools, Options, Compose tab.

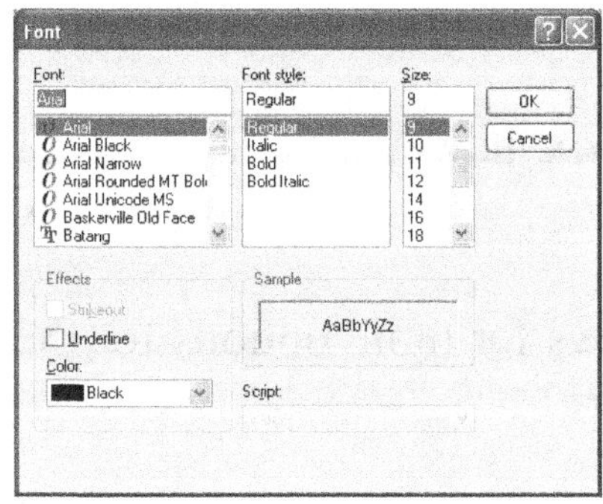

Figure 133 — Font, style, size, effect, and color.

There are a great number of fonts, several styles of the font, and various sizes to choose from. When you have decided, left click once on OK.

    Use any and all information at your own risk.

Blocking, Selecting, & Highlighting Text

To change any font, style, size, effect, or color for one message only, you must first block the text. This is also known as selecting or highlighting the text.

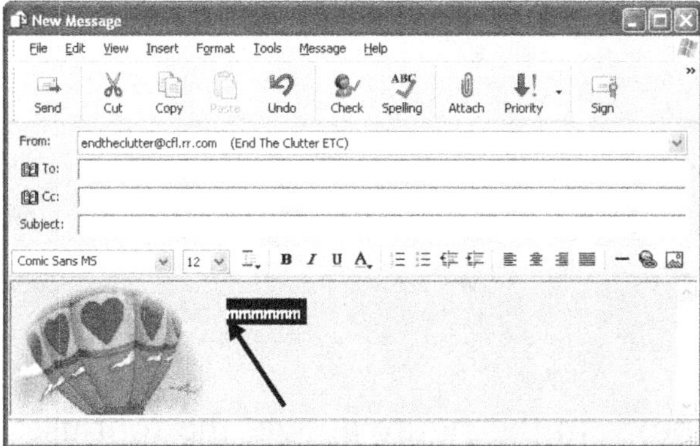

Figure 134 — Blocking, selecting, or highlighting text.

Create a new e-mail message by left clicking once on CREATE MAIL. Then type a little bit of text in the text box of your new e-mail message. *Without* clicking the mouse, move the mouse pointer until you get it just to the left of the text that you want to block — see black arrow above. When the mouse pointer gets near "text," it becomes what is called an I-beam because its shape looks like an I-beam. At that point in time when the I-beam pointer is to the left of the text you want to block, you left click the mouse once, HOLD the click and drag the mouse to the right until you get to the end of the text that you want to block. Let go of the mouse and the text is blocked. This takes practice. If you want to block a couple of lines of text, when you are dragging after holding the click, you also drag down as well as to the right.

Once the text is blocked, selected, or highlighted, you then select your changes for the font, the style, and size, etc. By blocking the text, the computer now knows what text it is you want to change.

If you want to make changes for an entire message, left click once on EDIT, and then left click once on SELECT ALL. This will "block" your entire message. A keyboard shortcut to "Select All" is to press the CTRL key, hold it down, and then press the "A" key; then let go of both keys. At this point, you can select your changes for the font, the style, and size. To unblock text, left click once in an area in the e-mail message that is not currently blocked.

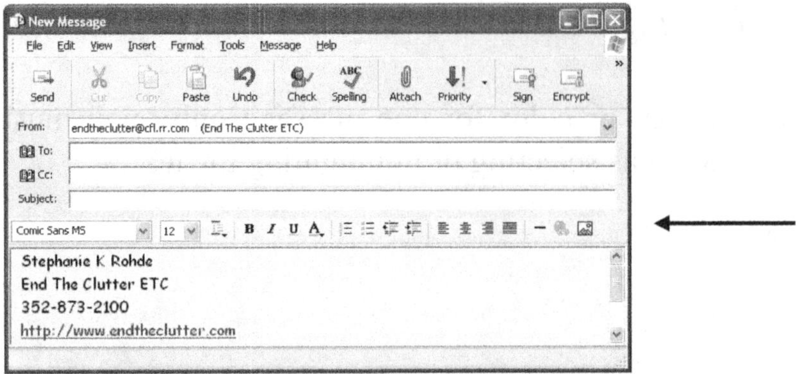

Figure 135 — Formatting or changing a new e-mail message.

Message Menu Bar

The first box in the menu bar is the "font" box. In the figure above, the font used is called "Comic Sans MS." Just before the right end of that font box is a little "directional down arrow." If you left click once on this directional down arrow, it will reveal many more fonts for you to choose from. To change a font in your e-mail message, remember that you must first "block" the text. After blocking the text that you want to change, you then left click once on the downward directional arrow in the font box. You then may scroll down to pick a new font. When you decide on the font you want, then you left click once on the name of the font. Voila! The new font has replaced the old font. To un-block the text, left click once in an unoccupied area of the e-mail message — a space that is not currently blocked.

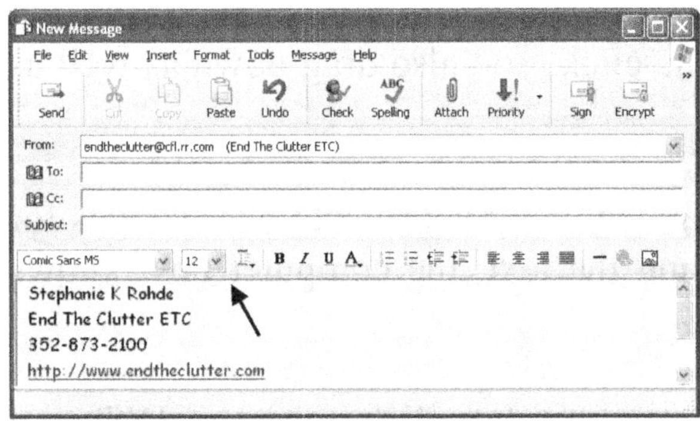

Figure 136 — Formatting an e-mail.

The size box is to the right of the font box on the menu bar. In the above example, the size is 12. This works the same way as the font box. Select the text first (block or highlight), and then change the size.

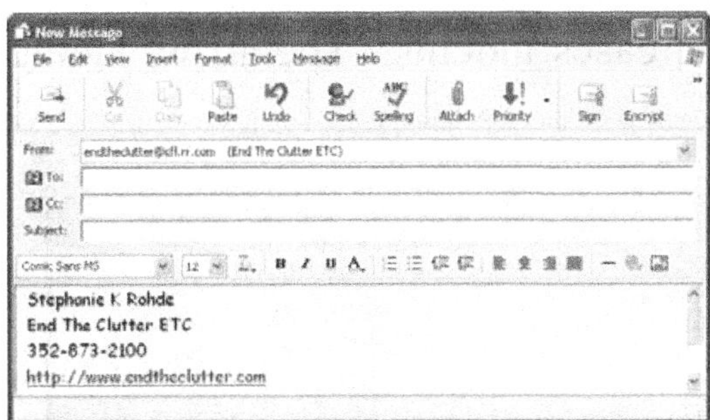

Figure 137 — Formatting an e-mail.

Continuing along to the right, we have the paragraph style (not necessarily for beginners), **Bold**, *Italics*, <u>Underline</u>, and Color of text. Block the text first, and then choose what you want.

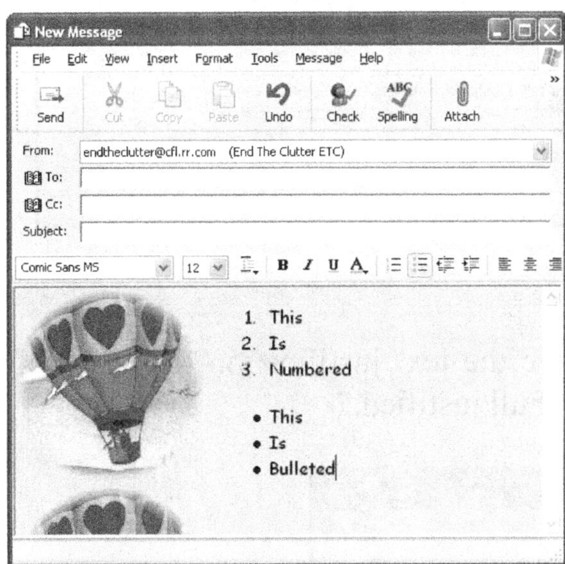

Figure 138 — Numbered and bulleted lists.

Next option for you is to insert a numbered or bulleted list. When the cursor is in the text box of an e-mail message and you left click once on the icon for numbered list, immediately after the left click, you will see a number "1." displayed. After you type your first item, press the "enter key;" the cursor will go to the next line and you will see a "2." displayed. To end the numbered list, press the ENTER key twice.

Bulleted lists work exactly the same way only instead of numbers appearing, you see bulleted icons. Please refer to the figure above.

Following numbered and bulleted lists on the menu bar is the increase and decrease indentation icons. The arrow facing the right increases indents. The arrow facing the left decreases the indentation.

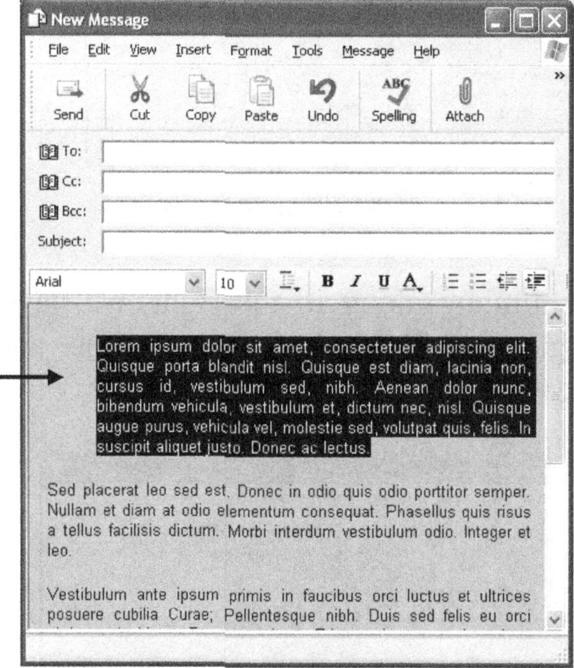

Figure 139 — Indentation.

To the right further on the menu bar, we have the text justification icons. "Left justified," "Centered," "Right justified," and "Full justified."

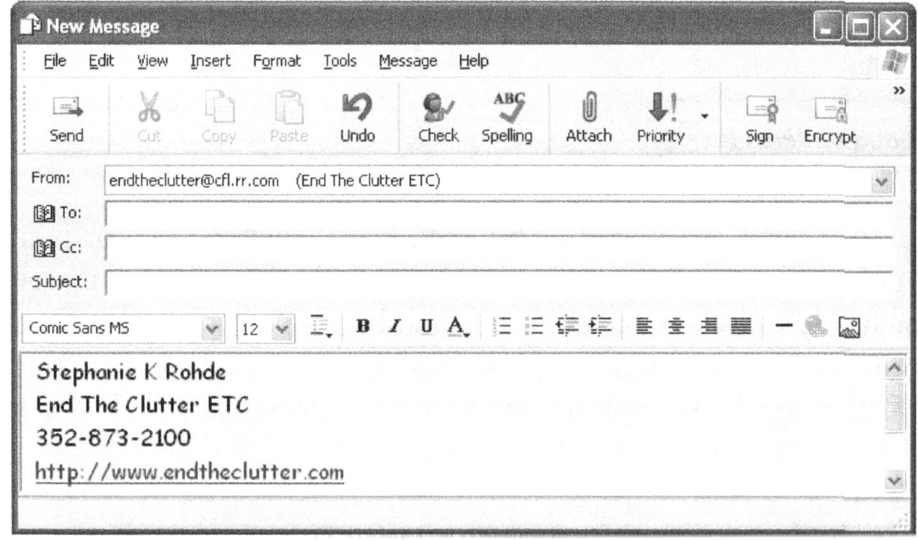

Figure 140 — Left Justified.

Use any and all information at your own risk.

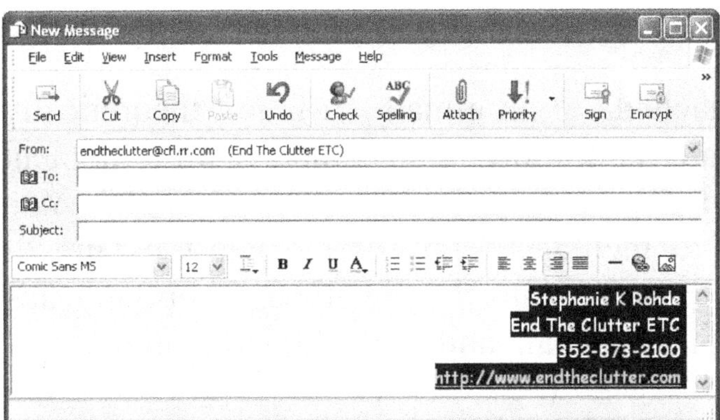

Figure 141 — Right Justified.

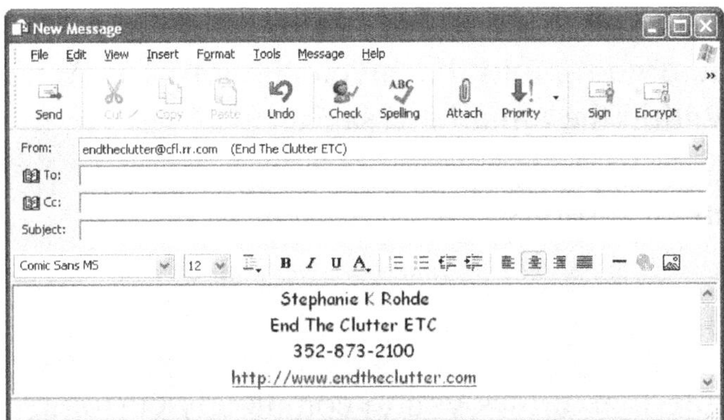

Figure 142 — Centered Text

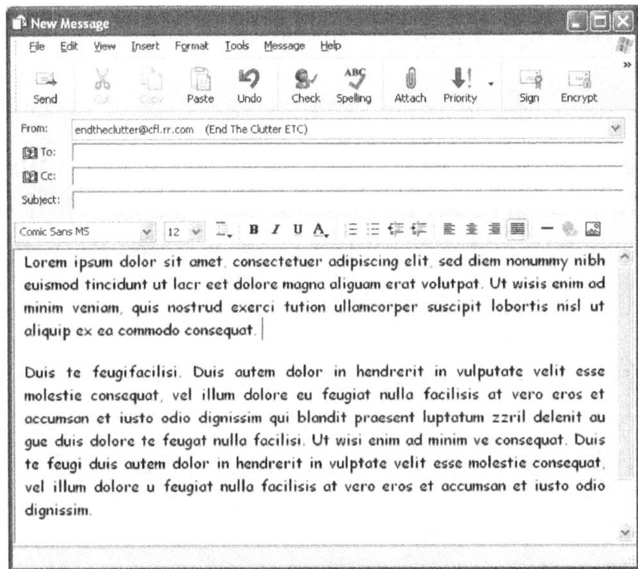

Figure 143 — Full Justified Text.

Attachments & Insertions

An attachment is something extra "attached" to an e-mail. It is not theoretically within the e-mail; it goes along with an e-mail. Forget the computer for a moment and think about writing an old-fashioned letter to a friend via "snail-mail." You write the letter and then you decide to include a copy of the latest picture of yourself. You have two separate items going into the envelope. Applying this scenario to the computer, the letter is an e-mail and the additional item, your picture, is the attachment.

Something *inserted* into an e-mail message on the other hand means just that. It is within and therefore part of the e-mail message. Using the example above of the snail-mail letter to your friend, imagine if you "taped" your picture right onto the letter. In this case, there is only one item going into the envelope, not two. With regard to e-mail, insertions are visible within the e-mail message.

There are many forms of attachments and insertions.

Stationery

Stationery is a wonderful insertion feature that allows you to completely customize your e-mail messages. It combines background images, graphics, fonts, and colors. You are limited only by your creativity. You can designate your own "default" stationery that will automatically be used with all your outgoing e-mail messages; and you always have the capability to change your stationery at any time for any reason in any e-mail message.

Please note that sometimes your messages with stationery get rejected by various places of business for various reasons. If you have an e-mail message rejected, try sending your message again using just plain text which has no formatting whatsoever.

There are many ways to use, obtain, and create stationery. A couple of techniques begin by using the COMPOSE tab. So to begin go back to the main screen of Outlook Express and left click once on TOOLS, then left click once on OPTIONS, and then once on the COMPOSE tab.

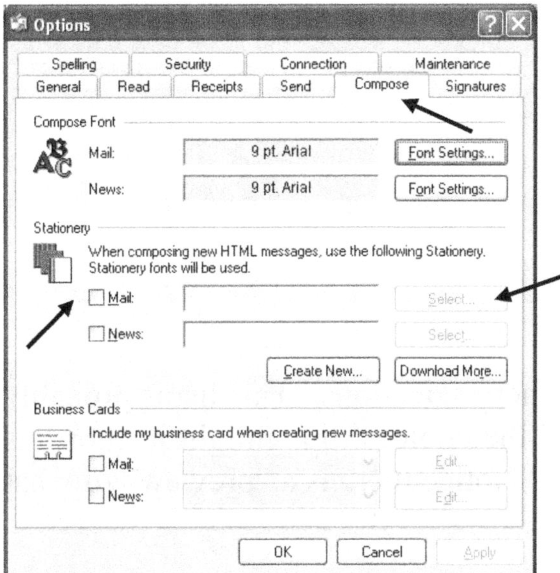

Figure 144 — Tools, Options, Compose tab.

One easy way to learn how stationery works is to use some that already exists on your computer. First place a check mark in the box directly to the left of "Mail" by left clicking once.

This action makes the "Select" button become active. Please refer to the figure below.

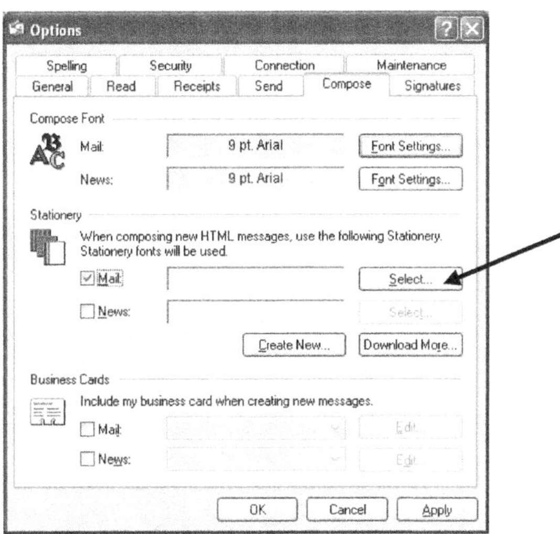

Figure 145 — "Select" button becomes active.

Left click once on the SELECT button. That action brings up the stationery folder.

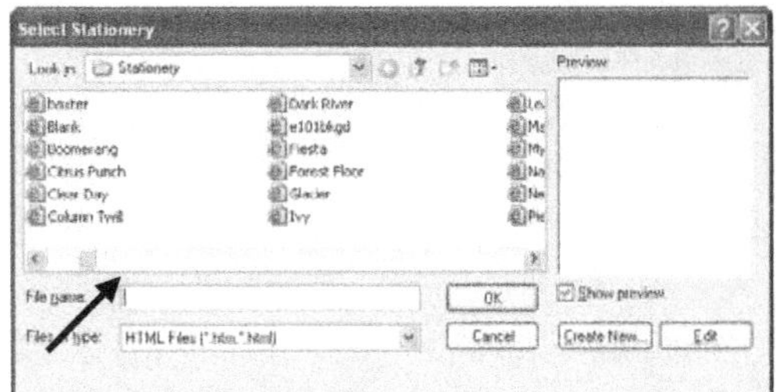

Figure 146 — Outlook Express Stationery Folder.

Use the scroll bar to see all the available stationery selections. This list is probably different on each computer. Left click one of the choices to highlight it. For this example, we use "Leaves" in the figure below. Notice there is a "preview" of what the selected stationery looks like.

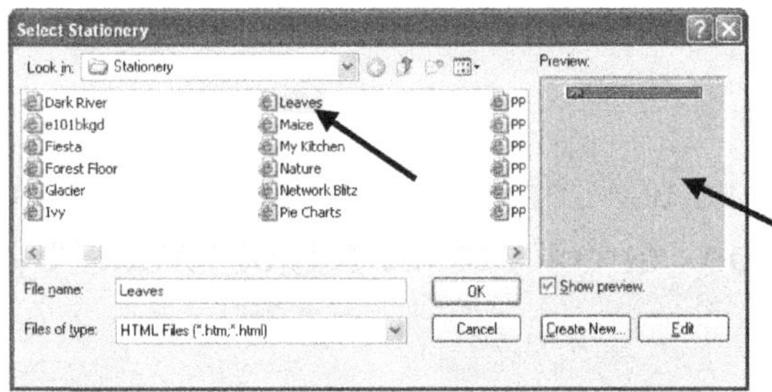

Figure 147 — Selection of LEAVES stationery.

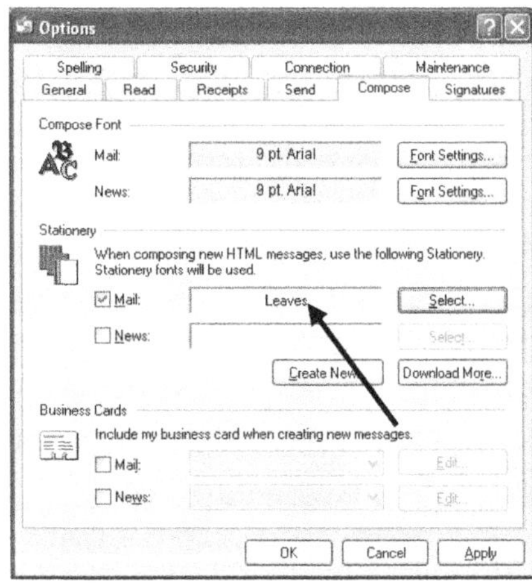

Figure 148 — "Leaves" is the chosen stationery.

Left click once on the OK button to close the COMPOSE tab in the Options window.

Now every time you create a new e-mail as per the previous example, "Leaves" will be the inserted stationery.

If you are feeling frisky, you can also create stationery from scratch. Go back to TOOLS, OPTIONS, and the COMPOSE tab.

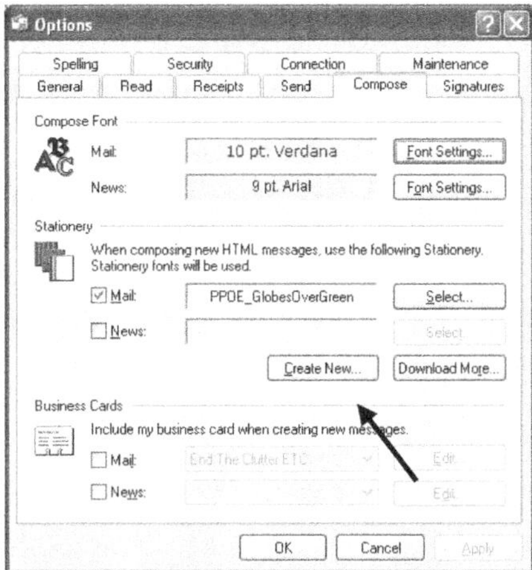

Figure 149 — "Create New" Stationery.

Creating stationery is a step up in difficulty than selecting already existing stationery. In the Stationery area left click once on CREATE NEW. This action will bring up the Stationery Wizard.

Figure 150 — Stationery Wizard.

The stationery wizard walks you through the "creating" stationery process. Take a deep breath; don't forget to exhale, and left click once on NEXT.

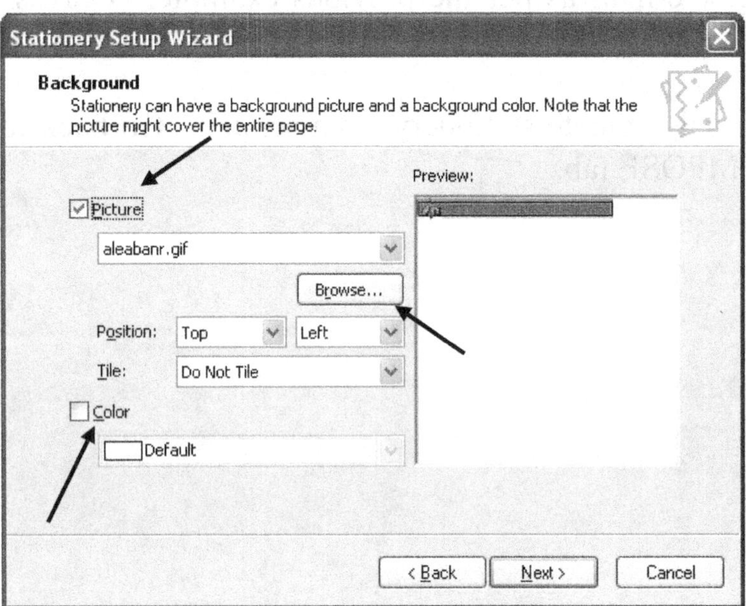

Figure 151 — Stationery Wizard Continued.

When creating stationery, you can have a background picture, a background color, or both as part of your stationery.

If you want a background picture, you have to know the location of the picture that you want to use; and then you have to tell the computer where the picture is. Left clicking once on the BROWSE button, helps accomplish this.

This process of locating "things" otherwise known as files is very important because it is used often; specifically when you want to insert your favorite family photo into an e-mail for example.

After you have told the computer the location of the background picture for your stationery via the BROWSE button, a preview of that picture will be displayed.

Any color you choose is previewed for you as well.

The *position* of the picture in this example is the top and left side. This means that the picture as part of your stationery will be located at the top left section of your e-mails.

When you are satisfied with the preview, left click once on NEXT.

                    Use any and all information at your own risk.

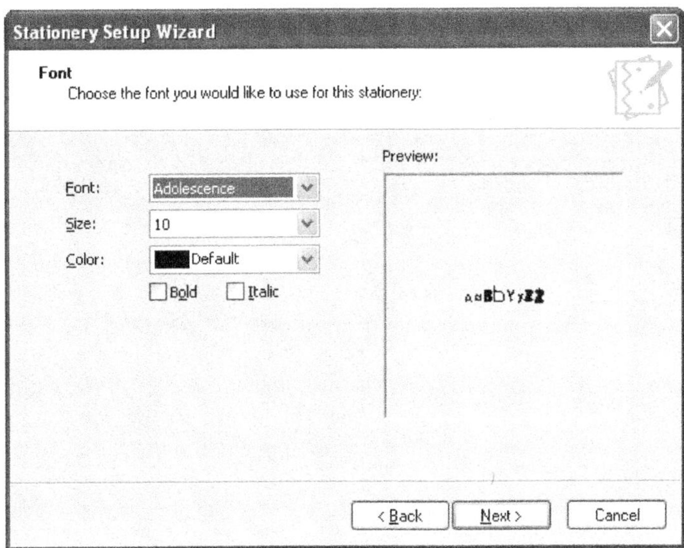

Figure 152 — Stationery wizard continued.

The above figure has to do with *text*. Select the font, size, and color. A preview of your font, size and color selections will be displayed in the "Preview" box.

The figure below has to do with text margins, not picture margins. Increase and decrease the left and top margins with the up and down arrows to see how the text margins move in the preview.

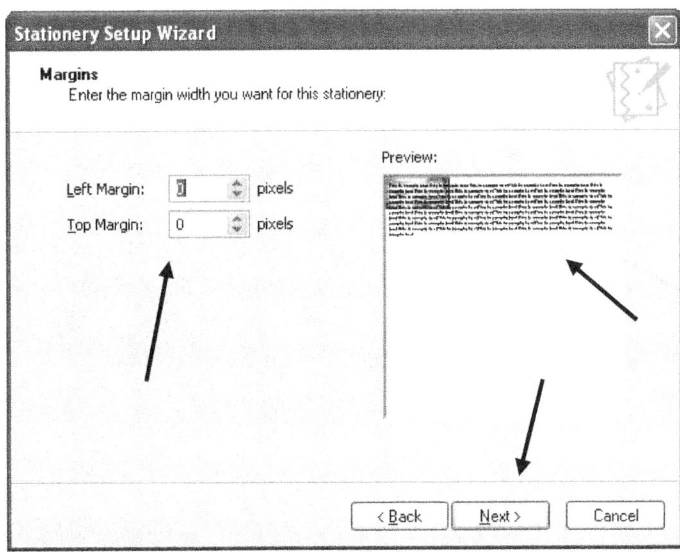

Figure 153 — Stationery wizard continued.

When you are ready, left click once on NEXT.

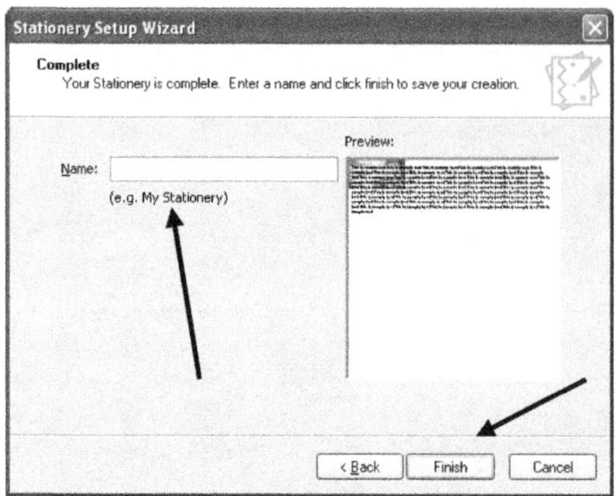

Figure 154 — Stationery wizard.

Choose a name for the stationery you have just created and left click once on FINISH.

You now know the difference between selecting stationery that already exists and creating new stationery.

You can also *download* additional stationery. Go back to the TOOLS, OPTIONS, and the Compose tab.

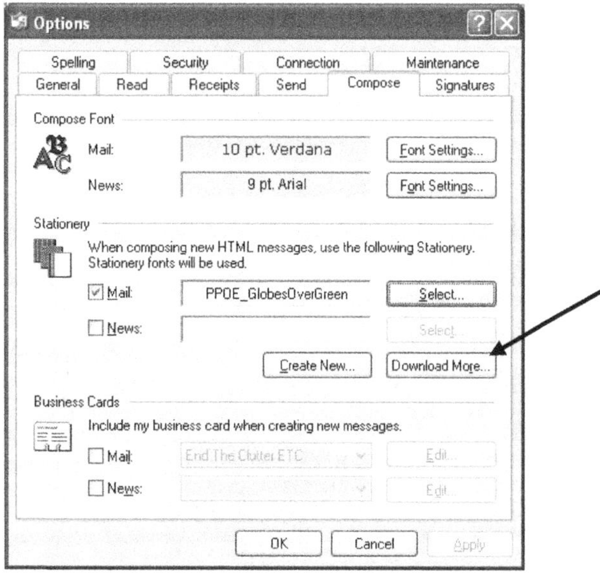

Figure 155 — Tools, Options, Compose tab.

Left click once on DOWNLOAD MORE.

Use any and all information at your own risk.

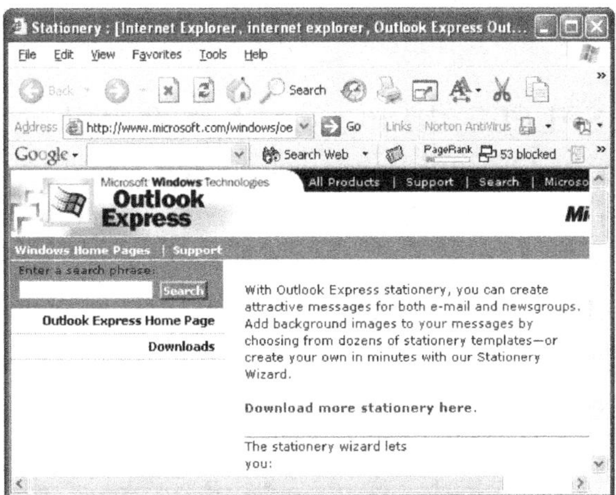

Figure 156 — Additional stationery from Microsoft.

After left clicking on the "Download More" button, something like the figure above will appear. You must be connected to the Internet for this window to appear.

Follow instructions to preview and download additional stationery from:

http://www.microsoft.com/windows/oe/features/stationery/default.ASP

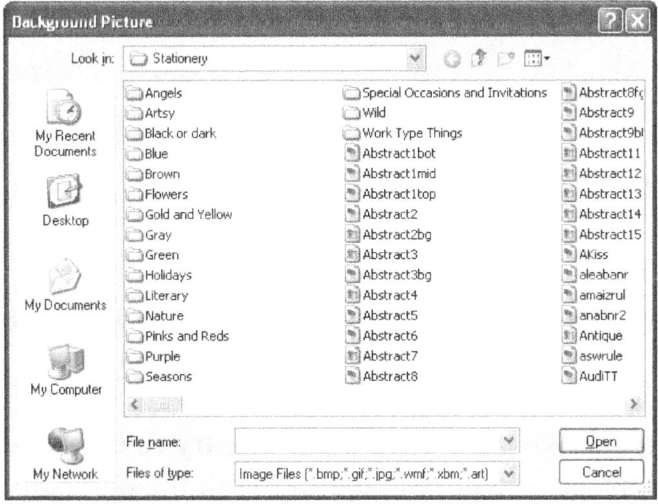

Figure 157 — Stationery Folder in Outlook Express.

If the Stationery Wizard or downloading additional stationery has temporarily placed you on "overload," remember you can always use stationery that is already provided on your computer.

As if all the above wasn't enough, you also have the option of using stationery that someone else has created or has used to send you e-mail.

If you like another's stationery, all you do is SELECT the message by left clicking once on the message in the main screen view of Outlook Express. Then left click once on FILE, and then left click again on SAVE AS STATIONERY.

You have the option to change or add stationery in the middle of an e-mail message. While you are within the e-mail message, left click once on FORMAT, then point the mouse to APPLY STATIONERY, and then select your choice. Just to keep you on your toes, the APPLY STATIONERY command works a little bit differently. When using this command, you only get the background color of the stationery. This won't look the same as the e-mail window that you get when you use the CREATE MAIL command or the MESSAGE, NEW USING command.

Please remember that stationery messages are created in HTML. None of this "fun stuff" can be done in the "plain" text mode.

Still don't have enough stationery? Companies produce HTML stationery for purchase. Go to any search engine on the Web and type in "Outlook Express Stationery" and you'll find a plethora of places to go to purchase.

Never purchase *anything* on-line unless you feel comfortable in doing so.

Don't download purchased software if you have the option to receive it on a CD or DVD. If you only download the software and you do not have it on a CD or DVD and something unthinkable happens to your computer, you may have lost the software forever.

Some software can be purchased via download as well as on a CD or DVD. This allows you instant access to the software with the backup copy on the way to you.

If downloading is the *only* way you can receive purchased software, try to copy the files to a CD so you have some kind of backup. Communicating with the company who sold you downloadable software to have them re-authorize a download can be difficult or sometimes impossible.

Signatures

When you first hear this term with regard to e-mail it may seem a bit confusing.

You don't physically take your pen and "sign your name."

What you actually do is create some text and/or graphics that explain or represent who you are or where you live.

The figure below gives an example of a signature inserted into an e-mail message that used the Valentine's Day stationery.

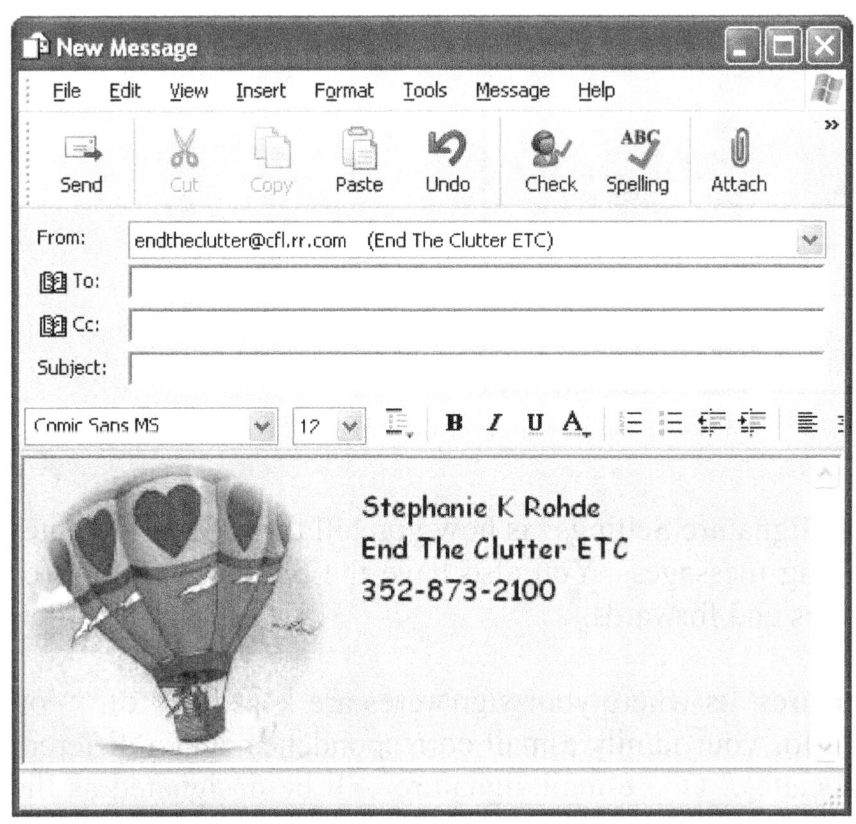

Figure 158 — New e-mail message with signature inserted.

Typing specific information at the end of every e-mail message — like your name and address for example is not only time consuming, there is always the possibility of a typing error or simply forgetting to include important information. By creating a "signature," you can have the correct information added every time.

To add your signature(s) to your outgoing messages, left click once on TOOLS, left click once on OPTIONS, and then left click once on the SIGNATURES tab.

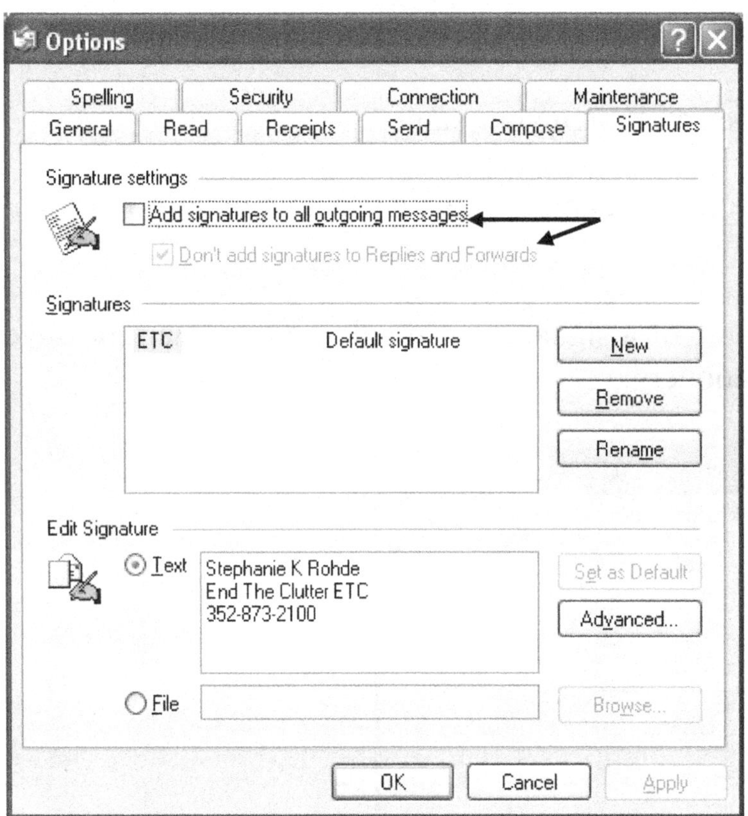

Figure 159 — Signature tab.

The top section of this tab "Signature Settings" is how you tell the program to enter your signature to all outgoing messages. You also have the option of adding (or not) signatures to your replies and forwards.

The middle section "Signatures" is where your signatures are kept track of. You might have a one signature for your family e-mail correspondence, and a different one for your business associates. One e-mail signature will be designated as the one you use most often, the *default* e-mail signature. If you only have one e-mail signature, that signature is the default signature.

The lower section "Edit Signature" is where you type in what you want your e-mail signature to be.

To create a signature in the "Signatures" block, left click once on NEW.

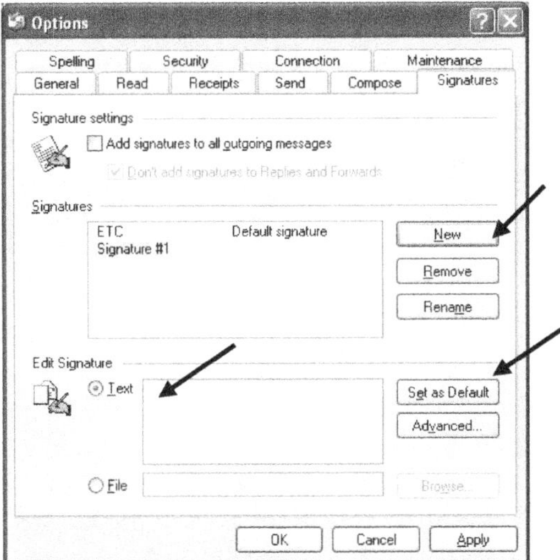

Figure 160 — Signatures tab.

As you left click once on NEW, the cursor will become active in the "Text" box in the "Edit Signature" area. Type in what you want for a signature. If you want this signature as the default e-mail signature, you must left click once on SET AS DEFAULT.

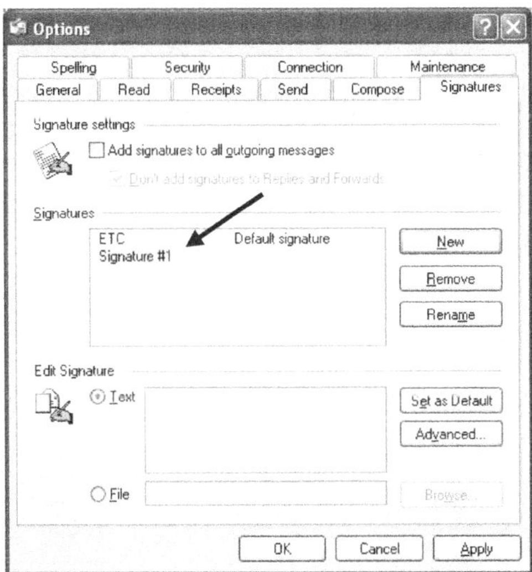

Figure 161 — Signatures tab.

You may "rename" "Signature #1" to something that makes more sense to you. If you have several physical addresses may want to have a separate e-mail signature for each physical address. Use what ever makes sense to you; and know that you can change it whenever you want.

For those who have more than one e-mail address account in Outlook Express, you can automatically use different e-mail signatures with different e-mail accounts by clicking the ADVANCED tab shown below.

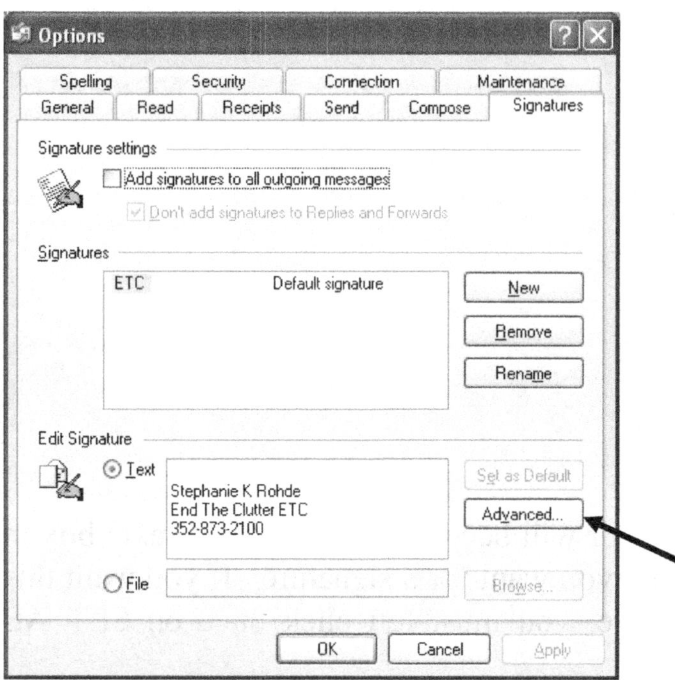

Figure 162 — Signatures tab.

Select an e-mail signature by left clicking it once. Left click once on the ADVANCED tab something like the figure below appears.

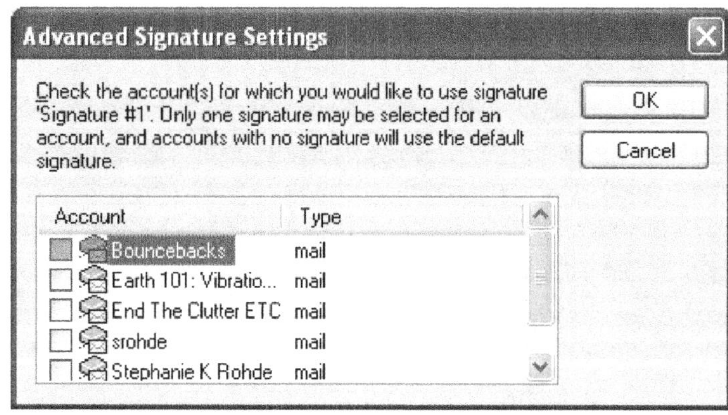

Figure 163 — Advanced signature settings.

Place a check mark in any box to the left of the account that you want to use the above figure "selected" signature for.

Signatures tab review.

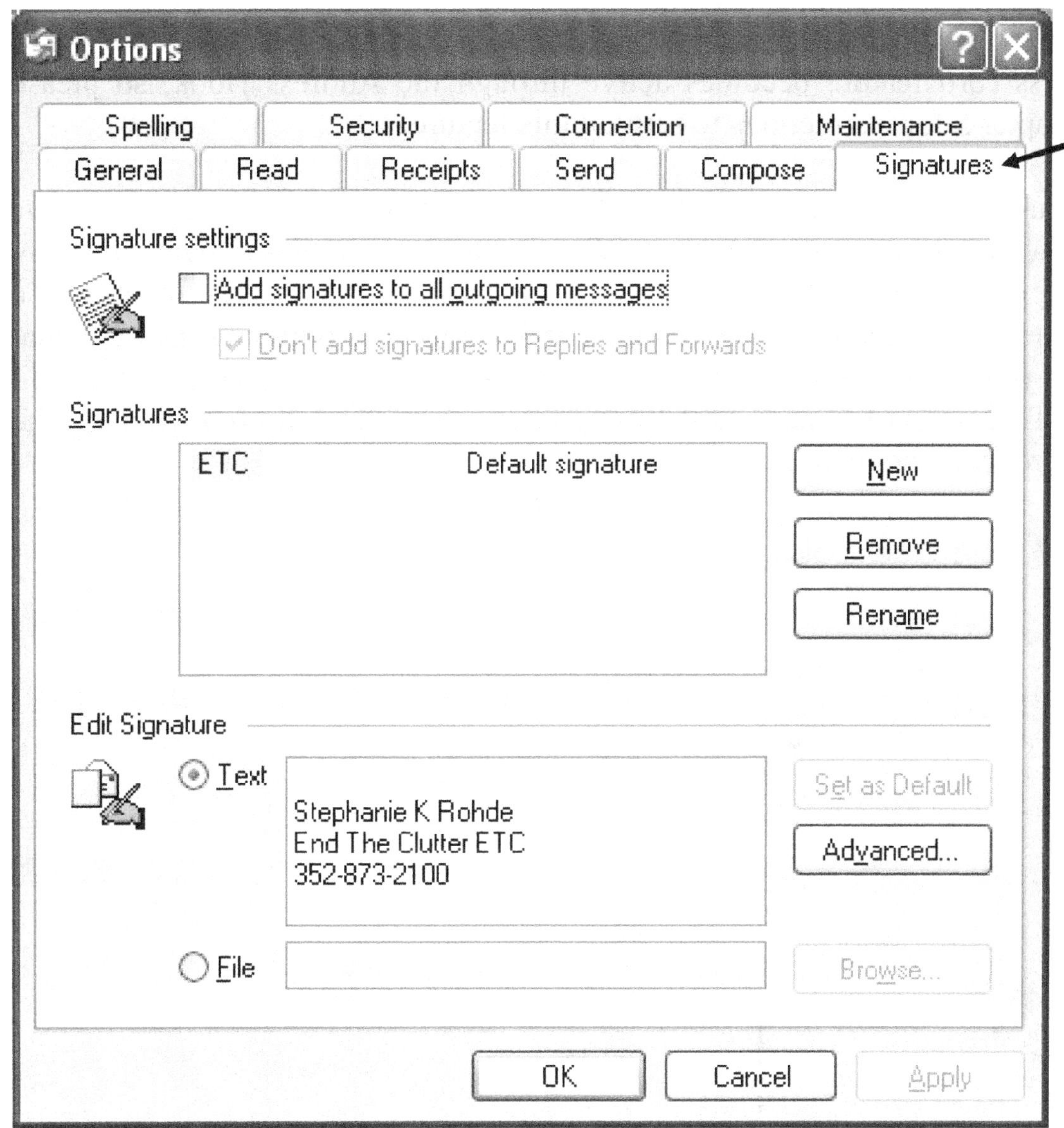

Figure 164 — Signatures tab.

This is where you tell the program to include signatures (or not) in your outgoing e-mail messages. You can place your signature in your original e-mails and in replies and forwards.

You can have as many signatures as you would like; if you have more than one, you must select one "signature" as the "default.

After you select a signature, you may modify, remove, or rename.

Electronic Business Cards

The business card feature becomes active through the Address Book, so please refer to Chapter 5 for instructions to turn on this feature.

Once the business card feature is active, you can send contact information for *any* individual with your outgoing messages. Please notice in the figure below directly to the right of the FROM block field is a little icon that looks very much like a little "business card" icon. When this icon appears in your outgoing message that means that you are sending an attached electronic business card with your e-mail message. To delete a business card from any one e-mail, right click once on the business card icon and then left click once on DELETE.

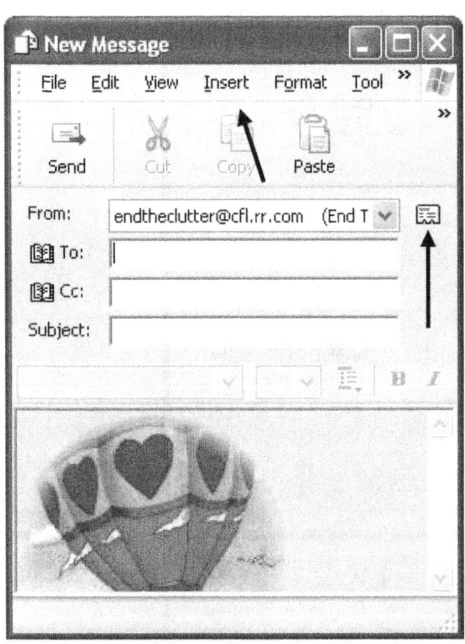

Figure 165 — Electronic business card.

To turn on or turn off the inclusion of the electronic business card, left click once on INSERT to see if there is a check mark (or not) to the left of where it says MY BUSINESS CARD. If there is a check mark beside it, the electronic business card is sent along by default with every e-mail message that you send. If you do not want the business card sent with every e-mail message you send, left click once on MY BUSINESS CARD and the check mark will disappear. To add your business card to one specific e-mail message only, left click once on INSERT, and then left click again on MY BUSINESS CARD.

To insert your business card into all messages, left click once on TOOLS, then OPTIONS, and then left click once on the COMPOSE tab.

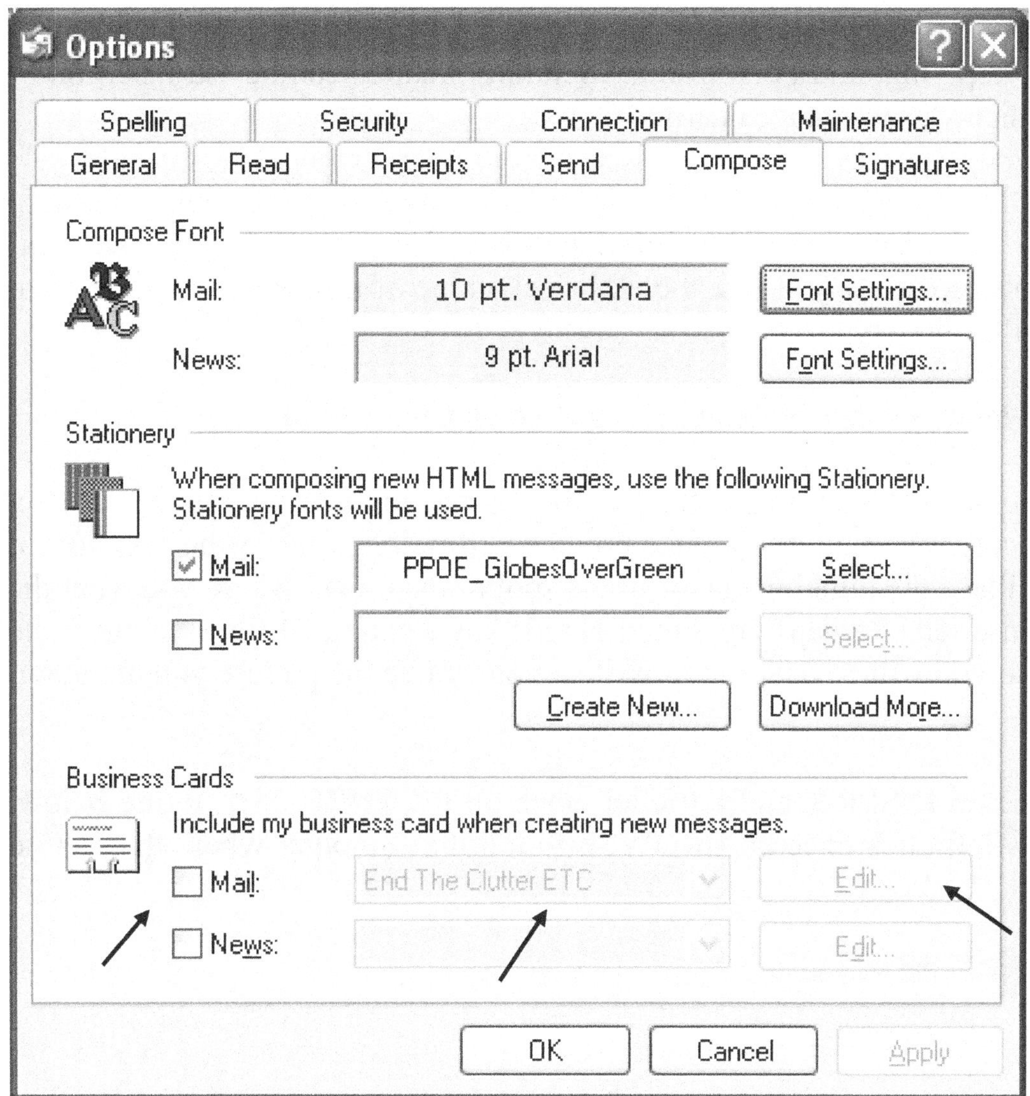

Figure 166 — "Compose" tab.

In the Business Cards section, place a check mark in the box to the left of "Mail" (left click once in the box), and choose your "contact of choice" information to attach as an electronic business card by left clicking once on the directional down arrow. You do have the option of including the business card of any individual in your Address Book.

To change information on any existing contact business card information, click EDIT.

Pictures

People love to send and receive pictures. *Receiving* pictures is covered in Chapter 7, Receiving, Replying, and Forwarding. Sending pictures can be via insertion or attachment which was introduced earlier.

Let's discuss "inserting" a picture first. In order to insert a picture into an e-mail message, you have to know where that particular picture is located on your computer. This process is just like the earlier example of inserting a picture when creating e-mail stationery.

Open a new e-mail message by left clicking once on Create Mail.

Left click once in the TEXT box of the e-mail message to make the text box active. An "I-beam" cursor and not the mouse pointer will be blinking in the text box of the message. Place the blinking cursor in the spot in the e-mail where you want the picture to be inserted. Perhaps press the ENTER key a couple of times to move the cursor down so you will have space to write a note above the picture you are about to insert.

Left click once on INSERT, and left click once on PICTURE. See figure below. You must now left click once on BROWSE to tell the computer where the picture file is located.

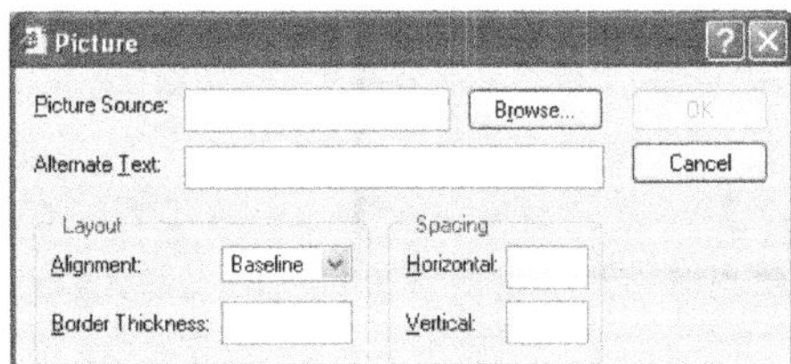

Figure 167 — "Inserting a picture" window.

If you don't know where the picture is you get stopped in your tracks right here. Think about this for a minute. Is the picture on a CD-ROM that you received from a photo development company? Have you scanned the picture to your computer? Is the picture sitting in your scanner? Is the picture in a folder located on your hard drive (C :) somewhere? Is the picture on your desktop? Was the picture e-mailed to you from someone else? You absolutely have to know the location of the picture.

If there are certain pictures you really like, you want to have them readily available to you for e-mailing at a moment's notice. Consider creating a new folder on your desktop to hold these pictures. This way you always know where your most adored pictures reside and you can locate them easily when the computer prompts you.

To create a folder on your desktop, right click the mouse once in a clear unoccupied area of your desktop. This will bring up a sub menu. Left click once on NEW, and left click once again on FOLDER.

The above actions create a folder on your desktop. The next step is to give this new folder a name. When the folder is created, the folder name is "New Folder" by default. This name "New Folder" is highlighted and it is waiting for you to type in the name you want to call this folder. A safe name for this folder is "your name" and the word PICS; like "Joe's PICS" or "Mike's PICS" for example.

As you begin typing the name for your folder, the blue-highlighted area will disappear. After you type in the name of your choice, press the enter key once. You now have your new folder on your desktop. If you want to "rename" this folder at any time, right click once on the name of the folder, and then left click once on RENAME. Then type in your new name for the folder and then press the enter key once.

Please do not use the name "My Pictures" as your new folder name because there already is a folder with that name included within the computer's operating system. This can cause great unnecessary confusion when you are learning.

If you place all your special pictures in this folder located on your desktop, you can tell the computer that the location is the "Desktop" whenever it asks you. In the following example and figures, the pictures are located on the DESKTOP in a folder called Joe's PICS.

If, in your e-mail message the "Picture" command is grayed out (shaded and unavailable for choosing), you need to verify your format mode. Remember that pictures are not available in the plain text mode. When you left click once on FORMAT, make sure there is a black dot next to Rich Text (HTML).

If your message recipients report back to you that they cannot view your insertions, go to TOOLS, OPTIONS, and left click once on the SEND tab. Then left click once on the HTML box. Make sure that the box next to "SEND PICTURES WITH MESSAGES has a check mark in it. From within a specific e-mail you can left click once on FORMAT and then left click on "Send Pictures with Message."

You also have the option to send an e-mail with your favorite picture as a background for the message. To do this, left click once on FORMAT, point your mouse to BACKGROUND, and then left click once on PICTURE. You must then left click once the BROWSE button and tell the computer where the picture is. Hopefully, the picture is located on your desktop, in a folder that you created.

Insert a Picture Step-By-Step.

Open a new e-mail message by left clicking once on CREATE MAIL.

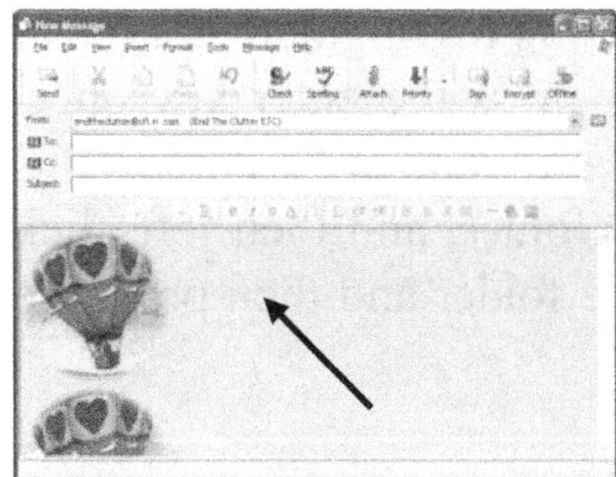

Figure 168 — New e-mail message.

To insert the picture of your choice, remember you first must have the cursor in the text box of the message. For this to happen, left click once in the text box of the message.

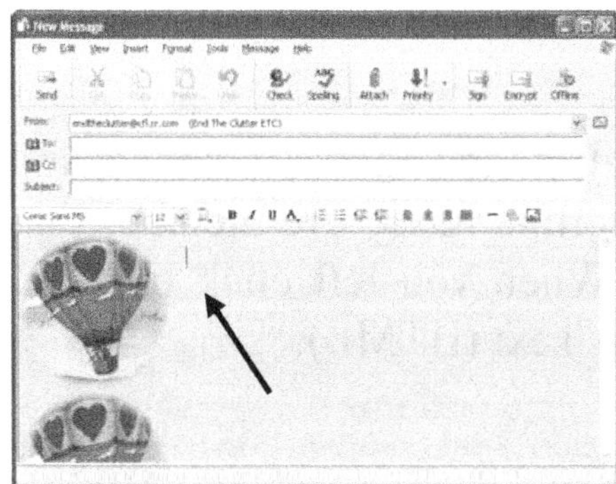

Figure 169 — Cursor or "I" beam in the text box of the message.

     Use any and all information at your own risk.

Figure 170 — Cursor or "I" beam in the text box of the message.

Left click once on INSERT, and then on PICTURE. That will bring up the figure below.

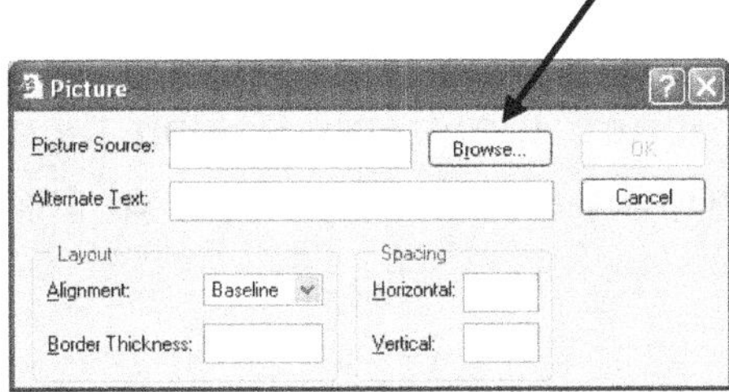

Figure 171 — Identifying the location of a picture.

Left click once on the BROWSE button. The window that appears looks differently on *every* computer. Left click once on the downward directional arrow.

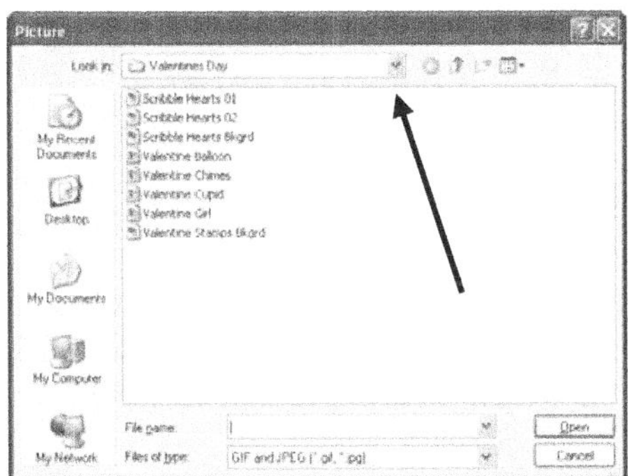

Figure 172 — Computer asking for location of a picture.

In this example, we will tell the computer that the location of the picture is on the DESKTOP in the folder named "Joe's PICS." When you left click on the directional down-arrow, a sub menu appears and you want to left click once on DESKTOP. That action brings up the next figure with "Desktop" being the place to look for the picture.

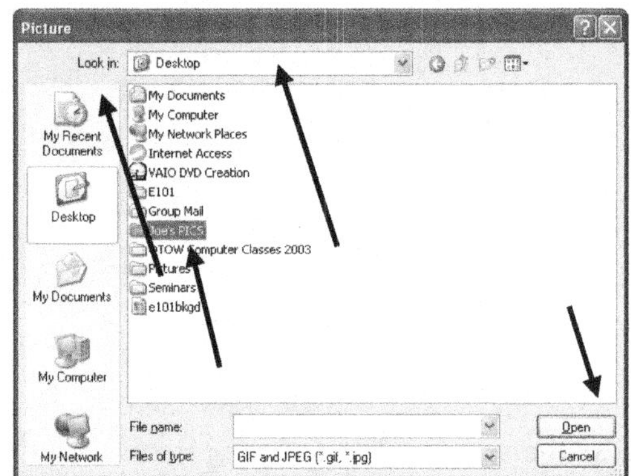

Figure 173 — Location of picture process.

Left click once on the folder named "Joe's PICS."

Once you have "Joe's PICS" highlighted (or your picture highlighted), you then left click once on OPEN. This action will allow you to see the contents of the "Joe's PICS" folder.

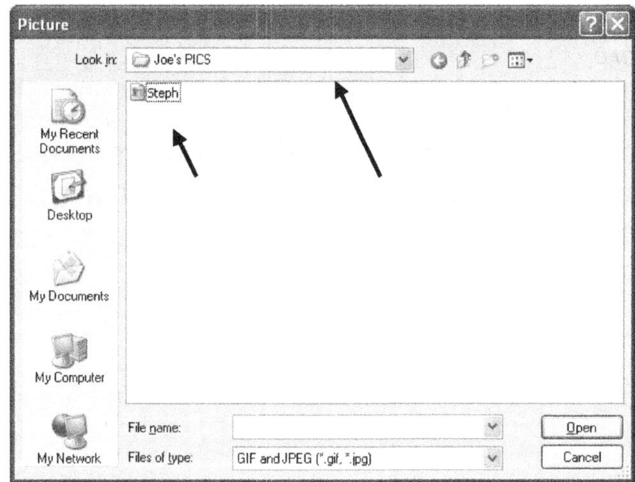

Figure 174 — Actual location of a specific picture(s).

The figure above is an idea of what "should" be appearing on your computer. All the pictures that you have placed in your new folder named "Whatever" (in this example, "Joe's PICS") should be listed as you reach this step. You then left click once on the picture you want; in this example "Steph." As we select "Steph," "Steph" will appear in the "File name" field. Then you left click once on OPEN. That brings you back to the window that originally asked for the location of the picture. It is now filled in with the correct file path (location of the picture).

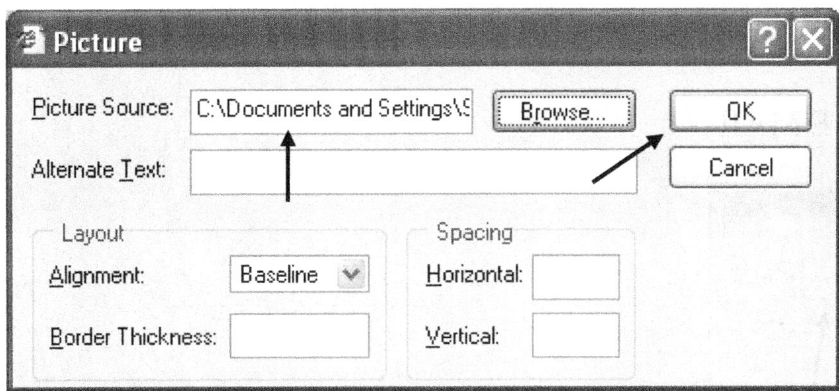

Figure 175 — Picture location in "Picture Source" box.

The computer has been told the location of the picture. The file path is listed to the right of "Picture Source." Now you left click once on OK.

As you complete that action, the picture of your choice *should* be inserted into the e-mail message like in the example below.

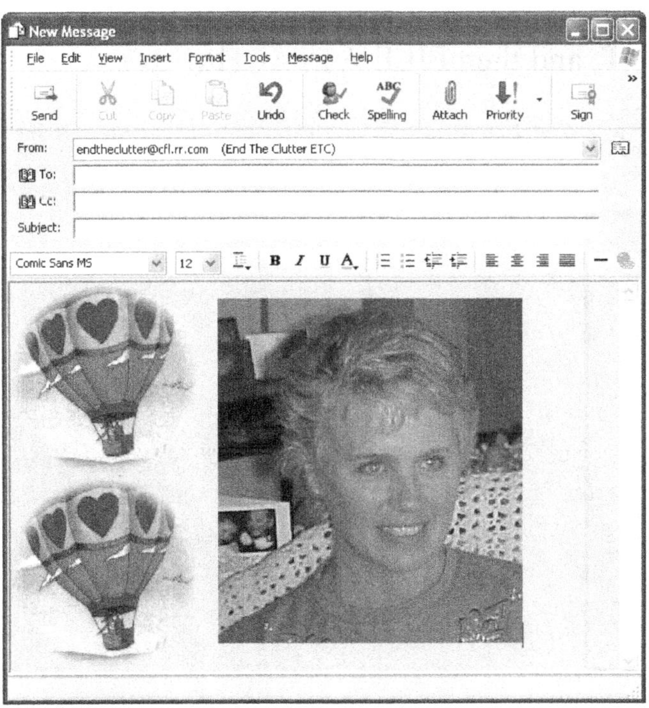

Figure 176 — Picture inserted into an e-mail message.

Your picture of choice has been inserted into your e-mail message. Don't get discouraged. This technique takes lots and lots of practice.

Attach a Picture Step-By-Step

Left click once on CREATE MAIL.

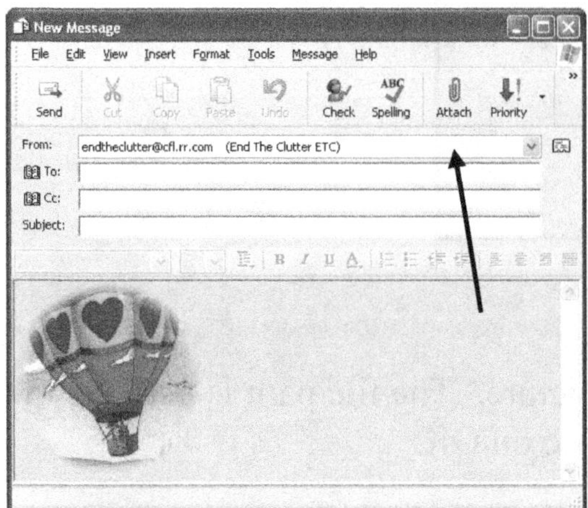

Figure 177 — New e-mail message.

Left click once on ATTACH. If the attachment button is not showing on your computer, then left click once on INSERT, and then FILE ATTACHMENT.

You are headed to your desktop and the folder that has your pictures in it.

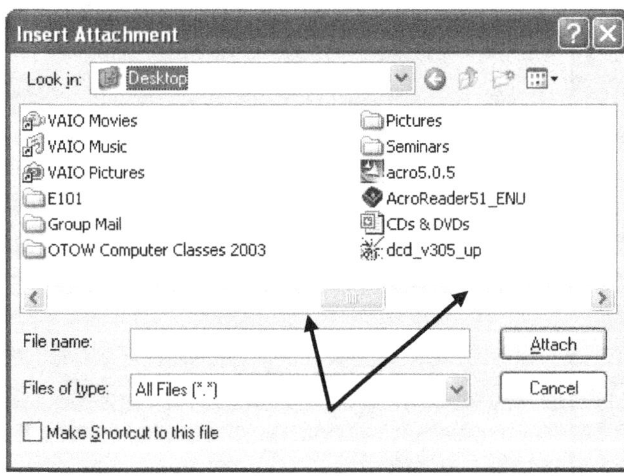

Figure 178 — Telling the computer a file location.

You may have to scroll over to see the entire list of what is currently on your desktop to find the folder you want; in this example we are looking for "Joe's PICS."

                    Use any and all information at your own risk.

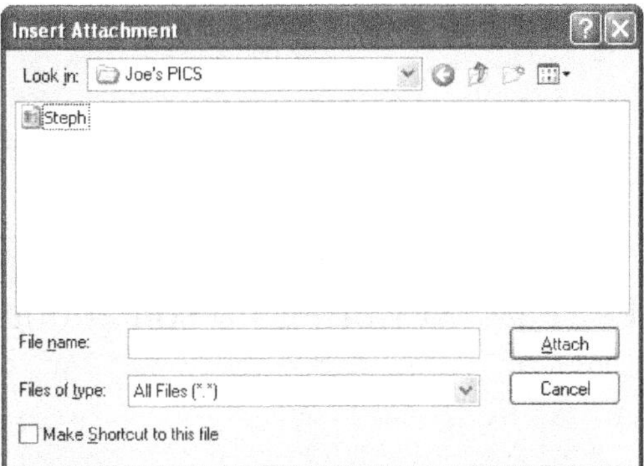

Figure 179 — Selection of picture to attach.

Left click once on the picture you wish to attach to your e-mail and then left click once on ATTACH (to insert you clicked on OPEN at this step).

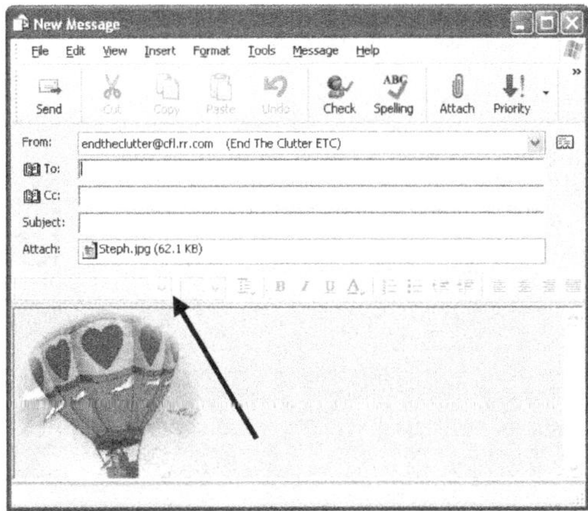

Figure 180 — Picture (file) attached to an e-mail message.

The file is attached. You don't see the picture inserted in the e-mail.

Many individuals insert *and* attach pictures in their e-mails. This allows for the greatest potential for recipients to "open" and view the pictures.

Understanding about the size of a picture file is important; especially if you or your e-mail recipients are using a telephone dial-up connection. In the example above, the attachment file size is 62.1 KB. This is nice and small; no problem for any connection speed. But if the file size was 3200 KB which is 3.2MB, it could take 10-15 minutes minimum to send via the telephone dial-up; so never send more than one picture of this size per e-mail if sending to individuals with a dial-up connection.

Sounds

Once you have mastered inserting and attaching pictures, inserting all kinds of other files becomes *almost* easy.

To begin, left click once on CREATE MESSAGE. That will bring up something like the figure below.

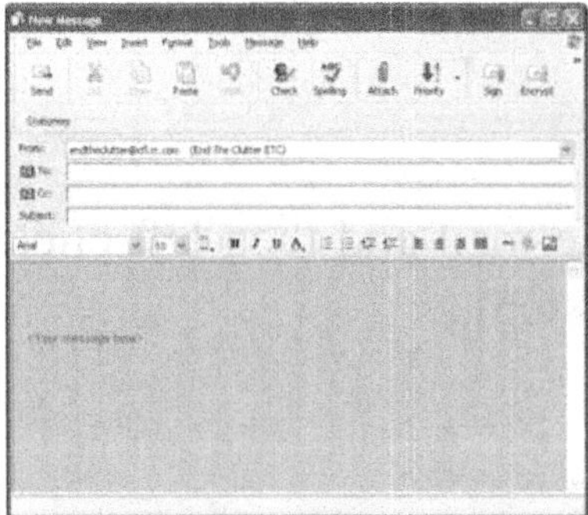

Figure 181 — E-mail message.

Left click once on FORMAT, point your mouse to BACKGROUND, and then left click once on SOUND.

Figure 182 — Entering a sound into an e-mail message.

In a similar fashion to inserting a picture, you must tell the computer the location of the sound file that you wish to insert. When you know the location of the sound that you want to play within your e-mail, you left click once on BROWSE and tell the computer the location. Once you give the location to the computer and left click once on OK, you will come back to something like the previous figure with the file path listed in the box next to "File." This is just like inserting a picture.

Figure 183 — Inserting a sound file.

You then decide how many times the sound will play, or to have it play continuously. You then left click OK and your sound has been inserted into your e-mail message. We recommend you do not choose "Continuously" as it can get annoying very quickly to the individual receiving the message.

As a precautionary measure, please consider sending *all* messages based on what you are learning to *you* first; many times if needed prior to sending to other humans. You will be glad you did in the long run. You want to see and hear how e-mail messages are arriving before you release them to the world.

Files

Once you feel comfortable with inserting and/or attaching a picture, or inserting a sound in your e-mail messages, inserting or attaching *any* file becomes second nature because it is exactly the same process as it is for the pictures and the sounds.

To insert "text" from any file located anywhere on your computer system, once again you must be in a new e-mail message. So, left click once on CREATE MAIL. Once you have a new e-mail message displayed, you need to have the cursor or I-beam in the text section of the message. To make this happen, left click once in the text portion of the e-mail message.

At this point left click once on INSERT, and then left click TEXT FROM FILE.

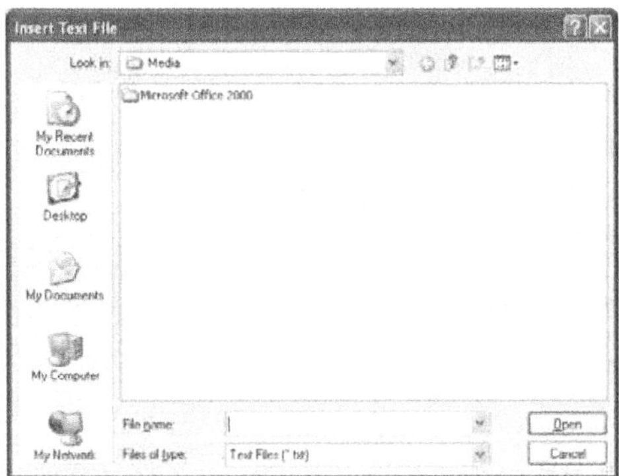

Figure 184 — Look for a file to insert or attach to an e-mail.

These kinds of windows like the one above should begin to look familiar to you now because the computer is always going to ask you where the location is of any file you want to insert into your e-mail message.

Regardless of whether you are inserting "into the e-mail message", or you are "attaching something to" an e-mail message, you must always be aware of the location of the "file" involved; you must know the location of the file. Remember that every computer system is different.

To attach any file (not just a picture) to your e-mail message, click on the "paper clip" icon in the tool bar of a new message. If the paper clip icon is not showing, left click once on INSERT, make your choice.

                    Use any and all information at your own risk.

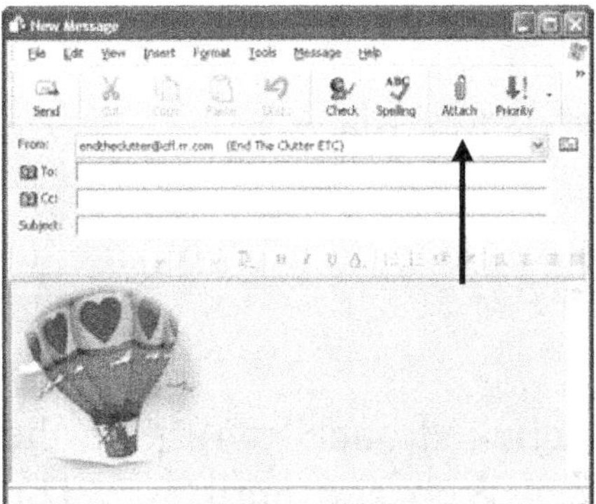

Figure 185 — New e-mail.

After you left click once on the "paper clip" icon, you will be asked the location of the file.

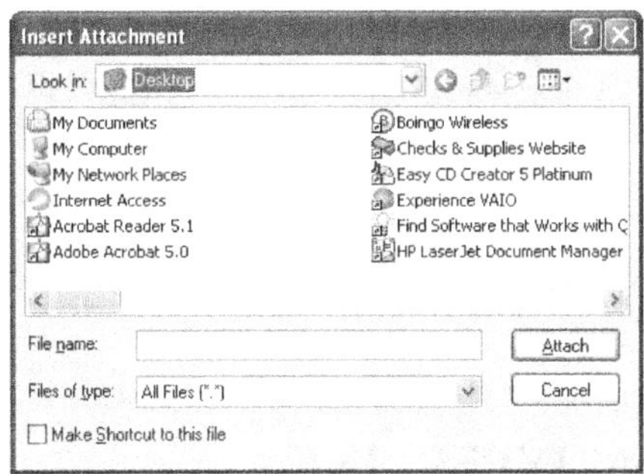

Figure 186 — Where's the file?

Hopefully you know the location of the file that you want to attach. In the beginning put things on the desktop so you can locate them easily. When you have eventually located the file, left click once on ATTACH. Then the file will be listed in the Attachment box in the e-mail message header.

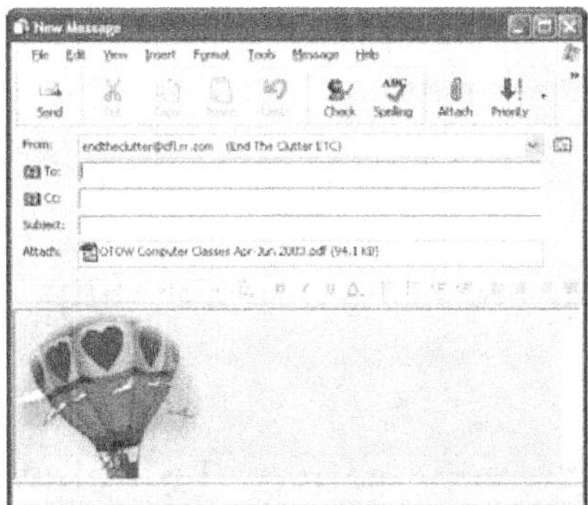

Figure 187 — Attachment successfully attached to an e-mail.

Hyperlinks

A hyperlink can be an icon, a graphic, or a word that exists in a file.

Hyperlinks can refer to a Web site address in an e-mail message, to a Web page, to a document, or to something completely different.

Web pages usually include hyperlinks that when "left clicked once" will take the viewer to another page on that Web site or to another Web site entirely. The mouse pointer often turns into a "hand" when it is around a "hyperlink."

Hyperlinks actually include the address and/or the name of the file, to which they point, but most of the time that information is hidden from the viewer.

To insert a hyperlink into an e-mail message, make sure you have a new e-mail message displayed. Left click once in the text portion of the e-mail message so that the cursor (I-Beam) is blinking in the text box.

Make sure the cursor is located at the position in the text box that you want to place the hyperlink.

Left click once on INSERT, and left click once again on HYPERLINK.

Figure 188 — Hyperlink insertion.

Some links begin with "http:" and some do not. If you are not sure, use "http:" which is the predefined setting (default).

Once you type in the Web address, the OK button will become active. Left click once on OK which will bring up something like the next figure.

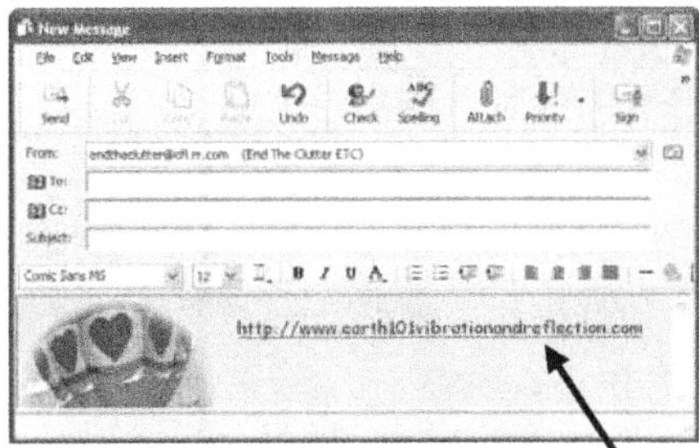

Figure 189 — Inserted hyperlink.

If for some reason, your attempt to insert a hyperlink does not work, perhaps the Rich Text (HTML) formatting is not selected. To check this, while you are in the e-mail message window, left click once on FORMAT and make sure a black dot is to the left of "Rich Text HTML" (• Rich Text HTML).

Instead of just inserting a hyperlink that points to a Web page, you can also insert a Web page into an e-mail message if you want to. The trick in this case is that you need to have already saved the Web page as an "HTML file" somewhere on your computer where you can locate it easily; like on the Desktop for example.

Left click once on CREATE MAIL and left click once in the message text box. Make sure the cursor is where you want to insert the actual Web page. Left click once on INSERT, and left click once on TEXT FROM FILE.

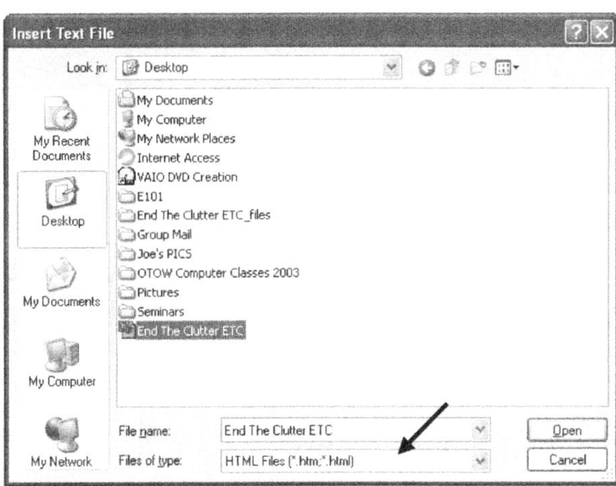

Figure 190 — Inserting a Web page into an e-mail.

The issue here is to make sure that the file type is (.HTML) and not "Text Files (*.txt), which may the default for this window on your computer.

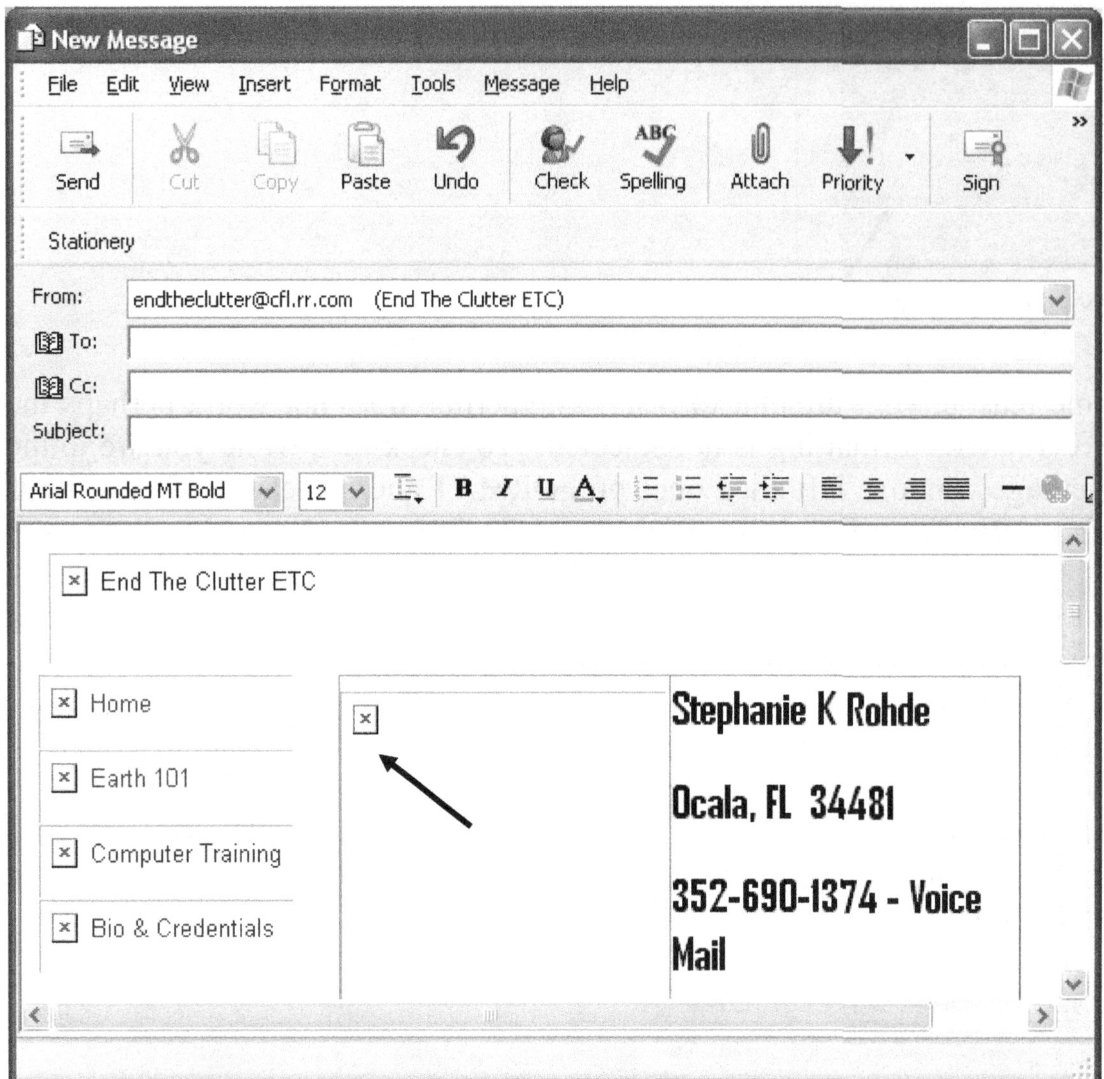

Figure 191 — Web page inserted in an e-mail message.

When you insert a Web page into an e-mail, it may not display correctly like in the above figure. That is why many just insert the Web page address rather than the Web page itself.

Every Web site can display differently on each computer system.

Chapter 7 — Receiving, Replying & Forwarding

It is strongly recommended that you have the latest updated version of a reputable Virus Protection software program installed on your system prior to playing with e-mail. It is also important to check for updates for this software daily before receiving or sending e-mail. New viruses appear all the time and keeping your software up to date provides you with the latest protection available. You can receive a computer virus in many ways — "previewing" an e-mail, opening an e-mail, opening an attachment, and via instant messages to name a few.

Computer Viruses & Hoaxes

A computer virus is a program of sorts that attaches itself to disks or to computer files. Remember e-mails, attachments, pictures, and sounds are all different types of computer files. A computer virus can replicate itself repeatedly; and usually does without the user's knowledge or permission.

Viruses can be on floppy diskettes, CDs, e-mail attachments, instant messages, shared network files, and the Internet.

All viruses are not necessarily damaging; many were created to annoy, to destroy data, or to halt system operations. Some however, do significantly hurt computer systems by completely destroying the hard drive or by taking up a lot of memory space.

Virus hoaxes also exist. You are led to believe that you have a virus when in truth you do not; you are given instructions on how to delete a file (sometimes crucial, sometimes not) from your system.

Virus hoaxes with attached viruses also exist. Not a happy place; this is why you want to invest in reputable Virus Protection software.

If ever you are in doubt about an e-mail message or its attachment(s), delete the e-mail message. You may want to block the sender as well.

The "Preview Pane"

The preview pane "previews" the message that is highlighted in the Inbox. Technically, when the preview pane is turned on and visible, the highlighted e-mail message is "sort of" open — "open" enough to allow a lurking virus to do its dirty work. Because of this, many prefer not to have the preview pane be active. But if you have good reputable daily updated virus protection software installed on your computer(s), having the preview pane active can be really helpful.

As always, if you are not comfortable with the "Preview Pane" being active, keep it inactive.

To allow the preview pane to be active or not, left click once on VIEW; then left click once on LAYOUT. This window should remind you of Chapter 2.

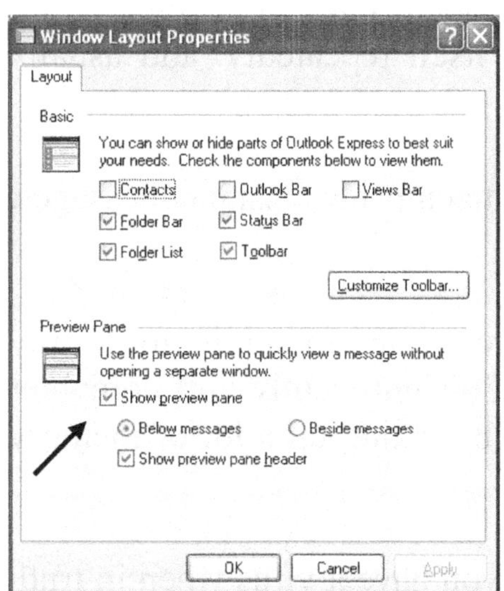

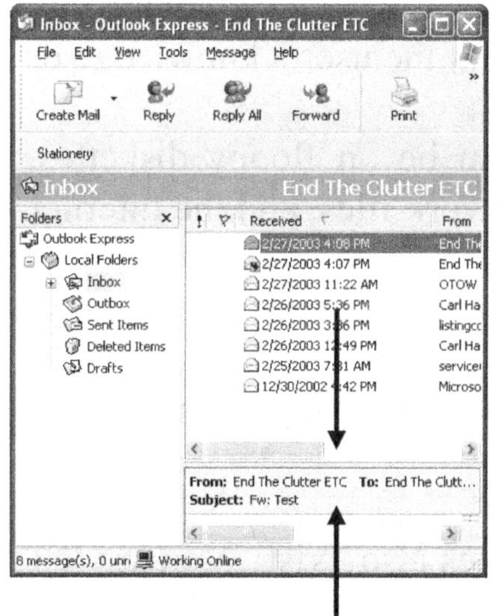

Figure 192 — Preview Pane

Uncheck or check the "Show preview pane." The preview pane can be to the right of your e-mail messages in your Inbox or below them.

You can change the size of the preview pane by moving the mouse pointer to the top (or side) edge — refer to the right figure above. At that time the mouse pointer changes to a double sided arrow at the edge. When the double sided arrows appear left click once, HOLD the click and move the edge to where you want it.

                                Use any and all information at your own risk.

The "Inbox"

If you want to see your inbox every time you open Outlook Express, left click once on TOOLS, and then on OPTIONS. Make sure you have a check mark in the box immediately to the left of "When starting, go directly to my 'Inbox' folder."

You can customize the way your incoming e-mail messages are displayed. Many individuals prefer to see the latest e-mail message displayed on the top (descending order) rather than displayed on the bottom (ascending order).

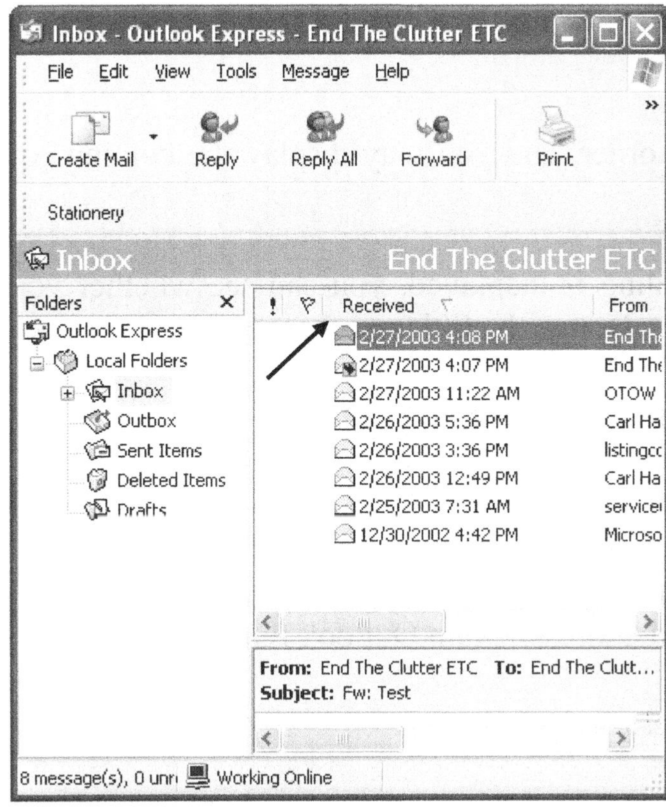

Figure 193 — Messages sorted in descending order of arrival.

To change how your e-mail messages are displayed from descending to ascending or vice versa, right click once in the middle of the "Received" column heading, and then left click once on ASCENDING or DECENDING.

You can also determine which column headings are displayed as well as their order. If you right click once on any column heading, you have a choice called "Columns" in addition to Ascending or Descending.

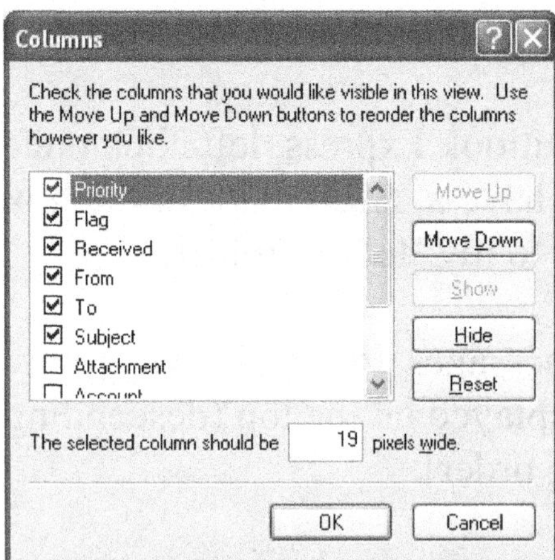

Figure 194 — Choices for column headings to view.

You may display the columns in any order, and you may display the columns of your choice.

- Flag — When this column heading is displayed, you can see whether you have "flagged" a message or not. Notice the little red flag.

- Received — The time your message was received.

- From — The individual who sent you the message.

- To — To which e-mail address the message was sent. This can be important if you have more than one e-mail address within Outlook Express.

- Subject — The subject of the message.

- Attachment — Lets you know if there is an attachment with your e-mail message.

- Account — To which account in Outlook Express the message was sent to.

- Size — The file size of the e-mail.

   Use any and all information at your own risk.

Checking for New E-mail Messages

Each time you open Outlook Express, the program will automatically check for new e-mail if you set it up to do this task for you.

Figure 195 — Send and receive messages at startup.

To have Outlook Express automatically check for messages each time you open the program, left click once on TOOLS, then left click once on OPTIONS, and the above figure should appear. Make sure there is a check mark in the box next to "Send and receive messages at startup."

The box beneath when checked allows you to tell Outlook Express how often you want it to check for new messages; every ten minutes for example.

When you receive an e-mail, you have many choices. You can "preview" e-mail without ever technically opening it via the Preview Pane. If you do not have the Preview Pane showing and you want to turn it on, left click once on VIEW, and then left click once on LAYOUT. Make sure there is a check mark in the box directly to the left of "Show preview pane."

Often directly from the "Preview" pane, you immediately know what it is you want to do with a particular message. If the e-mail message is something you do not want, you can "delete" it immediately. You may want to "Block" the sender in addition to deleting the message so you never have to be bothered again from that particular e-mail address. When blocking an e-mail address it is added to the "blocked senders" list.

You can also left click once on the SEND/RECV button in the main screen toolbar to have the program check for e-mail when ever you want.

Priority of Incoming Messages

As mentioned in Chapter 6, e-mail messages can have low, normal, or high priority.

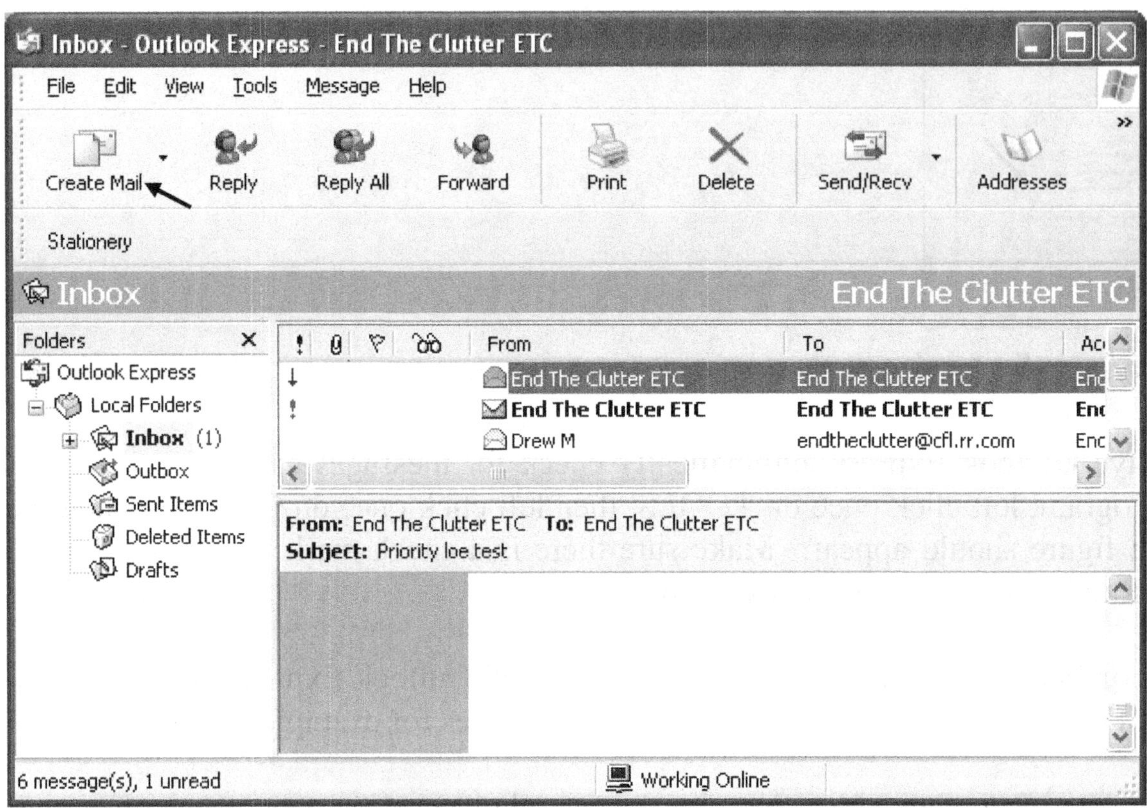

Figure 196 — Message Priority.

Low priority messages arrive with a blue arrow pointing down. High priority messages arrive with a red exclamation point. Normal priority messages do not have a priority icon associated with them.

The priority column must be active in the column view in order to see any priority icons. Right click once on any column heading and then left click on "Columns." Select the column headings you want to be showing as well as their order of placement.

Send e-mail messages to yourself using low, normal, and high priority so you can see how this works.

                                    Use any and all information at your own risk.

Flagging a Message

Sometimes when an e-mail arrives, it requires some action on your part for some reason. If you would like this e-mail message to stand out in your inbox, you can flag the message.

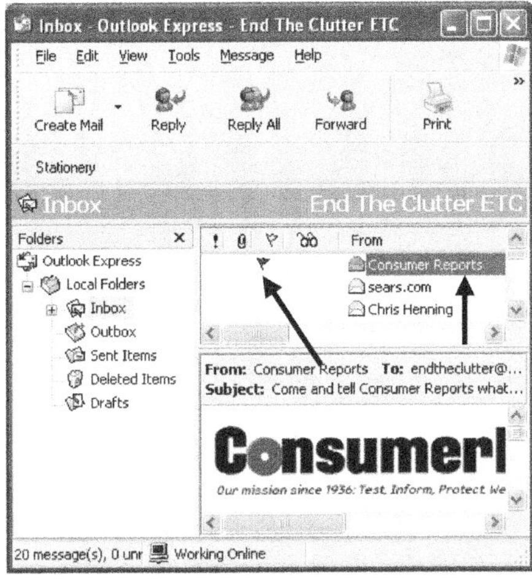

Figure 197 — Flag an e-mail message.

To flag an e-mail message, highlight it. Then left click once on MESSAGE in the message toolbar. Then left click once on "Flag Message." This action places a little red flag next the e-mail address that you highlighted. If the flag does not display for you, it may be because you don't have the *column* that displays the flag available to you in the main screen. Right click once on the column headings, and left click once on COLUMNS.

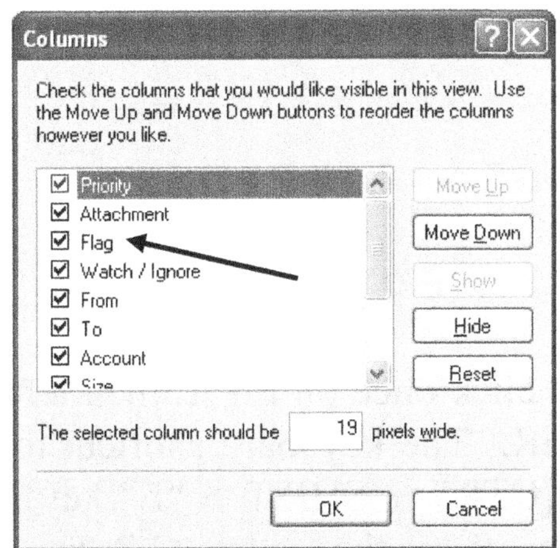

Make sure there is a check mark in the box to the left of "Flag."

Use the "Move Down" or "Move Up" buttons for toolbar placement.

Figure 198 — Customizing the columns showing in the main screen.

Creating Folders

One purpose for folders is to organize e-mails that you want to keep. To keep e-mails in the "Inbox" can be cumbersome. Some individuals like to keep the "Inbox" clean so they can deal with e-mails as they arrive. To create a folder within Outlook Express make sure the program is open and that you are viewing the main screen.

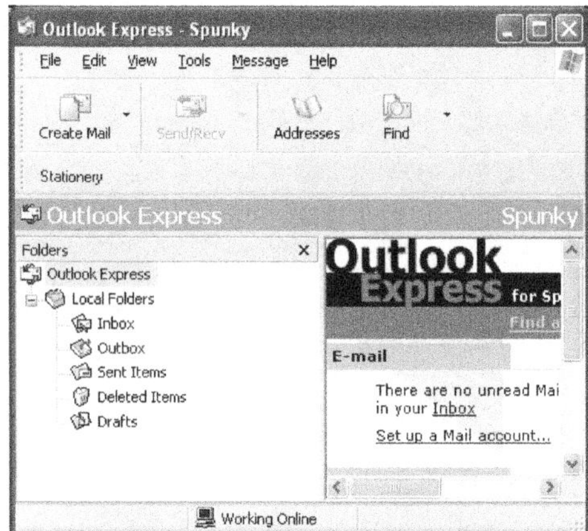

Figure 199 — Main screen view.

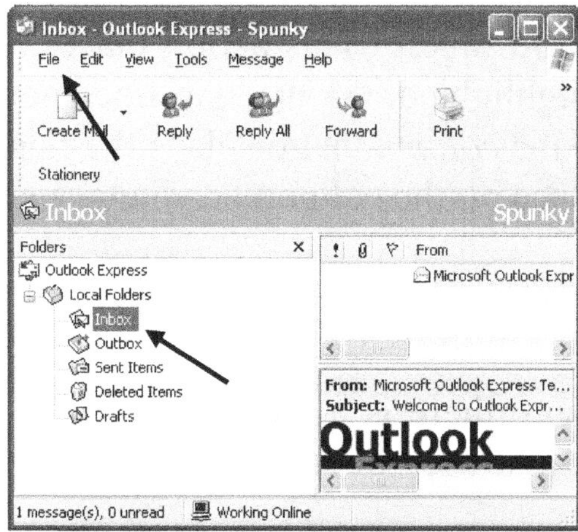

Figure 200 — Highlight "Inbox."

Left click once on INBOX to highlight it. Then left click once on FILE; then left click once on NEW; then left click once on FOLDER. The keyboard shortcut to create a new folder after "Inbox" is highlighted is [CTRL + SHIFT + "E" key]. Hold the CTRL and Shift keys down and then press the letter "E" key. Immediately after pressing the "E" key, let go of all the keys.

         Use any and all information at your own risk.

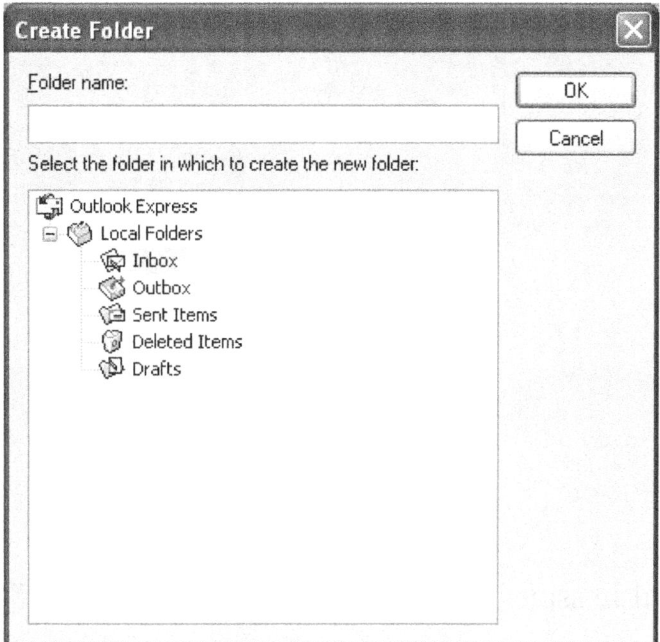

Figure 201 — Naming your new folder.

For this example we will name the folder "Steph's E-Mail Lessons."

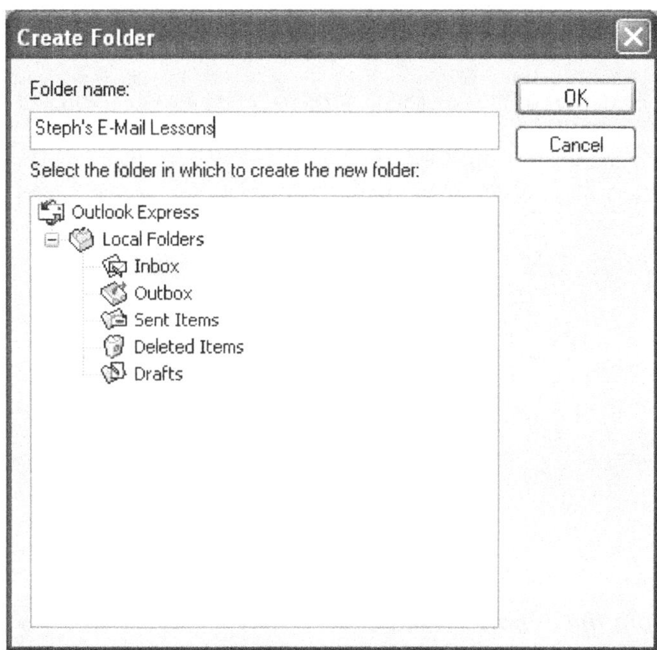

Figure 202 — Steph's E-Mail Lessons.

After you have typed in the name of the folder, left click once on OK.

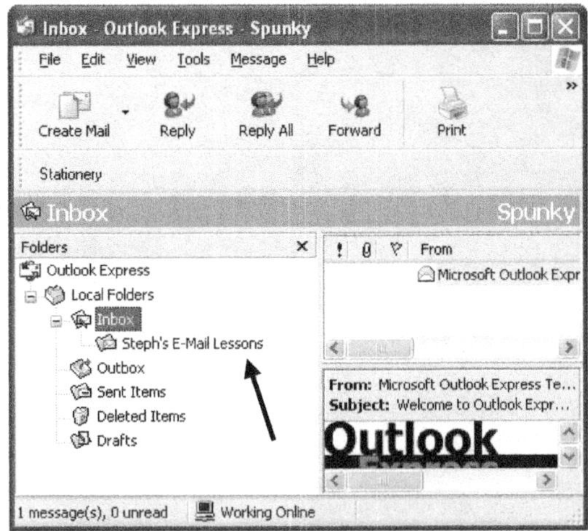

Figure 203 — New folder created.

The new folder entitled "Steph's E-Mail Lessons" is listed underneath the "Inbox."

When future e-mails come in from Steph, we can just move them to the new folder and leave the "Inbox" empty to await future e-mail.

To move a message from the "Inbox" to a folder, left click once on the e-mail to highlight it. Then right click once on the choice MOVE TO FOLDER. The computer will ask you "what" folder.

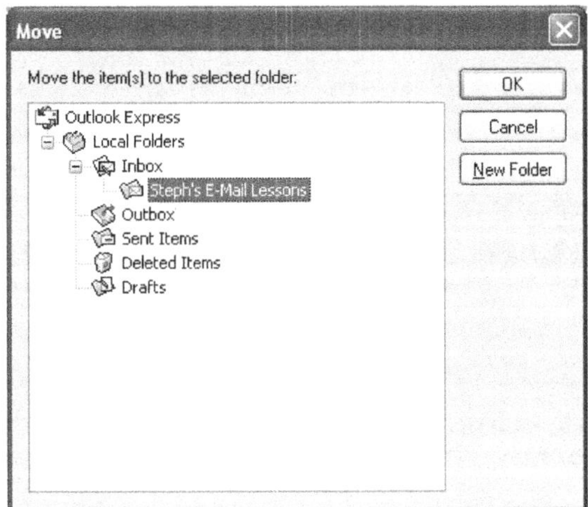

Figure 204 — Telling the computer where to put the e-mail message.

You highlight the folder where you want the e-mail message to go and then left click once on OK.

                    Use any and all information at your own risk.

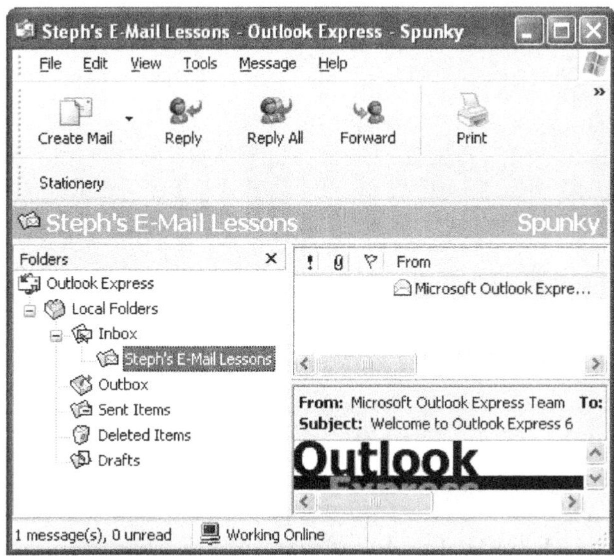

Figure 205 — Message moved to Steph's E-mail Lesson folder.

By highlighting "Steph's E-Mail Lessons" folder on the left side of the window, the contents of that folder are displayed on the right hand side. The message was moved from the "Inbox" to "Steph's E-Mail Lessons."

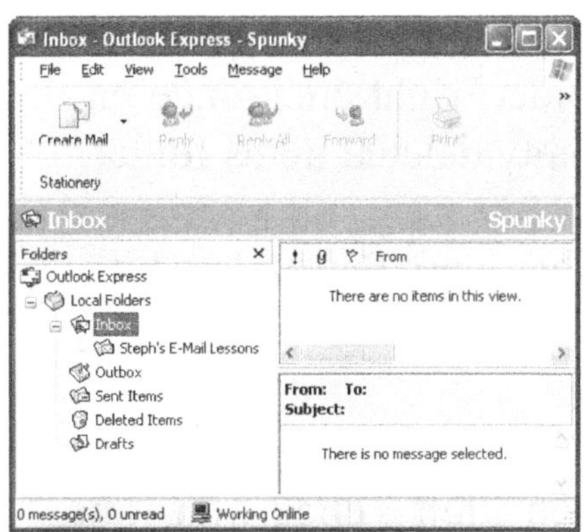

Figure 206 — The "Inbox" is now empty.

As your expertise improves, you can move multiple messages simultaneously to the same folder. Using the CTRL key, select the messages you wish to move. Then right click in an area that is highlighted, and choose MOVE TO FOLDER. The process is the same as moving one e-mail message.

The SHIFT key works as well when you have many e-mail messages grouped together that you want to move.

Deleting an E-mail

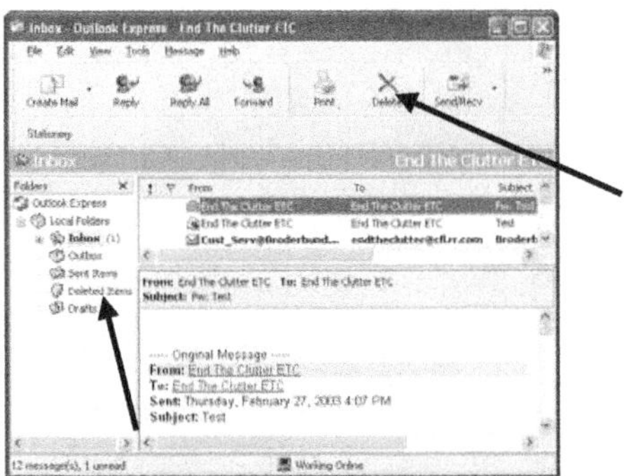

Figure 207 — Inbox.

In the figure above, the top e-mail message is highlighted.

To delete this message only, left click once on the "Delete" button. The message then goes to the Deleted Items folder. Recommend you delete e-mail messages from the Outlook Express main screen view and not while the message is open.

Just in case you accidentally delete a message by mistake the "Deleted Items" folder is a holding bin of everything you delete in Outlook Express. To permanently delete the items in the "deleted items" folder, right click once on the "Deleted Items" folder, and then left click once on "Empty deleted items folder."

You can also program Outlook Express to automatically empty the "deleted items" folder when you close the program.

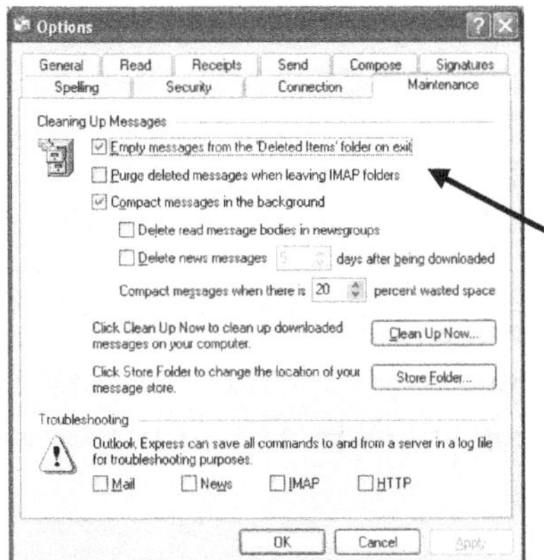

Left click once on TOOLS, then left click on OPTIONS, and then left click on the MAINTENANCE tab. To have Outlook Express automatically empty the "deleted items" folder when you close the program make sure there is a check mark in the box immediately to the left of "Empty messages from the 'Deleted Items' folder on exit."

Figure 208 — Tools, Options, Maintenance tab.

Use any and all information at your own risk.

Blocking a Sender

To block future messages from the sender of a highlighted message like in the figure below, left click once on "Message."

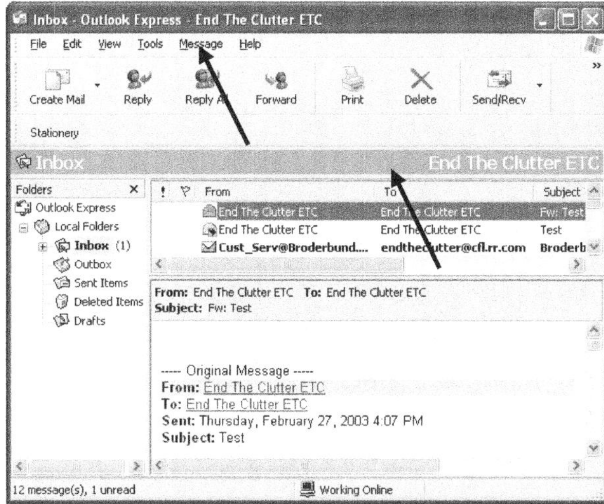

Figure 209 — Inbox.

After you left click on "Message," left click once on BLOCK SENDER. That action will bring up the next figure. The e-mail address that is about to be blocked is listed in the window.

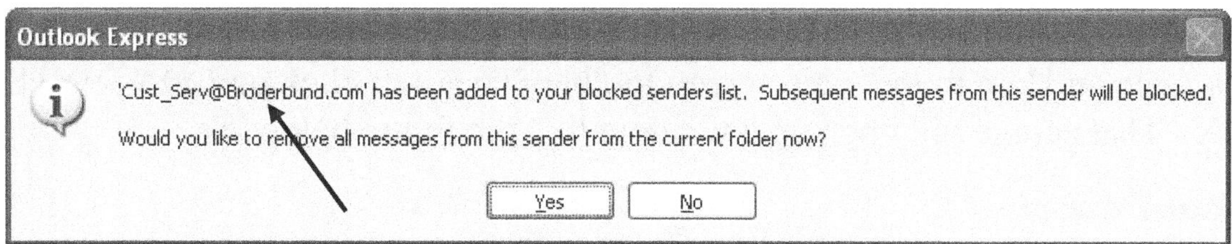

Figure 210 — Blocked sender notification.

In addition to blocking the sender, the program will also remove any additional messages currently in your "inbox" from this sender if you desire.

Periodically check to make sure *you* are not in your blocked senders list. Weird stuff can happen and some bulk e-mail telemarketers are pretty smart; they fool the program into thinking some messages are from you when they are not. This is one way *you* can end up in your "Blocked Sender's List." If this happens any messages you receive, go directly into the "Deleted Items Folder.

To view the "Blocked Senders" list, left click once on TOOLS, then left click once on MESSAGE RULES, and then left click once on BLOCKED SENDERS LIST.

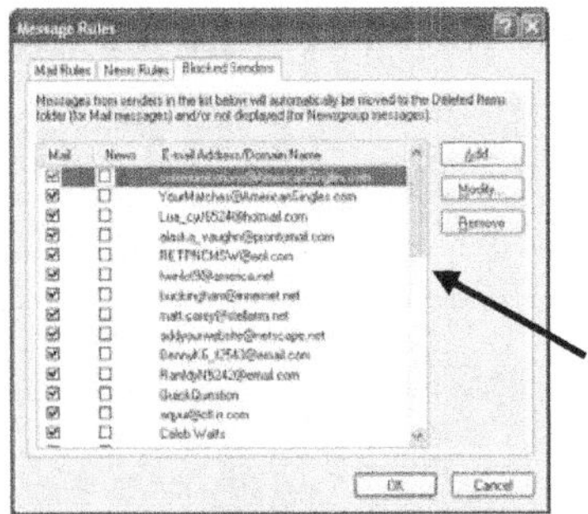

Figure 211 — Blocked Senders list.

Scroll down using the "scroll bar" to make sure *you* are not listed in your "Blocked Senders" list. To remove an e-mail address from this list, highlight the address with a left click and then left click once on REMOVE.

Message Rules

Message rules are just that. You can have Outlook Express automatically do something with messages that come in. For beginners this function can create far more confusion than it solves. For those wanting to delve into this topic, or any topic for that matter not mentioned in this book, please refer to the existing "Help" section within Outlook Express.

Left click once on Help in the main screen toolbar. Then left click on CONTENTS & INDEX. That action will open up a window like the figure below.

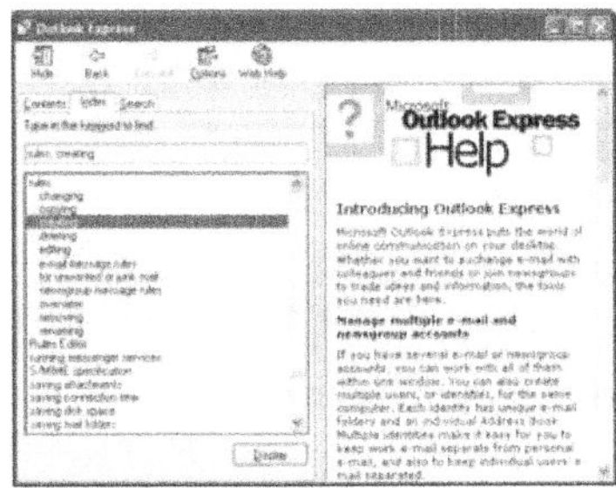

Figure 212 — Outlook Express Help

To receive help about "Message Rules" for example, type in RULES. You can refer to this section when you need help.

     Use any and all information at your own risk.

Sender Properties

When you receive an e-mail, you don't always see the actual e-mail address of the sender; sometimes you see their actual name displayed as in the figure below.

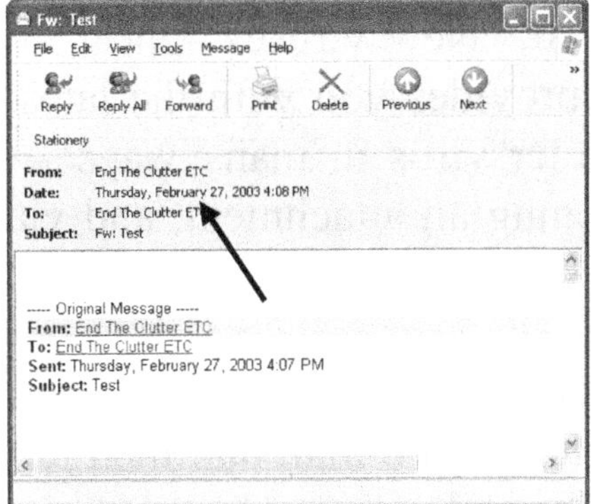

Figure 213 — An open received e-mail.

If you would like to see the actual e-mail address of any sender, place the mouse pointer in the vicinity of the text immediately to the right of the "From:" portion of the message. As the mouse pointer gets near "text," (in this case End The Clutter ETC), the pointer will turn into the I-beam. At that point, *right* click once, and a sub-menu will appear. Then left click once on PROPERTIES. That action will bring up a "Properties" window like the figure below. This window should remind you of entering contacts into the Address Book covered in Chapter 5.

Figure 214 — "Properties" window.

Add Sender to Address Book

To add that sender to your Address Book, again right click once on the name of the sender and left click on "Add to Address Book.

Opening an E-mail without Attached Files

It is strongly recommended that you have the latest updated version of a reputable Virus Protection software program installed on your system prior to playing with e-mail. It is also important to check for updates for this software daily before receiving or sending e-mail. New viruses appear all the time and keeping your software up to date provides you with the latest protection available. You can receive a computer virus in many ways — "previewing" an e-mail, opening an e-mail, opening an attachment, and via instant messages to name a few.

You can "open" an e-mail message by double left clicking on the e-mail that you want to open. Or, you can right click once on the highlighted e-mail and then left click once on OPEN. The following figure is an open e-mail message without any attachments.

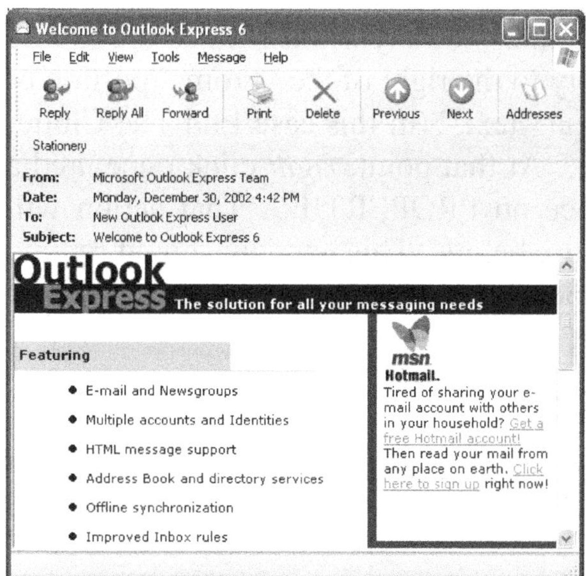

Figure 215 — Outlook Express Welcome Letter.

Reply

With regard to e-mail, "Reply" means to respond to an e-mail message that you have received from another. To reply you left click once on the REPLY button. That will bring up something like the next figure.

                      Use any and all information at your own risk.

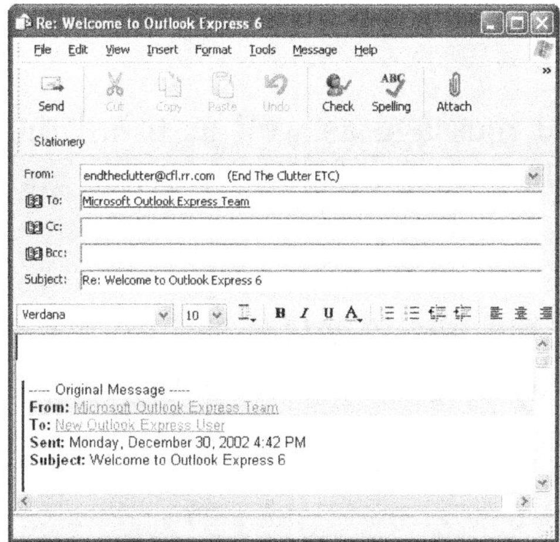

Figure 216 — Message reply.

This looks very similar to an e-mail created from scratch. The difference is that the original message that you received can be placed in the text box for you as reference material.

You can control whether the original message is included in the reply through the "Send" tab. (TOOLS, OPTIONS, SEND tab).

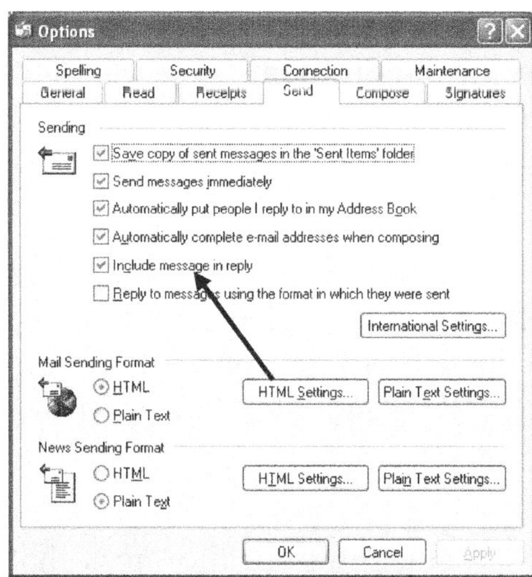

Figure 217 — "Send" tab.

In the "Sending" section (top), the fifth choice down is "Include message in reply." Whether or not you have a check in this box will determine whether the original messages will be included in your reply.

Reply All

If you choose to reply to the author of the original message as well as to all the other recipients of the original message, you left click once on REPLY ALL, and not REPLY. This is not recommended.

If you must reply to all, please consider copying the e-mail addresses from the "To:" field into the "Bcc:" field for respectful e-mailing and place *your* e-mail address in the "To:" block.

Forwarding E-mail

Forwarding an e-mail is just like "sending" e-mail from scratch covered in Chapter 6. The major difference is that it arrived to you from another; you did not create it. Another difference is that forwarding e-mail to others is usually of an unsolicited nature on your part. Unsolicited doesn't necessarily mean "unwanted" however. Unsolicited e-mail of *any* kind can be considered SPAM by some and is regarded about as highly as are telephone telemarketers and junk "snail mail" senders.

Often times we receive forwarded e-mails with many e-mail addresses displayed on them along with other extraneous and unnecessary information. Here is your chance to be part of the solution rather than to be part of the problem.

Respectful E-mail Forwarding

When you create an e-mail from scratch, you now know how to do it respectfully (Chapter 6). To review briefly, if you are sending the e-mail to one individual, use the "To:" or "Bcc:" block. If you are sending an e-mail to more than one individual, send the e-mail "To:" yourself and "Bcc:" everyone else. Or, just use the "Bcc:" for every e-mail address.

Respectful forwarding involves two additional steps — cleaning up the mess that was forwarded to you and removing all those e-mail addresses.

This is another reason why sending your "created from scratch" e-mails and now forwarded e-mails to *you* first comes in very handy. You are able to see if you cleaned up the e-mail the way that you wanted to before forwarding it to your immediate world. Sometimes if you do too much cleaning up, you can lose the cute animations that are within a received message. Again, this is why you want to send it to you first, several times perhaps to make sure you are sending it the way that you think you are.

Here we go. You have received an e-mail that you think is cute, or noteworthy of forwarding to a number of select individuals. Here is one way to make this work. Open the message that you want to forward. This does not mean view the message through the "preview pane." Double-left click on the message or the attachment to open it. Hopefully you are looking at exactly what it is you want to forward after some minor corrections or additions. With this received message open, create a brand new clean e-mail message by left clicking once on CREATE MAIL. Copy just the part that you want from the message that you received and paste it into the new e-mail that you just created. If you are not familiar enough with CUT, COPY, & PASTE, please stop here and study Appendix D — Block Text, Cut, Copy, & Paste.

Once you have copied and pasted the material you want to forward into the new e-mail message, type in the subject. If you are sending to just one person, use the "To:" or "Bcc:" block; if you are sending to more than one e-mail address, send the message to yourself, and "Bcc:" everyone else. In the beginning, recommend you send this "newly created message" only to you to make sure it arrives the way that you want. You may have to practice this five, ten, twenty times or more. It takes as long as it takes. But perseverance is truly rewarded. Before you know it, others will be asking you "How did you do that?" And then you can happily explain.

If you don't want to create a new e-mail to copy and paste, and you want to use the FORWARD command, here is what you can do.

When you are actively viewing an open e-mail message, left click once on the FORWARD button. This action automatically brings up a new e-mail message with an entire copy of the original e-mail inserted. Here, you can delete what you don't want by blocking and/or by pressing the "delete" button or the back space key. You forward what is left to you only first, to see how it arrives to you. When you are ready repeat the process and send to your designated individuals; send the forwarded message "To:" yourself, and "Bcc;" everyone else.

Opening E-mail Attachments

It is strongly recommended that you have the latest updated version of a reputable Virus Protection software program installed on your system prior to playing with e-mail. It is also important to check for updates for this software daily before receiving or sending e-mail. New viruses appear all the time and keeping your software up to date provides you with the latest protection available. You can receive a computer virus in many ways — "previewing" an e-mail, opening an e-mail, opening an attachment, and via instant messages to name a few.

True attachments are not part of an e-mail message; they are separate files. Some attachments require a specific program (often referred to as the "native" application — the program with which the document was created) to be opened or edited. Let's say a document file is prepared in PageMaker, a very high end business publishing program and that this file is e-mailed to you as an attachment. If you do not have PageMaker installed on your computer, you will not be able to open the file. Many have experienced the frustration of attachments not opening. This is one common reason why; you may not have the same software installed on your computer that created the attachment.

Sometimes in Outlook Express you suddenly can't open *any* attachments. If you want to open attachments and the program is preventing you from doing so, left click once on TOOLS, then left click once on OPTIONS, and then left click once on the SECURITY tab.

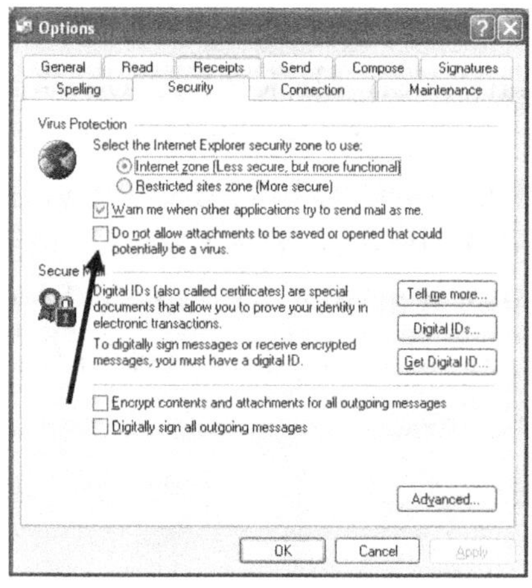

If there happens to be a check mark in the box "Do not allow attachments to be saved or opened that could potentially be a virus," you won't be able to open *any* attachments in Outlook Express.

To remove an existing check mark, left click on it once.

Figure 218 — "Security" tab.

Often you think you have an attachment but when you double left click nothing appears to happen. The attachment is most probably there but you have to keep opening it again and maybe again; you may have to open it many times before you get to the actual attachment. This happens when things are forwarded many times prior to arriving to your inbox.

There are a couple of ways to open e-mail attachments.

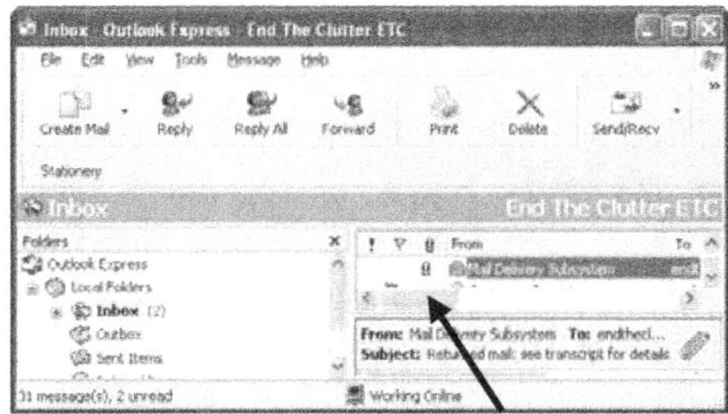

Figure 219 — Opening attachments.

The highlighted message in the inbox in the above figure has an attachment represented by the paperclip icon. Double left clicking the message opens the message and brings up a window something like the figure below.

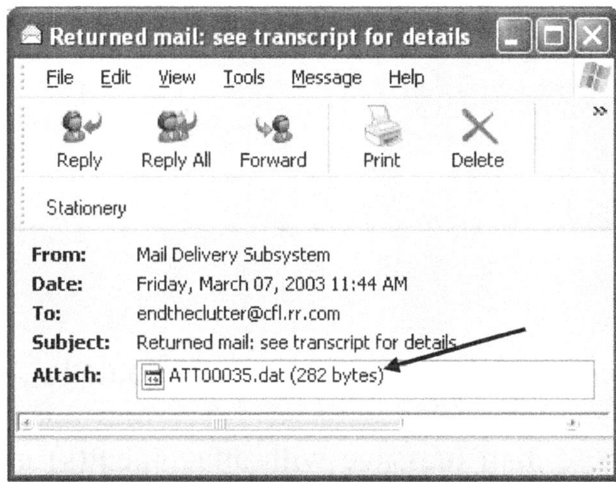

Figure 220 — Opened e-mail with attachment.

Double left click the attachment icon to open the attachment. Remember you may have to open some attachments again and again when the attachment has been forwarded many times.

You may open attachments another way as well.

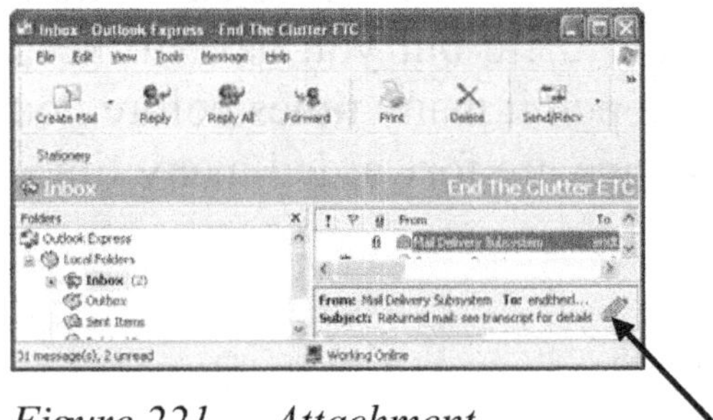

Figure 221 — Attachment.

Left click once on the paper clip icon.

Opening up any attachment will probably bring up the following window unless you have turned it off. Please leave the check mark so you will be prompted about opening attachments in the future.

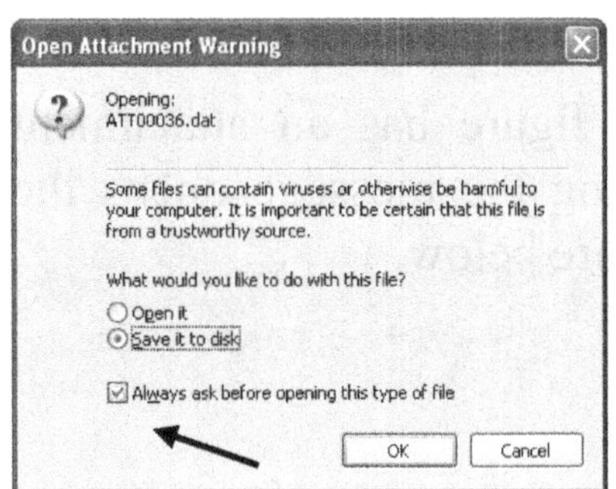

You get to choose whether you want to open the attachment or save the attachment.

Recommend you open the attachment and then decide if you want to save it or not.

Figure 222 — Opening an attachment warning.

Saving E-mail Attachments

When you want to save an e-mail attachment there are a number of ways to do it.

The easiest is probably to leave the entire e-mail message with attachment(s) in your inbox.

If you get more than one e-mail per month, the above action may not suit your needs. As explained earlier, you can create a folder within Outlook Express to organize your e-mails.

If the document is really important to you, consider saving it to a floppy or to a CD as well as on the computer hard drive so you have several backups available.

                    Use any and all information at your own risk.

Printing E-mail Attachments

When the attachment is open, left click once on FILE, and then left click on PRINT. The printer window is different on every computer.

Figure 223 — Printer window.

Make your selections and left click on OK.

"CTRL + P" is a keyboard shortcut that also brings up the Print Window.

You can also use the "Print" icon.

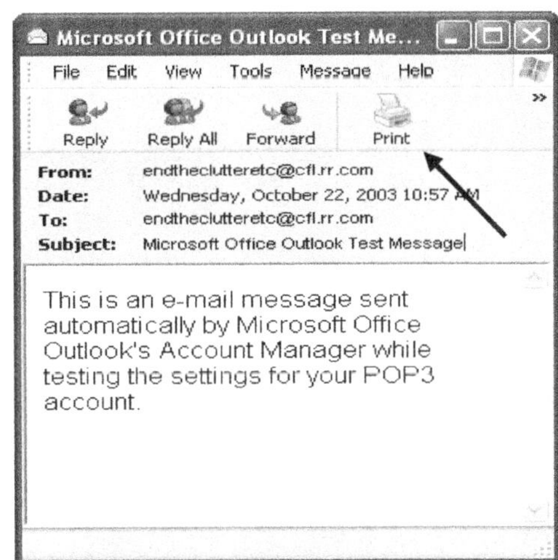

Figure 224 — Using printer icon.

Every computer is different and the printer icon works differently on each one as well. On some computers, the print window is completely bypassed and the entire document is printed. Using FILE, PRINT or CTRL + P gives you the most control over printing.

E-mail Message Icons

The following are excerpted directly from the HELP section in Outlook Express.

Icon	Indicates that:
	The message has one or more files attached.
	The message has been marked high priority by the sender.
	The message has been marked low priority by the sender.
	The message has been read. The message heading appears in light type.
	The message has not been read. The message heading appears in bold type.
	The message has been replied to.
	The message has been forwarded.
	The message is in progress in the Drafts folder.
	The message is flagged.

Figure 225 — E-mail message icons.

Keyboard Shortcuts

Outlook Express Help	F1
Send & Receive E-Mail	CTRL + M
Select all E-mail messages	CTRL + A
Print a Selected E-Mail Message	CTRL + P
Print a Selected E-Mail Message	Right click once; left click Print
Delete a Selected E-Mail Message	DEL
Delete a Selected E-Mail Message	CTRL + D
Delete a Selected E-Mail Message	Left click "Delete" button in toolbar.
Open a new E-Mail	CTRL + N
Open a new E-Mail	Left click once on CREATE MAIL
Open the Address Book	Left click icon in toolbar
Open the Address Book	CTRL + SHIFT + B
Reply to E-Mail Message Author	CTRL + R
Forward an E-Mail Message	CTRL + F
Go to the Inbox	CTRL + I
Go to the next E-Mail Message	CTRL + >
Go to the next E-Mail Message	CTRL + SHIFT + >
Go to the next E-Mail Message	Use Arrow Keys
Go to the previous E-Mail Message	CTRL + <
Go to the previous E-Mail Message	CTRL + SHIFT + <
Go to the previous E-Mail Message	Use Arrow Keys
View Properties of a selected E-Mail	ALT + ENTER
Go to next unread E-Mail Message	CTRL + U
Go to a folder	CTRL + Y
Open a received selected E-Mail	CTRL + O
Open a received selected E-Mail	ENTER
Mark an E-Mail as read	CTRL + ENTER
Mark an E-Mail as read	CTRL + Q
Close an E-Mail Message	ESC
Find an E-Mail Message	CTRL + SHIFT + F
Check Names	CTRL + K or ALT + K
Check Spelling	F7
Insert a signature	CRTL + SHIFT + S
Send an E-Mail Message	CTRL + ENTER
Send an E-Mail Message	ALT + S

Appendix A — Windows Taskbar

The Taskbar Defined

The taskbar is a horizontal or vertical bar located on your computer screen desktop. Often this bar is pre-defined (a default setting) to be a horizontal bar at the bottom of the desktop screen. The placement of the taskbar can be customized by each individual. In addition to being a horizontal bar at the bottom of the desktop, it may also be a horizontal bar on the top of your desktop; it may be a vertical bar located on the left side of the desktop; or it may be a vertical bar located on the right side of the desktop.

You can use the taskbar to:

- Switch between open programs.
- Arrange windows.
- Control programs.
- Access the Web.
- Access your desktop.
- Change your system date and time.
- Change your speaker volume.
- Schedule tasks.

Moving the Taskbar

Take hold of the mouse (laptop users place your finger on the pad) *without* clicking and slowly place the mouse pointer in an unoccupied space on the taskbar. Once the pointer is there, left click, HOLD the click, and drag the mouse up, down, left, or right to the location of your choice (up, down, left, or right). As you drag the mouse (holding the click) you should see a line indicating the new location of the taskbar; at this point release the click (let go of the mouse) and the taskbar *should* move to its new location. You may have to try this several times before you get the taskbar to move. Occasionally the taskbar gets moved unintentionally. Now you know how to move it wherever you want. The XP operating systems have a "lock taskbar" function which must be unlocked before the taskbar can be changed. Right click in an unoccupied space in the taskbar to reveal the menu to "unlock" it. Left click on "Lock the taskbar" to remove the check mark that represents that the taskbar is currently locked.

Sizing the Taskbar

Make sure the taskbar is unlocked. Take hold of the mouse without clicking and point to an edge of the taskbar that is closest to the center of the desktop. In other words:

If the taskbar is on the bottom—point to the top edge of the taskbar.
If the taskbar is on the top—point to the bottom edge of the taskbar.
If the taskbar is on the left—point to the right edge of the taskbar.
If the taskbar is on the right—point to the left edge of the taskbar.

As you point the mouse to the taskbar edge, the white arrow pointer will change to a "two-directional" sizing pointer. You will see two smaller black arrows facing opposite directions (up and down ↕, or left and right ↔) depending upon where your taskbar is located at that time. When you see these two opposite facing arrow sizing pointers, left click, hold the click, and drag the edge (up, down, right, or left respectively) to the new *size* of your choice. Release the click and let go of the mouse. You may have to try this several times in order to become comfortable with changing the size of the taskbar. Be careful when you make the taskbar smaller. If you move the mouse too quickly or too far, the taskbar may get so small, it may seem like it has magically disappeared. It has not. To make the taskbar larger again, slowly move the mouse pointer to the edge. As you then receive the two-directional sizing pointer, click, hold and drag the edge up, down, left, or right.

Hiding the Taskbar

You can intentionally hide the taskbar regardless of its size. This is accomplished by:

Right click in an empty space on the taskbar.
Left click on "Properties."
Place a check mark (✓) in the "Auto Hide" box.
Click "Apply."
Click "OK."
Close Taskbar Properties Box.

                                    Use any and all information at your own risk.

Taskbar Components

The taskbar can contain the following items:

The Start Button — contrary to popular belief, all "Start" buttons are not located in the lower left-hand side of the desktop. This is only true when the taskbar is horizontal and at the bottom of the desktop; this is usually the pre-defined or default setting for many computers. The "Start" button lets you carry out many "Windows" tasks. Some of the many things this button allows you to do are:

- View all programs on your system.
- Start programs.
- Open the "Favorites" folder.
- Open documents.
- Change computer settings.
- Find files and folders.
- Get help.
- Shut down the computer.

Please note that the XP operating system start menu has two panes unlike earlier operating systems which only have one.

Quick Launch Toolbar (which may or may not be showing at any given time) is located to the right of the Start button when the taskbar is at the bottom of the desktop screen. It contains buttons for the frequently used features and programs; Internet Explorer (the blue "e"), Outlook Express (envelope icon), and a "desktop" icon for example. Quick launch is a nice feature because all you need is one left click on any of these icons to open the desired feature or program.

If you are not familiar with what a particular icon stands for, you can use the mouse and slowly point (no clicking) to the icon you are wondering about. A small pop-up box, called a tool tip displays the name of and information about a button or an icon.

A way to tell if your quick launch toolbar is showing on the taskbar is to right click in an open area of the taskbar and then left click on "toolbars." If there is a check mark (✓) next to "quick launch," then it should be showing in your taskbar.

The Taskbar Button Area — when the taskbar is located on the bottom of the desktop, the taskbar button area is located to the right of the Quick Launch Toolbar, which is to the right of the Start button. Taskbar buttons represent an "open" program; each button has an icon representing the open program.

The System Tray — when the taskbar is located at the bottom of the desktop, the system tray is located at the right end of the taskbar. This tray displays system icons, and offers easy access to (and information about) what each icon represents. This system tray can get overloaded and can cause a drain on system resources; particularly on operating systems prior to XP. To turn off (not take off) items in this system tray is covered in our book entitled Computer & Internet Basics Step-By-Step.

Appendix B —Desktop Shortcuts & Icons

An icon is a small graphical image of some sort that can represent many different things. Often icons represent programs like Outlook Express for example.

There is a very huge difference between a desktop "shortcut" icon and an actual program icon. Shortcuts are a link to something like to an application program or to a Web page.

Figure 226 — Shortcut icon for Outlook Express.

In the figure above, the icon representing Outlook Express is a shortcut icon. The way you can tell that it is a shortcut icon (or not) is by the lower left hand corner of the icon. If it is a shortcut, there will be a square with a black arrow pointing diagonally up and to the right as part of the icon.

The purpose of a program shortcut icon is to make the opening of a program easier for you. It is usually easier and faster to double left click an icon located on your desktop rather than going to START, PROGRAMS, and then OUTLOOK EXPRESS. You can also right click once on a shortcut icon, and then left click once on OPEN.

Icons are also the buttons that you see when you open a new e-mail message in Outlook Express by left clicking on CREATE MAIL.

Please refer to the figure on the next page.

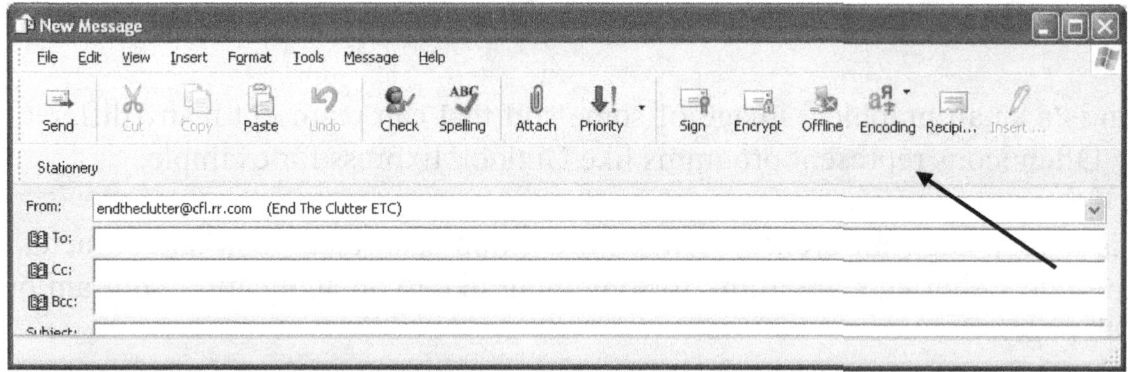

Figure 227 — Buttons are also icons.

The buttons at the top of an e-mail message are also icons as in the figure above.

On Web pages icons often represent information about a different Web page. Often those icons are hyperlinks.

A company logo can take the form of an icon.

To create a shortcut for any program on your computer here is what you do:

Left click once on START. Left click once on PROGRAMS or ALL PROGRAMS. Right click once on the program you want to make a shortcut for. Left click once on SEND TO. Left click once on Desktop (create shortcut).

Don't confuse a shortcut icon with a shortcut key(s). Shortcut *keys* execute a command within a program that is open and running.

For example, in Outlook Express, to select all the text in an e-mail message, you press and hold down the CTRL key and press the letter "A" at the same time. This is an action within the program.

The F1 key when pressed in Outlook Express opens the HELP menu.

For more information about Outlook Express shortcut keys, please refer back to Keyboard Shortcuts.

Appendix C — Minimize, Maximize, & Close

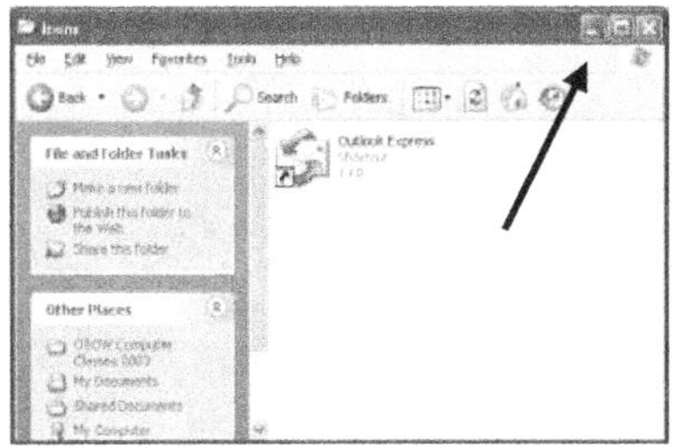

Figure 228 — Minimize, maximize, and close buttons.

Minimizing a window means to reduce the size of the window while at the same time keeping the program (application) open and running. In the figure above, the black arrow is pointing to the minimize button. As you left click once on a minimize button, the program or application that you have currently open and running will become reduced to a button on your taskbar. When left clicking once on the button in the taskbar, the program will become visible to you once again via your computer screen.

Often you may have a file open within a program, so in the upper right hand corner of the computer screen you may see two or more minimize buttons indicating more than one window is available. Left clicking a minimize button minimizes the window with the button that was left clicked.

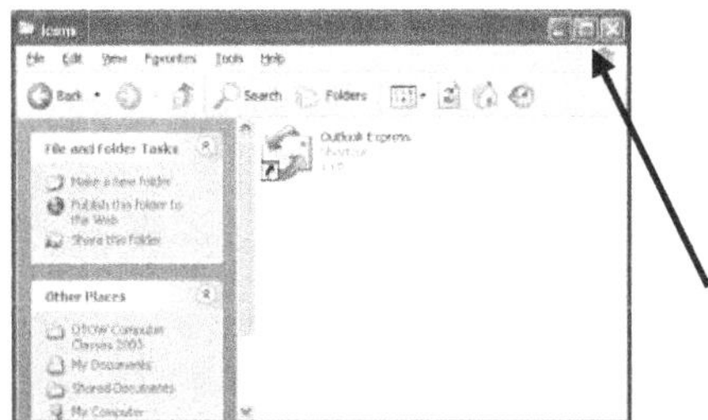

Figure 229 — Maximize button.

The maximize button located to the right of the minimize button enlarges a window to its maximum size, usually filling your computer screen. After clicking a maximize button once, the button's image changes to an icon that resembles two windows cascading over one another. When you left click on that icon (two windows cascading over one another), that action returns the window size to whatever size it was before the first left click on the maximize button.

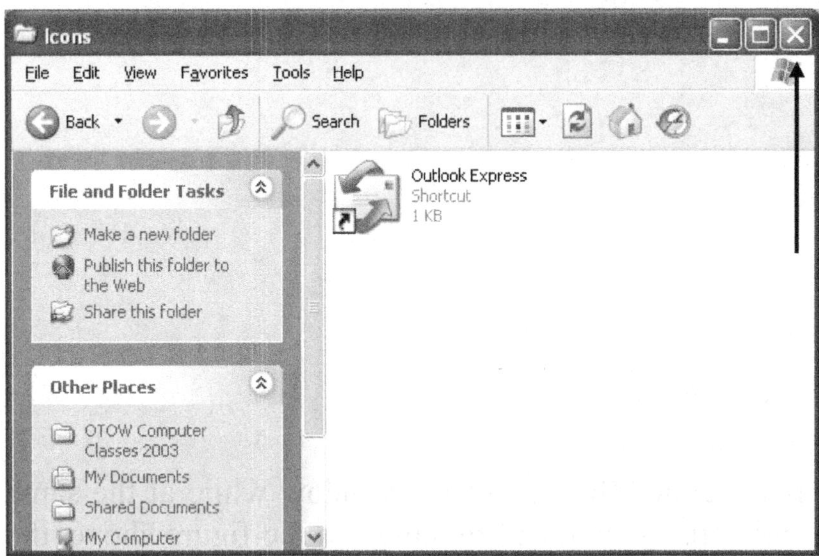

Figure 230 — Close button.

The box with the "X" in it is the close button. Left clicking this button once will close a window or a program; this action does *not* send it to the task bar as does the minimize button.

                                   Use any and all information at your own risk.

Appendix D — Block Text, Cut, Copy, & Paste

Blocking otherwise known as selecting and highlighting text is a really important part of using a computer especially when sending e-mail.

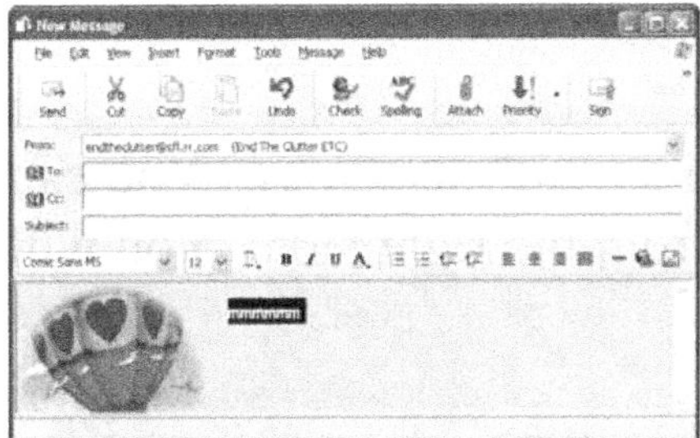

Figure 231 — Blocked text.

When you are learning to block text, start with one line or word at a time until you feel comfortable with the process. Blocking large amounts of text can be extremely useful to copy information from one e-mail so you can paste it into another prior to forwarding for example.

The mouse pointer (usually white) turns into an "I-beam" cursor when it gets around "text." Slowly move your mouse in an e-mail without clicking and watch how the pointer changes as you "slowly" move the mouse around. If you happen to move it near a hyperlink, the cursor turns into an icon that looks like a hand. When this "hand" is visible, one left click will take you somewhere if you are currently connected to the Internet.

You cannot cut, copy, or paste without knowing how to block text first because "blocking" the text alerts the computer that a change of some sort is coming.

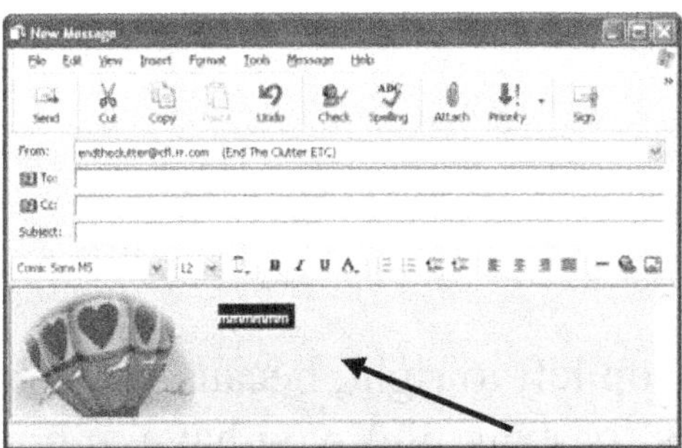

Figure 232 — Blocking text.

You can practice blocking text just about anywhere — within an e-mail, on a Web page, in a word processing, spreadsheet, or database document.

Let's use an e-mail in Outlook Express as an example. Open a new e-mail (CREATE MAIL). Left click once in the text box to place the cursor there. Make sure you have HTML formatting turned on. (FORMAT, Rich Text HTML is selected).

Type in one word, or like in the previous figure, the letter "m" six times. You can block from the left side of the word or you can block from the right side. You will soon learn which side you prefer.

We will start the process from the left first. Without any clicking, move the mouse pointer to the left of the text that you wish to block. As the pointer gets near the text, it will take the I-beam shape. At that point, left click once, HOLD the click, and drag the mouse to the end of the word — in the previous figure to the right of the last "m." Then let go of the mouse completely. The text *should* be blocked. You may have to do this a few times before you feel comfortable with it.

You may also block from the right side of the word. In this case you place the cursor to the right of the last letter of the word, wait for the I-beam to appear, left click once, HOLD the click and drag left. Please refer to the figure below.

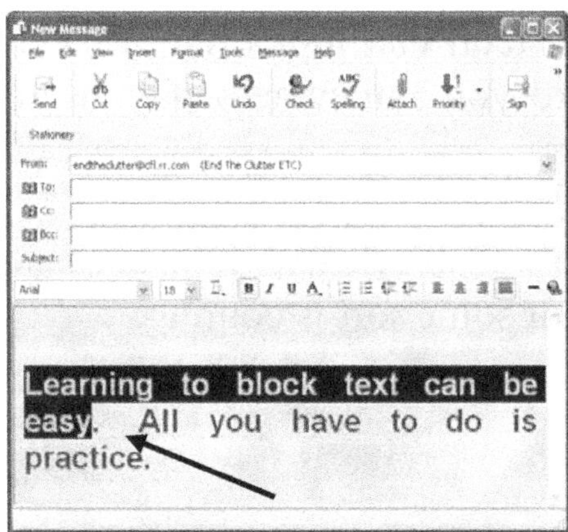

Figure 233 — Blocking more than one word of text.

When blocking text, many prefer to block from the top left to right, because as you want to block more than one word, (like a few lines for example), you have to not only drag the mouse to the right, you also must drag the mouse diagonally downward to the right to include more than one line of text.

          Use any and all information at your own risk.

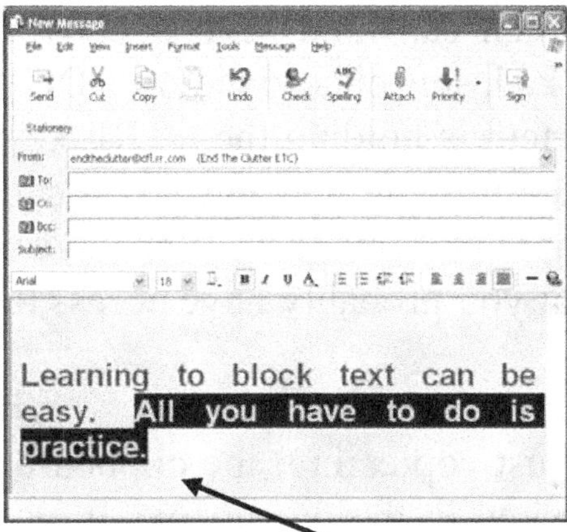

Figure 234 — Blocking text from the lower right to upper left.

You can block the text from the right, but then you would be dragging upward diagonally to the left.

If you want to block an entire e-mail message or an entire document, you can left click once on EDIT, and then left click once on SELECT ALL. A keyboard shortcut to this is to press and hold down the CTRL key; then press the "A" key; and then let go of all the keys.

If you have a larger document and you want to block several pages, but not the whole document, one way to do this is to begin blocking at the top left hand side of what you wish to block, block a few lines, and let go of the click. This blocks only a part of what you want. Then without clicking scroll down (or get to) the end of the passage you wish to block, press and hold the SHIFT key down. At this point left click at the end of the passage or lines that you wish to block. Let go of all keys. This action, if done correctly should block the entire portion of text that you want.

Once you know how to block text, you get to decide whether you want to "cut" vs. copy. When you "cut" you remove the blocked text from its current location. The items that you previously blocked in the document are no longer visible. They have been transferred to what is known as the "clipboard" which is a memory system included with all Windows Operating Systems and is somewhat temporary in nature. The clipboard is shared among all applications (programs) installed on a particular computer system. The clipboard accepts a wide range of data formats and file extensions. The clipboard per se usually only holds one item at a time so if a second item is cut or copied the previous one is erased.

The Operating System clipboard is not to be confused with the Microsoft Office Clipboard found in Microsoft Word for example which can hold several cut (or copied) items at a time. To cut after you have blocked, left click once on EDIT, and then left click once on CUT. The keyboard shortcut is holding the CTRL key down and pressing the "X" key. If nothing is blocked nothing gets cut. You can only cut documents that *you* have created. You cannot cut items from Web pages; you can only copy from Web pages. Don't forget that you probably have access to the UNDO command if you cut something in error.

Copying text (or items) differs from "cut" in that it just copies into the clipboard. It leaves your blocked text exactly where it was blocked in the document. It just *copies* it to the clipboard. To copy text after you have blocked, left click once on EDIT, and then left click on COPY. The keyboard shortcut for this is CTRL and the "C" key.

To paste a cut or copied item first involves placing the blinking cursor where you want the text to go (left clicking once in the spot where you wish to paste the information). When ready, left click once on EDIT, and then left click once on PASTE. The keyboard shortcut for this is CTRL and "V."

Appendix E — Suggested PC Maintenance

Daily

1. Check for virus and firewall protection software updates. If any are available, download and install.

Weekly

1. Spybot & Adware to remove spyware — explanation follows.
2. Disk Cleanup — explanation follows.
3. Disk Defragmenter — explanation follows.
4. Backup files you have created that you don't want to live without.

Monthly

1. Scan Disk or Error Checking in XP — explanation follows.
2. Check for Windows Updates — see Chapter 1.
3. Full Anti Virus Scan of all computer files.

Spyware & Adware

Spyware is yet another kind of software that is most probably on your computer without your knowledge. It tracks your behavior and finds its way into your computer in various ways. It can be virus type software but more often unfortunately it comes as part of *legitimate* software applications. Companies installing Spyware on your computer with or without your consent, do so to track your browsing habits to later relay them to advertisers.

Adware technically is not Spyware although often they are linked together. Adware is usually just a pop-up or pop-under. While Adware can be somewhat exasperating, it isn't as covert in nature as spyware; the ads are in your face designed to get your attention; and unfortunately they do. The ads via Windows Messenger in the XP operating systems are usually Adware.

Many are familiar with the term *cookie* which is a small file placed on your computer hard drive by a company for identification purposes. Cookies make it possible for you to be welcomed by name when you access a Web site.

Cookies also can contain information about your login name, password, and preferences. On subscription sites, cookies can make it unnecessary for you to login every time. Users can configure their computer browsers to accept or decline cookies. All cookies are not bad; from reputable and ethical Web sites they are extremely helpful.

Spyware goes further than any cookie infringing on your right to privacy. Spyware is specifically designed to be sneaky. And if you have spyware on your computer, you may have unintentionally agreed to it in one way or another. For example, many of us have been conditioned to just click *accept* regarding end user license agreements (EULAs) because we have found out if we don't agree, the software won't install. BUT, sometimes within that EULA that we have no desire to read or necessarily agree to, are "permission statements" to install spyware. There also may be boxes that have check marks already inserted for you. If you don't notice them or know to "uncheck" them, Spyware can be automatically installed.

Reputable, ethical companies usually place "permission statements" and boxes in clear view *without* any check marks placed in the boxes allowing you the conscious choice of saying "Yes" or "No" by default if you didn't happen to notice the boxes.

The line between legitimate, useful computer user tracking software and Spyware will probably remain blurred in the years to come simply because everyone's definition of the word *legitimate* can vary greatly.

Receiving more pop-up ads than you would like could be Spyware; but maybe it's just Adware. If you like to download FREE software frequently, your computer maybe loaded with Spyware. If undesirable Web sites end up in your Favorites it could be Spyware. If your "home page" isn't the one you want and magically changed one day, it could be spyware. If you have had your computer for several years and have never checked for Spyware, you probably have lots of it; and it may be slowing your system down considerably.

We currently use two programs once a week to check for and remove spyware from the computer. They are Spybot Search & Destroy 1.3 and Ad-ware 6.0. We use the Google toolbar and pop-up blocker to handle a good majority of "popups" and "popunders."

Here is a link to download Spybot 1.3:
http://www.safer-networking.org/en/download/index.html

Here is a link to download Adware 6.0:
http://www.lavasoftusa.com/support/download/

Here is a link to download the Google pop up and pop under blocker:
http://toolbar.google.com/

All of these downloads are currently free. Links are current and active at the time of publication.

As always please do *nothing* unless you feel comfortable in doing so.

Disk Cleanup

Disk Cleanup is one way to "End The Clutter ETC™" on your computer. Lots of "no longer needed files" can pile up unbeknownst to you. The computer creates spare or temporary files for many reasons; many have to do with Web pages while you are browsing. Some however, are created while the computer is performing certain tasks — printing, downloading, and installing files. Even if *you* are not consciously creating files, be assured that your computer is.

This feature became available with Windows 98; you won't see it on Windows 95 or on earlier operating systems. And you really can't do anything wrong unless you consciously choose to use your recycle bin as a storage container. Please do not place anything in the recycle bin unless you want to get rid of it, because when you perform the Disk Cleanup utility, the recycle bin is one of the items on the list to be emptied as it should be. Your computer recycle bin needs to be cleaned out; this is no different than taking out the trash from your home.

It is optimal to *manually* perform disk cleanup weekly. While automating this task is well intentioned and may work for some, to be sure it gets done, just do it; and do it prior to ScanDisk/Error Checking, and the Disk Defragmenter utility.

Disk Cleanup is a System Tool, and can be found by left clicking once on START, Programs (or All Programs), Accessories, System Tools, and then Disk Cleanup.

Suggest you *"pin this item to your startup"* (for XP users) and/or make a shortcut icon for your desktop (for XP and non-XP users).

As soon as you open Disk Cleanup, a figure *similar* to the one below on the left should appear. Please remember that these diagrams were created with the XP Home operating system and will vary slightly on each computer.

If you have more than one hard drive, recommend you perform this utility on each drive, at least weekly.

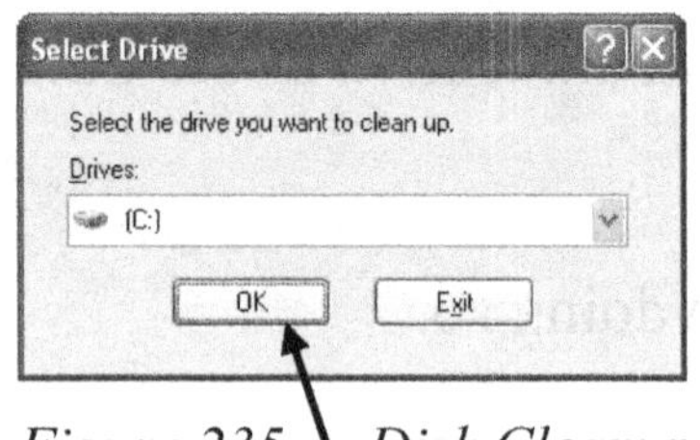
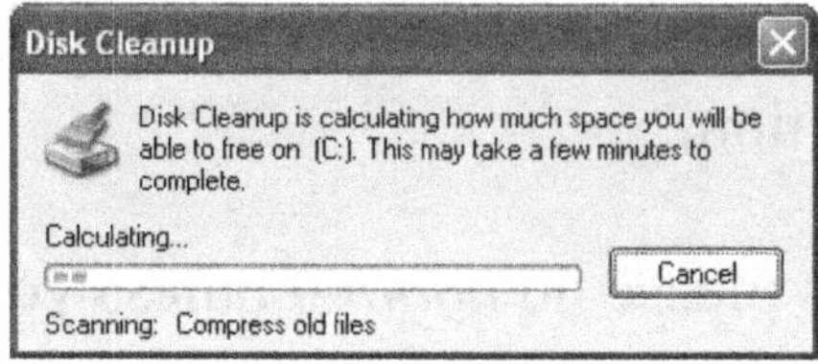

Figure 235 — Disk Cleanup.

When you click on OK, something similar to the above right appears. Please have patience while the computer is deciding what is available to delete. Then you get a figure like the one below on the left:

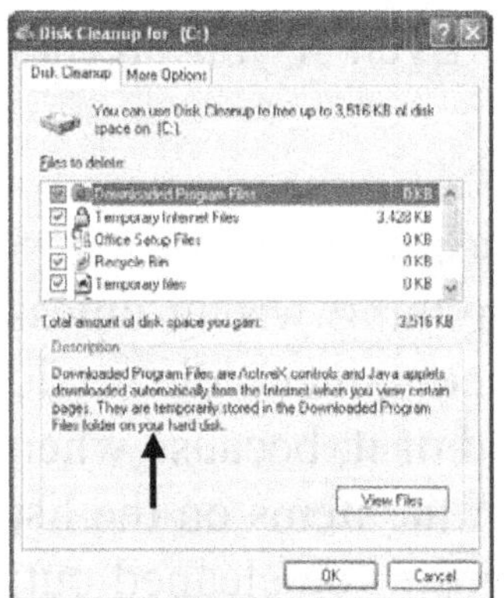
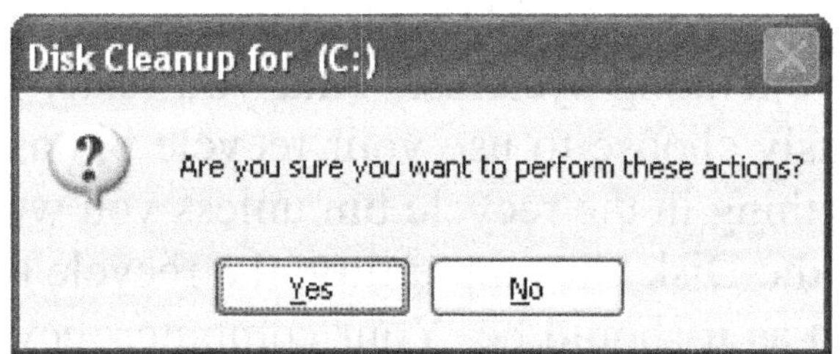

Figure 236 — Disk Cleanup.

Everyone's list in the top left side figure will be slightly different. In this example, "Downloaded Program Files" is highlighted. A description of what that means is in the description box.

Generally speaking, (and this varies with computer and user), you place a check mark (if one is not already there) in the boxes on the left side that have numbers greater than "1" on the right side. As always, if you have doubts and are not sure,

          Use any and all information at your own risk.

do nothing; ask for clarification and instruction from someone you trust. If you don't want to empty the recycle bin this time around, make sure there is not a check mark in the box to the left of it. Keeping the recycle bin full keeps the computer sluggish. When the check marks are where you want them, left click once on OK. That action will bring up the previous page figure lower right box. Left click once on Yes. Then WAIT for the utility to finish. When it is done the disk cleanup utility boxes disappear.

ScanDisk & Error Checking

ScanDisk (Windows 95, 98, Me) and Error Checking (XP) is another system utility like Disk Cleanup and Disk Defragmenter. It does not have to be run as frequently though, for regular preventive maintenance. Perform this after Disk Cleanup, but before Disk Defragmenter when you do it.

It looks for and hopefully corrects any errors on the disk — usually the hard drive; but it also can check floppy diskettes, and removable drives. ScanDisk/Error Check cannot be used with CDs or DVDs.

Windows 95, 98, & Me

For these operating systems, you have two choices; *basic* and *thorough*. A *basic* ScanDisk happens (or should) each time the computer has not been shut down optimally. To manually perform the *thorough*, see below.

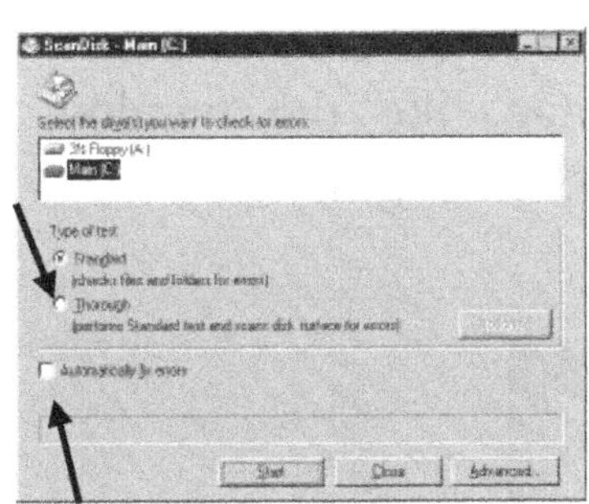

Start, Programs, Accessories, System Tools, ScanDisk. Highlight the drive you want scanned by left clicking it once. Click once in the circle to the left of the word *thorough*. Also place a check mark to automatically fix errors.

Figure 237 — ScanDisk

Then left click once on Start. This can take considerable time especially if you have never run it before, if you have many files, or a very large hard drive. Do a *basic* at least once a month and a *thorough* once each quarter. On many computers when you choose *thorough*, you have to manually change it back to *basic*.

Error Checking in Windows XP

Left click once on START. Left click once on MY COMPUTER. Right click once on the "LOCAL DRIVE C:" (Or any other drive you want to error check). Left click once on PROPERTIES. Left click once on the TOOLS tab.

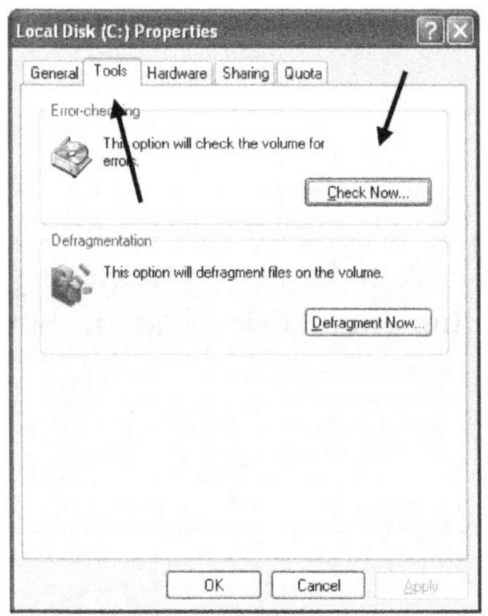

Figure 238 — Error Checking.

Left click once on CHECK NOW. That action brings up the figure below.

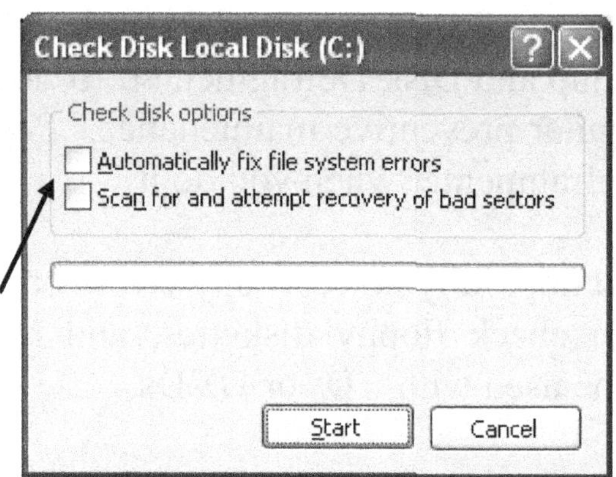

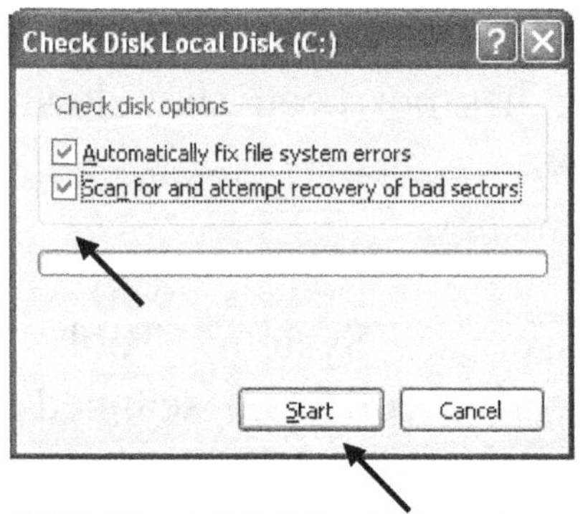

Place a check mark in both boxes above by left clicking once in each box. That action should produce a window like the figure to the left. Then left click once on START. That action may bring up a message like the window below or the error check will begin.

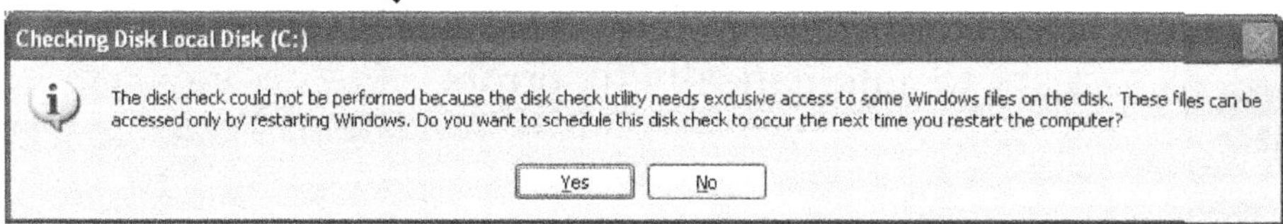

If you receive the above message, left click once on YES and restart the computer. The RESTART command shuts the computer down and automatically starts it up again. Left click once on START. Left click once on TURN OFF COMPUTER. Left click once on RESTART. When the computer restarts, do nothing; you will see a blue screen background. The process can take 30 minutes or more.

              Use any and all information at your own risk.

Preferred Subscriber Program

Receive a weekly e-mail from End The Clutter ETC™ — custom computer instruction specifically designed for those over the age of 50.

Sample #1: Removing an Application Program

When & Why?

1. The program stops working completely.

2. The program is not working correctly.

3. The program causes your computer to malfunction or *crash*.

4. The computer might be running low in space on its hard drive.

5. The computer may require more RAM (random access memory).

6. You may have outgrown the program completely.

7. You may want to replace the current version of the program with the newest available version.

Caution

Before removing a program, it is a good idea to back up (if you haven't already) any files that you have personally created with this program. In other words, make sure you have a copy of any documents that you have created with this program on a floppy disk, a CD, or a DVD in addition to being on the computer's hard drive. This might not be applicable if you are removing a computer card game like *Scrabble*; but definitely is important if you are removing a greeting card, word processing, spreadsheet, database, desktop or Web publishing program. When any program is removed, lots of files are deleted and if the wrong file(s) gets accidentally deleted, you are protected when you have your material on external medium like a floppy, CD, or DVD in addition to the computer's hard drive.

How?

This varies with each computer, each operating system, and each *version* of a computer operating system. You want to get into the CONTROL PANEL. Windows XP users, left click once on START, and then left click once on CONTROL PANEL. Operating systems prior to XP left click once on START, then on SETTINGS, and then on CONTROL PANEL. Once in the Control Panel, double left click (or single, depending upon your computer setup) on ADD/REMOVE PROGRAMS. Please WAIT for the list of programs to appear.

Carefully look at the list to locate the program that you wish to remove. If you are not sure, please remove nothing and consider having someone actually show you how or talk you through this process on the telephone.

If you are sure of the program you want to remove, select the program by highlighting it (left click the program name once). When the program is selected, left click once on the box that says ADD/REMOVE or something to that effect.

Carefully follow instructions from the computer. If you are asked about "shared files" don't delete them (click "*No to all*") because shared files can be used by more than one program and you don't necessarily know what those programs are. You could unintentionally delete a file that another program needs.

If at any time, you get confused or don't understand, stop the process and write down what happened, didn't happen, or what the confusion is. This can also be a place when you might consider asking for clarification — call the program Tech Support, a friend, family member, computer club member. Don't ever accept any answer from anyone unless it makes sense to you. No one knows your computer system better than you.

After the computer has removed the program it is important to RESTART the computer so your operating system can finish deleting any stray files that remain from the un-installation.

When you are learning, remove one program at a time.

<table>
<tr><td>

Become a Preferred ***Subscriber***

✓ Weekly Computer Tip from **ETC**

✓ E-mailed to you each Friday

✓ Cost is less than US$1 per week

</td></tr>
</table>

*This page may be torn out
and/or copied for
subscription purposes.*

The annual fee is US$50

Methods of Payment: Checks, Money Orders, & Credit Cards via PayPal

Checks & Money Orders:	Make US$50 Payable to:
	End The Clutter ETC or ETC
Remit funds and this completed form to:	8961D SW 96th Lane, Ocala, FL 34481-6670

Credit Cards via PayPal:	E-mail US$50 to:
	endtheclutter@cfl.rr.com

*You must have an account with PayPal to pay in this way.
Include the information below with your PayPal payment.

Print all letters and numbers clearly to assure proper delivery.

First Name:	
Last Name:	
E-Mail Address:	
Area Code & Telephone:	

Information will not be sold or given out.

Weekly e-mail tips will be coming from **endtheclutter@cfl.rr.com**.

Please insure the above address is <u>NOT</u> on your blocked senders list.

Subscriptions are non-refundable.

Table of Figures

                                Use any and all information at your own risk.

                                   Use any and all information at your own risk.

                    Use any and all information at your own risk.

Bio & Credentials

Stephanie Keller Rohde was born June 13, 1952, and raised on Staten Island, New York. A graduate of Port Richmond High School in 1970, she then earned her undergraduate degree in mathematics and education from Springfield College, MA, in 1973. Upon graduation, she worked for Brown Brothers Harriman in Manhattan in the Foreign Exchange Advisory Department until September 1976 when she joined the United States Air Force. Her first assignment following Officer Training School (OTS) was nine months of communications-electronics instruction in Biloxi, MS, which prepared her for the next tour of duty located at Kelly AFB in San Antonio, TX. While at Kelly AFB, she worked with Operations and Maintenance divisions in the base Communications Squadron. In her next assignment — her early claim to fame she was the first lady to ever command a site for the Air Force in the "European" theatre. Actually it was in Malatya, Turkey (Asia) — a most remote tour on a mountaintop during 1980 and 1981. She taught mathematics while there as an extension of the University of Chicago. She later obtained her Master's Degree from the University of Texas at Austin, courtesy of the United States Air Force in math and computer science education in 1983. She then was assigned to the United States Air Force Academy (USAFA) as an Assistant Professor of mathematics where she taught the cadets' trigonometry, calculus, differential equations, and statistics from 1983-1987. She attained the rank of Major, which she declined, and separated from the Air Force in 1987. Remaining in Colorado Springs, she worked for the Prudential Insurance Company until mid-1990, managed and also taught for the Kaplan Educational Test Prep Center into 1995. She then became the personal assistant and secretary to Dr. Hal A. Huggins, DDS through 1997. In 1998, she managed the office for Aspen Painting Inc., Aspen, CO. She moved to Ocala, Florida in 1999 to be close to her Dad, as her Mom died in 1996. Stephanie, in addition to her mathematics and educational training also has nearly 30 years of varied computer experience (personal and business) including IBM compatibles (PC) and Mac equipment. A computer, office management, and business-consulting professional, she owns and runs her own custom computer instruction business. Stephanie published a correspondence course entitled *Learning Outlook Express ETC — Respectful E-Mailing Step-By-Step* dedicated to the "Over 50 Crowd" in March 2003. That work evolved into this book you have in your hand. Stephanie is also the author of *Computer & Internet Basics Step-By-Step* also published in 2004. Additionally she is the author of *Earth 101: Vibration & Reflection — Living Life To The Fullest At Any Age*, which explains in complete detail via physics why anyone's life is the

                                    Use any and all information at your own risk.

way that it is for each individual uniquely. This book explains in detail a new application to an old physics application called wave theory. With this knowledge in hand, everyone can take *real* control of their life from this moment on. Stephanie had "things" happen to her in her life that she did not consciously want or choose, but nonetheless happened anyway. This book was originally published in September 2001 and was the result of nearly 20 years of intense personal research for the answer of *Why Stuff Happens* which is the title of her latest edition (2004). This re-write now includes information regarding disease, over weight, under weight, and human health in general.

Stephanie can be reached via e-mail at: endtheclutter@cfl.rr.com.

Made in the USA
Monee, IL
07 July 2026